What people are saying about Alan Elsner's

Gates of Injustice

"Alan Elsner's vivid accounts provide a frightening and realistic glimpse into the brutality of life behind bars. Elsner exposes the dark underbelly of the American prison system, where rapes, assaults, and deaths are regular occurrences. As long as U.S. prison officials are able to operate in secrecy and without accountability these abuses will continue."

—*Elizabeth Alexander, Director,*
National Prison Project of the American Civil Liberties Union

"Alan Elsner has written an enormously compelling book. His lucid and informative analysis provides a framework for understanding why the crisis has occurred and what can be done to end it. This book should be read by everyone who cares about America's future."

—*Jean Maclean Snyder, MacArthur Justice Center,*
University of Chicago Law School

"*Gates of Injustice* provides a rare and poignant glimpse of the cruelty our society has permitted to fester in the name of 'criminal justice.' A prerequisite for the obvious proliferation of blatant human rights abuses behind bars is the blindness and silence of the American people. Alan Elsner describes the horrors of the current imprisonment binge for anyone who is willing to open their eyes. In fact, this book should be required reading for all who care about the future of democracy and humanity."

—*Terry A. Kupers, M.D., author of* Prison Madness

"Alan Elsner's powerful book demonstrates that our $40 billion corrections system for both adults and juveniles is badly broken. Our jails and prisons and penitentiaries are failing us at enormous cost in money and in danger to society. Elsner makes an overwhelming case for reform, and his many sensible proposals deserve to be implemented. This book should be a wake-up call for federal, state, and local governments across America."

—*Senator Edward M. Kennedy*

GATES OF INJUSTICE

GATES OF INJUSTICE

THE CRISIS IN AMERICA'S PRISONS

ALAN ELSNER

PEARSON
Prentice
Hall

An Imprint of PEARSON EDUCATION
Upper Saddle River, NJ • New York • London • San Fransico • Toronto • Sydney
Tokyo • Singapore • Hong Kong • Cape Town • Madrid
Paris • Milan • Munich • Amsterdam

Library of Congress Number: 2004043293

Hardback Edition
Editorial/Production Supervision: *Jane Bonnell*
Cover Design Director: Jerry Votta
Cover Design: Mary Jo DeFranco
Cover and Title Page Photo: *REUTERS/Shannon Stapleton*
Interior Design: *Gail Cocker-Bogusz*
Manufacturing Manager: *Alexis Heydt-Long*
Executive Editor: *Jim Boyd*
Editorial Assistant: *Richard Winkler*
Marketing Manger: *Martin Litkowski*

Paperback Edition
Vice President and Editor-in-Chief: *Tim Moore*
Executive Editor Editor: *Jim Boyd*
Editorial Assistant: *Susie Abraham*
Development Editor: *Russ Hall*
Director of Marketing: *John Pierce*
Marketing Manager: *Martin Litkowski*
International Marketing Manager: *Tim Galligan*
Cover Designer: *Alan Clements*
Managing Editor: *Gina Kanouse*
Project Editor: *Rebecca Storbeck, and Kayla Dugger*
Indexer: *Larry Sweazy*
Senior Compositor: *Gloria Schurick*
Manufacturing Buyer: *Dan Uhrig*

© 2006 by Pearson Education, Inc.
Publishing as Prentice Hall
Upper Saddle River, New Jersey 07458

Prentice Hall offers excellent discounts on this book when ordered in quantity for bulk purchases or special sales. For more information, please contact U.S. Corporate and Government Sales, 1-800-382-3419, corpsales@pearsontechgroup.com. For sales outside the U.S., please contact International Sales at international@pearsoned.com.

Company and product names mentioned herein are the trademarks or registered trademarks of their respective owners.

Printed in the United States of America

First Printing

ISBN 0-13-188179-5

Pearson Education LTD.
Pearson Education Australia PTY, Limited
Pearson Education Singapore, Pte. Ltd.
Pearson Education North Asia Ltd.
Pearson Education Canada, Ltd.
Pearson Educación de Mexico, S.A. de C.V.
Pearson Education—Japan
Pearson Education Malaysia, Pte. Ltd.

To Shulamit, who keeps me honest.

CONTENTS

PREFACE TO THE
SECOND EDITION

J ust as the first edition of this book was published in 2004, shocking video emerged of U.S. military personal abusing Iraqi prisoners at Abu Ghraib prison. The images produced a wave of
revulsion among Americans. The scandal also placed increased attention on the U.S. prison system, especially after it became clear that two
of those mostly deeply involved in the Abu Ghraib abuses had been
employed as correctional officers here at home. Suddenly, some Americans began to question conditions in the U.S. prison system. They
asked themselves whether we should not be at least as concerned about
the mistreatment of U.S. prisoners as we were about the abuse and torture of Iraqis.

Unfortunately, that wave of attention and concern did not sustain itself
for very long. Soon enough, it was back to business as usual. The story
receded from the headlines while the steady, relentless growth of our
giant prison system continued unchecked.

That is not to say there have not been some positive developments in
the past two years. An independent bipartisan Commission on Safety
and Abuse in America's Prisons was established and began holding
public hearings. I testified at the first of them. The Commission's even-
tual report could focus much-needed attention on the issue of prison
abuse. Drug courts are spreading around the nation, diverting more
and more non-violent offenders away from prison and toward treatment. There are also signs that the federal government is finally taking
the scourge of prison rape seriously. Meanwhile, a group of congressional members of both parties began a new effort to pass a bill that
would dismantle some of the barriers that prevent released prisoners
from being reabsorbed into society.

On the negative side, the costs of incarceration are exploding, despite the
efforts of states and counties to explore alternatives to incarceration for
non-violent offenders. Lawmakers continue to invent new mandatory

sentences, which as usual will fall disproportionately on young African Americans and Hispanics. A good example is the so-called "Gangbusters Act" passed by the House of Representatives in April 2005. The act condemns juveniles to 10- or 20-year prison sentences or even the death penalty for a long list of so-called 'gang crimes.' Judges no longer have the ability to weigh the individual circumstances of the crime before passing sentence. A gang is defined as any group of three or more people who commit two crimes. The congressional budget office estimated that this bill alone would increase the prison population at a cost of $62 million for the first four years, growing exponentially after that.

Gates of Injustice points out two fundamental problems. Our prison system is too big and it remains too abusive. What can we do about this? As members of a proud democracy, we have the right and the responsibility to make sure that our elected representatives hear our voices about subjects that matter to us. But first, we need to educate ourselves. I hope once again that this book will play a part in that process.

Alan Elsner, Washington, D.C.
July 2005

PREFACE TO THE FIRST EDITION

This book is a guide to a land that most readers will never visit—the world of U.S. prisons and jails. Like any travel book, it profiles the people that live in this land, outlines their customs, history, geography, and language and lists the many dangers that lurk. It also provides key facts about the local currency, food, and health care.

Readers may ask, Why would anyone want to visit this forbidding land, even in a book? After all, we're never going there. Why should we want to know what really goes on in America's prisons? Why should we care about the massive growth of the U.S. penal system over the past quarter century? Why should we worry about the racial inequalities? Why do we need to be told about the abuses? Why should we bother about the plight of the hundreds of thousands of mentally ill people kept behind bars, about the thousands of men subjected to rape, about women abused and harassed, about those left in solitary confinement for months and years on end with virtually no human contact? What has all this got to do with us?

I offer three answers. First, this book is not in fact about some remote foreign country that has nothing to do with us. It is about the United States, the global superpower. For those of us who live here, if we believe that we are all, in a deep sense, one nation and one family, then how can we ignore the plight of so many of our brothers and sisters, our cousins, our neighbors, our fellow citizens?

President George W. Bush acknowledged this in his State of the Union Address on January 20, 2004. Asking Congress for $300 million to help prisoners who had served their sentences reintegrate into society, the

President said, "America is the land of the second chance and when the gates of the prison open, the path ahead should lead to a better life."

Bush's words showed that prisons and the plight of prisoners are climbing higher on the nation's agenda. Unfortunately, as this book shows, America too often is not the land of the second chance for those behind bars, and when the gates open, there is no path ahead.

Second, try as we might, we Americans cannot separate ourselves from the world of jails and prisons. Ten million people cycle through our jails every year. The abuses they endure, the diseases they contract, the traumas they suffer inevitably come back to haunt the rest of society. There is no Iron Curtain separating them from us. They *are* us.

Third, as members of an old and proud democracy, respect for human rights is a central and vital part of who we are. We champion human rights all around the world. It's one of the most important American values. Yet, increasingly, other people do not take us seriously. We are seen as self-righteous and hypocritical. We criticize others but not ourselves.

Each spring, the State Department issues a report on the state of human rights in every nation on the globe. Secretary of State Colin Powell wrote these words in the introduction to the report issued in March 2003 (U.S. Department of State, Country Reports on Human Rights Practices for 2002. Bureau of Democracy, Human Rights, and Labor. Washington. March 31, 2003):

> We gain little by ignoring human rights abuses or flinching from reporting them. ... But in truth, no country is exempt from scrutiny, and all countries benefit from constant striving to identify their weaknesses and improve their performance in this less-than-perfect world.

The report covered 196 countries, but it left out one—the United States of America.

This book holds up a mirror for us to examine one aspect of our nation. It does not always make for comfortable viewing. The face staring back at us is not the perfect, unblemished image we would all wish to see. But it is better to confront the truth without flinching than to behave like Oscar Wilde's Dorian Gray, who concealed his ugliness behind a false veneer of physical perfection. We must acknowledge our imperfections.

As the Scripture teaches us, "You shall know the truth and the truth shall set you free" (Gospel of St. John, 8:32).

Alan Elsner, Washington, D.C.
January 2004

ACKNOWLEDGMENTS

Many people have helped in the production of this book, and it would be impossible to list them all. Thanks are due to my colleagues Bernd Debusmann, Alisa Bowen, Peter Millership, Steve Jukes, and Janie Gabbett. I spent two wonderful days with Shannon Stapleton as guests of Sheriff Arpaio shooting pictures in Arizona. At Prentice Hall, thanks go to Jim Boyd, Jane Bonnell, and Carol Lallier. I would also like to acknowledge Rob Dver for generously sharing his time and expertise, and Chris Nugent for his support. Margaret Winter, David Fathi, and Jean Snyder opened some of their files. Thanks to Steven Kirstein for constructing my Web site. My sons, Micha and Noam, are my greatest source of pride. I hope I make them proud. My wife, Shulamit, is a shining moral example to all who know her as well as my best friend and most reliable critic.

"The degree of civilization in a society can be judged by entering its prisons."

Fyodor Dostoyevsky, The House of the Dead ◼

"Open to me the gates of justice; I shall enter through them, I shall give thanks to the Lord."

Psalms 118:19 ◼

1

THE SECOND TOUGHEST SHERIFF IN AMERICA

"The liberal approach of coddling criminals didn't work and never will."
President Ronald Reagan[1] ■

Sheriff Gerald Hege liked to boast that he ran the toughest—and pinkest—jail in America. It was definitely the pinkest but maybe only the second toughest. From his sleepy, small-town base in Lexington, North Carolina, self-described Barbecue Capital of the World, Hege turned himself into a national TV personality by striving for the unofficial title of meanest, baddest, roughest, toughest sheriff in America. He was also possibly the only one to have his own theme song, "The Man in Black."

> All you bad guys had better leave town
>
> Sheriff Hege's not fooling around
>
> Your days of breaking the law are through
>
> When the Man in Black comes after you
>
> (*Spoken*) That's right. He's got that big stick.
>
> Go 'head and make his day.
>
> He sure loves the smell of handcuffs in the morning.[2]

Hege was narrowly elected sheriff of Davidson County, a mainly rural area located in the middle of the state, in the big national Republican landslide of 1994. He quickly made a mark by painting the inside of the 300-bed county jail bright pink with blue pictures of weeping teddy bears on the walls to make inmates feel like "sissies." It was the height of the "get tough on crime" movement sweeping the nation, and Hege's testosterone-soaked image perfectly fit the moment. He wore a black, paramilitary-style uniform and was often photographed wielding a five-foot-long stick or a semiautomatic. He designed a new logo for the sheriff's department—a spider's web with a big arachnid in its center—and he had a giant silver spider painted on the hood of his personal squad car, a souped-up, Nascar-style 1995 Chevy Impala with a Corvette engine.

On his Internet site,[3] Hege sold a line of posters featuring himself in various threatening attitudes. There was Hege and his men busting a drugs trafficker on the interstate; Hege standing by his spider car brandishing a semiautomatic while prisoners wearing striped uniforms cleaned up trash; Hege wearing dark glasses and holding his stick with three officers similarly dressed arrayed behind him with assault rifles; Hege about to lead a squad of police dressed in full riot gear into action. It was all part of his pledge to make what he called "Hege country" a safe and fine place to live for law-abiding citizens and a living hell for "scumbags."

The posters had slogans like "Do the crime, scumbag, and you'll do the time" and "Resistance is futile." There was also a variety of other merchandise for sale on the Internet site: spider web T-shirts, toy spider cars, Hege statuettes and coffee mugs, CDs with the theme song—even Sheriff Hege's Lexington-style barbecue dip. The proceeds went to a police charity.

A county sheriff is the closest thing America has to a feudal baron. As long as he keeps public confidence and doesn't mess up too badly, there are few constraints on his powers. He has no boss; he reports directly to the voters. Residents of Davidson County liked Hege's style and reelected him in 1998 by more than 5,000 votes. In 2002, after three of his own trusted deputies were busted by federal agents for dealing in cocaine, marijuana, anabolic steroids and Ecstasy, he still won by about 1,700 votes. All three deputies were convicted and sent to prison.

While cultivating his own macho image, Hege feminized inmates of his jail by making them wear striped uniforms—baby blue for those charged with misdemeanors, lime green for sex offenders, pastel orange for accused felons and black for the road crew that worked outside the jail. He kept many inmates locked in their cells 23 hours a day. There were no exercise facilities, no television, no cigarettes, no coffee, no pencils or pens and no magazines. Books were censored: only Bibles and other approved texts were allowed. Family visits were limited to 10 minutes a week with no physical contact between the inmates and their loved ones.

Never mind that many inmates had not been convicted of anything and were in jail awaiting trial because they could not make bail. Never mind that many of those who had been convicted were serving relatively short sentences for misdemeanors. "It's not my responsibility as sheriff to be concerned about whether they are guilty or innocent," Hege said. "Ninety-nine percent of the people I have in my jail are guilty of whatever they've been charged with. Very few can be rehabilitated and it's not worth trying."[4]

Sheriff Hege first came to my attention in 1999 when Court TV gave him his own late-night talk show, *Inside Cell Block F*, which was filmed live in the jail with inmates as the "guests." The sheriff seemed to personify several different trends in U.S. society all at once. He was a poster boy for the "get tough on crime" crowd, but he was also a relentless self-publicist. And his show, which commanded a regular national audience of around a million, fit the fashion for "reality" TV. "The show is compelling because the inmates' stories are compelling," said Court TV producer Andy Regal. "It's not just reality TV; it's harsh reality TV."

In my role as National Correspondent for Reuters News Agency, I was interested in the political and social forces that lay behind the explosive growth of U.S. prisons in the 1980s and 1990s. By the turn of the century, the richest country on the planet also had the world's largest prison population, with more than 2 million of its citizens held behind bars. How did it happen that the United States, with only 5 percent of the global population, had a quarter of all the world's prisoners?[5] And what was life like for those inside this giant penal system? What was really going on behind the prison walls?

While investigating these issues, I had the opportunity to visit many prisons and jails around the country. I met murderers and rapists, prison wardens and corrections officers, sheriffs and police chiefs, prosecutors and defense attorneys, gang members, doctors, psychologists, child abusers, rape victims, mothers and juveniles behind bars. This book draws heavily on those experiences.

So it was that I found myself in Lexington on a warm spring day, interviewing Sheriff Hege, who looked a bit like Darth Vader in a baseball hat. He explained why he had painted the jail pink. "We have a lot of musclebound, tattooed guys in here who have done silly things. The pink and the teddy bears brings them down a bit," he said. "I was aiming for a day-care atmosphere—something like a girl's bedroom, a little feminine touch. The color pink has a soothing effect on the inmate population."

Hege would have loved to have been called the toughest sheriff in America, but that was one title that eluded him. There was a lawman out west in Arizona who claimed to be even meaner, even rougher, even badder, and even more publicity-conscious. His name was Sheriff Joe Arpaio of Maricopa County, which includes Phoenix and the surrounding area. When it came to media appeal, Arpaio always seemed one step ahead. He was elected in 1992, two years before Hege. He presided over the fourth largest jail system in the country with over 7,500 inmates, which made Davidson County seem strictly bush league. Hege had a pink jail; Arpaio made inmates wear pink underwear and streamed live images of convicts from the jailhouse to the Internet for almost three years until a judge ordered him to stop.[6] Hege started a road crew; Arpaio had "the world's first female chain gang" removing graffiti, picking up trash and burying paupers. Hege locked inmates in cells. Arpaio made hundreds of them live in tents under the hot desert sun, fed them only twice a day on green bologna and charged them money for the privilege. "Our meal cost is 45 cents a day for an inmate. Our dogs cost more to feed than the inmates," Arpaio told me in October 2003.

When a searing heat wave hit Phoenix in July 2003, with temperatures exceeding 130 degrees, Sheriff Arpaio allowed inmates one concession: they were permitted to take off their striped jail suits and roam around their tents in their pink underwear. Arpaio toured the facility and rejected inmates' complaints. He told them, "It's 120 degrees in Iraq and the soldiers are living in tents and they didn't commit any crimes, so shut your mouths."[7]

Three months later, when I visited in mid-October, the temperature was still above 100 degrees. Arpaio took me on a tour of the tent city. Inmates, dressed in convict stripes, gathered around. The sheriff gleefully told them he was cutting their rations from 3,000 calories a day to 2,500. "I'm on a diet myself. I'm taking away your food because I'm trying to help you. You eat too much fat," he said. He shrugged off prisoners' complaints that their food was often rotten. But it quickly became clear during our tour that the inmates in the tents were not the worst off by any means. Anyone committing a disciplinary offense was thrown into a punishment cell measuring 8 by 12 square feet that they had to share with three other prisoners for 23 hours a day.

Reporters and TV crews from as far away as New Zealand and Japan beat a path to Phoenix to cover Arpaio, who welcomed them all with open arms. "We have nothing to hide and nothing to fear," he said. Soon, images of inmates, chained around the left ankle in groups of five, flashed around the world. When one needed to go to Johnny-on-the-Spot, the rest all lined up in a row outside until she had finished.[8]

They worked picking up trash or burying the bodies of indigents who had died penniless on the streets or in the hospital at a county cemetery out in the desert. On the day I joined them, there were six bodies, two of them babies. The prisoners hauled the coffins out of vans and placed them above their final resting place. A young Catholic priest said a few brief prayers for the deceased. "We commit this baby boy back to earth and back to the custody of God who made him," he said, as one body in a tiny white casket was lowered into the ground. The baby did not even have a name. One or two of the women on the chain gang shed a tear. Then they got to work filling the hole.

As Arpaio never tired of saying, the public loved it. The more that prisoners suffered, the better. But why was it necessary? The men and women on the chain gang posed little or no escape threat; most were serving relatively short sentences for relatively minor crimes.[9] They were little more than faceless props in Arpaio's political psychodrama.

Over the years, Arpaio also attracted less welcome visitors—investigators from the Department of Justice and Amnesty International—as well as hundreds of lawsuits. The Justice Department forced him to agree in 1997 to improve conditions in the tents, reduce the use of "improper restraints," stun guns and pepper spray and identify officers "who may be prone to using excessive force."[10] Most of the lawsuits came to nothing, but not all. There was the case of Scott Norberg who died of asphyxiation in a Maricopa County jail in 1996 after being forced into a "restraint chair" with a towel stuffed in his mouth. The autopsy report showed he suffered many scratches and lacerations to his head, face, neck and limbs, as well as burn marks that suggested he was repeatedly fired at from close range with a stun gun. The death was ruled accidental, but the county settled a lawsuit brought by Norberg's parents for $8.25 million.[11]

Then there was Richard Post, a wheelchair-bound paraplegic with no criminal record who was arrested after exchanging insults with the owner of an Irish pub on St. Patrick's Day, 1996.[12] He alleged officers ignored his request for a catheter and put him in an isolation cell. Desperate to empty his bowels, he blocked the toilet to get some attention and caused a minor flood. Officers then strapped him in a "restraint chair" for several hours. They tightened the straps so tightly that he suffered permanent nerve damage to his spinal cord and neck and lost the ability to propel his own wheelchair. They also refused to let him sit on his gel cushion. As a result, he suffered a severely ulcerated anus. Post accepted a settlement of $800,000.[13] Asked about these payouts, Arpaio was unrepentant. "The insurance company paid that. Not the taxpayers," he said of the Norberg case. "I'll put my record against anybody. They can sue me all they want. But I'm not going to close the tents. I will still run a tough jail system."[14]

Hege clearly admired Arpaio and even displayed a framed letter from him in his office. The tone was friendly but dismissive. "Yup, you look mean, but where are your tents?" the Arizona lawman wrote.

Still, nobody could deny that Hege also had a flair for the dramatic. In 2001, a few weeks after the attacks on the World Trade Center and the Pentagon, he sent out Christmas cards showing himself standing in a desert with a camel and a Humvee in the background, holding the severed head of Osama bin Laden in one hand and a raised sword in the other. At the bottom of the card was the message: "Happy Ramadan! Merry Christmas and Happy Holidays! Sheriff Gerald K. Hege."[15]

Despite such stunts, Hege was a determined and crafty politician. He had first worked in the Davidson County Sheriff's Department as a deputy in the early 1970s but was terminated after he kicked an inmate, leaving a size 11-1/2 boot print in his chest.[16] Hege vowed to return—as sheriff. He ran in the Republican primary in 1986 and 1990 but lost both times. Hege realized he would never win without a firmer political base, so he got himself elected as chairman of the Davidson County Republican Party in 1991. Finally, in 1994, he won the prize he had sought for over twenty years.

"When I took over in 1994, the prisoners spent their time watching color TV, smoking and playing poker for money. They could get their girlfriends in for the night for $50. I changed all that," the sheriff said. "I want prisoners in my jail to have a bad time. If prisoners have a bad experience, hopefully they won't come back."

But who were the "scumbags" he kept referring to? Was violent crime really out of control in Davidson County? Hege posted the county's 10 Most Wanted on the Sheriff Department's Web site. When I checked in mid-2003, there were only nine individuals on the list: no murderers, no rapists, no drugs traffickers, no child molesters. The most serious case was a man accused of first-degree burglary, kidnapping and robbery. The rest did not seem particularly menacing—a couple of suspected embezzlers, one man wanted for possession of stolen goods and one wanted for failure to pay child support. They hardly seemed worthy of Hege's tough rhetoric.

The highlight of my visit to Davidson County came at nine o'clock, when it was finally time for the TV show to air. Cameras rolled into position inside the cell block. Producers were dashing around, and the sound guys checked levels as the "studio audience"—around 40 convicts wearing striped uniforms in various colors—filed in and sat on wooden benches. The klieg lights went on. Hege took his place and started to speak.

To my surprise, he was far from a TV natural. He spoke in a low, dull monotone and kept repeating himself. The featured "guests" were a sister and brother, Jodi and Jackie, who were both incarcerated in Hege's jail at the time. Under jail rules that banned any contact between men and women, they spoke from cells on separate floors and were not allowed to see one another. They were dull as well. Jodi told a long and involved story about how her abusive parents drove her to alcohol and drugs. Her brother, Jackie, described how he took his first steps on a path to crime after his father tried to shoot him when he was 13. Hege didn't waste much sympathy on them. "Should it be the taxpayers' responsibility to rehabilitate you? They should just put you in prison and forget about you," he told the unhappy pair.

I had caught Hege at the height of his power and influence. But things turned bleak for the "man in black" in 2003. On September 15 he was indicted on 15 counts, including embezzlement and obstruction of justice, and suspended from his post. By then, Court TV had dropped his show, and the former publicity-seeker had retreated to the old farmhouse where he lived, refusing to speak to the media. The indictments accused Hege of taking $6,200 from a fund used for undercover drug buys, some of which he was alleged to have used for reelection celebrations. He also allegedly had deputies do repairs on his home during work hours and threatened to fire anyone who cooperated with investigators looking into his practices. Half a dozen deputies came forward to testify that Hege had a racial policy when it came to pulling over drivers. He allegedly instructed them to pull over anyone who was "darker than snow."[17] Hege came up with $15,000 in bail to avoid being sent to his own pink jail. And on May 17, 2004, Hege agreed to resign as sheriff and pleaded guilty to two felony counts of obstruction of justice. He received a six-month suspended sentence, three months of house arrest and three years of probation but avoided jail time. [18]

"He was a fun story for a while," wrote *Charlotte Observer* columnist Tommy Tomlinson. "You always like to see someone with flair. And Hege was smart enough to see that throbbing vein in the public's forehead. Millions of people think criminals get off too easy, inside jail and out. But you always got the feeling with Hege that the point wasn't punishing criminals or reducing crime or making a better place for the people who provide his paycheck. The point was Hege. The point was to make him a star."[19]

In 2001, as I drove away from Lexington, all this was still in the future. But I did have several concerns. To what extent did Hege's reality TV reflect actual reality? He had certainly made the lives of his prisoners a lot more miserable. But were people safer than before? What actually lay behind the "get tough on crime" slogan that had swept America in the 1980s and 1990s? And one last question: what *do* handcuffs smell like in the morning?

2

BECOMING A PRISON NATION

You've got the innocent victims who are taxpayers who have to pay for more and more prisons, and more and more prisoners, and more and more police."
Nobel Economics Prize Winner Milton Friedman[1] ∎

On April 6, 2003, the Bureau of Justice Statistics (BJS), a division of the U.S. Department of Justice, issued its semiannual report on the U.S. prison population.[2] The first paragraph began blandly: "At midyear 2002, the Nation's prisons and jails incarcerated 2,019,234 persons. Prisoners in the custody of the 50 States, the District of Columbia, and the Federal Government accounted for two-thirds of the incarcerated population (1,355,748 inmates). The other third were held in local jails (665,475)."

These figures, although impressive, did not include more than 100,000 minors under age 18 held in juvenile facilities and lockups around the country.[3] Nor did they include almost 4 million individuals on probation and another three-quarters of a million on parole. When all the figures were added up for 2001, the Justice Department arrived at a grand total of 6,627,322 human beings under the supervision of the U.S. criminal justice system.[4] The cost to local, state and federal governments was almost $57 billion,[5] considerably more than President Bush's proposed 2006 budget for homeland security, which totaled only $32.2 billion.[6] In all, the United States was spending an astounding $167 billion a year on police, corrections, and the judiciary.[7]

Reverend Jesse Jackson observed, "We are often tempted to think of China as an oppressive country, but we incarcerate 500,000 more people in this country—despite the fact that we have less than one-fourth the population of China. We lock up our poor, our uneducated, our unruly, our unstable and our addicted, where other countries provide treatment, mental hospitals and care."[8]

The U.S. incarceration rate as a proportion of the population is 5 to 10 times greater than that of other democracies. Today there are more Americans behind bars than working on farms[9] or in higher education or on public welfare.[10] There are more Americans behind bars than the combined populations of metropolitan Boston, San Francisco and Washington, D.C.[11]

The media in the United States paid some attention to the Justice Department's April 2003 press release but did not appear to regard it as a major story. Both the *New York Times* and the *Washington Post* buried it in their inside pages. Still, despite the matter-of-fact tone, the report was historic. It marked the first time that the number of people incarcerated in America had pushed through the 2 million barrier. Despite falling crime rates, the prison population continued to grow through 2003 and 2004. By the middle of 2004, the BJS reported that the number of people behind bars had risen to 2,131,180.[12] And there were other nuggets hidden in the dry, bureaucratic text. Of the 2 million behind bars, 596,400 were African American men in their 20s and 30s. In total, African Americans accounted for more than 40 percent of prison and jail inmates, although they make up only about 12 percent of the total U.S. population. Around one in eight African American men in their 20s and early 30s was behind bars. The figure for Hispanics in the same age group was 4 percent; for whites, it was 1.6 percent.

In some states this racial disparity was even more dramatic. African Americans make up only 2 percent of the population of Iowa but 20 percent of the prison population. In Florida they make up about 15 percent of the population and 48 percent of prison inmates; in Alabama, 26 percent of the population and 62 percent of those in state prisons.[13]

What does this mean in practice? It means, according to Department of Justice statisticians, that almost one in every three black men (28.5 percent) and almost one in every five Hispanic men (16 percent) can expect to spend time in prison during his lifetime;[14] that young black men in California are five times as likely to go to prison as to a state university;[15] that in 1999, in the middle of the greatest economic boom in U.S. history, the state of Illinois had 10,000 more African Americans in prison than in college. For every four African Americans in college in Illinois, 10 were in prison or on parole.[16] For many young black men, prison is their college. Serving that first stretch has become a twisted rite of passage some even look forward to and welcome.

"Prison loomed in my future like wisdom teeth; if you lived long enough you got them. Prison was like a stepping stone to manhood...Your 'work' (as a gang member) brought you into contact with the police and, since jail was part of the job description, you simply prepared ahead of time," said Sanyika Shakur, a former Los Angeles gang member who went by the street name Monster Kody Scott.[17]

Successive generations of black men, and increasingly women as well, now attend prisons in a grotesque parody of the way in which the children of elite families follow in their parents' footsteps at Ivy League universities. Take the case of Baba Eng, described by *New York Times* correspondent Fox Butterfield in 1999:

> Baba Eng had been a prisoner at Sing Sing for 22 years, serving a life sentence for murder, when a new inmate walked into the shower room one day and stared at his face.
>
> "Dad," the stranger exclaimed. The man was his son, whom Mr. Eng had not seen since his arrest, and who now was in prison himself for armed robbery.[18]
>
> Eng said that day was the worst of his life.

Mass incarceration also meant that at the time of the 2000 election some 1.4 million black men, or 13 percent of the total, had permanently lost the right to vote under legislation adopted in several states that disenfranchised ex-felons for life.[19] Gone was the concept of paying one's debt to society. In many ways the debt could never be paid. Given that African Americans overwhelmingly vote Democrat, their enforced absence was a big help to Republicans in closely fought state and congressional elections. At least 200,000 disenfranchised African Americans live in Florida, one of four states where a quarter of all black men have been cast out of American democracy forever. Had they been allowed to take part in the 2000 presidential election, the winner might well have been Al Gore and not George W. Bush. In 2003, despite opposition from Governor Jeb Bush, Florida state officials decided to restore the voting rights of around 20,000 to 30,000 former prisoners.[20]

In describing the U.S. prison system, it is easy to fall back on statistics. The BJS is just one of many agencies within and outside the government devoted to the purpose of generating literally millions of numbers each year on every aspect of crime and incarceration imaginable. Figures are sliced and diced for insights on race, gender, age and educational attainment. However, what is often missing from the mass of facts and figures is the human cost. Numbers tell us nothing about the sheer brutality of life for many thousands of people in U.S. prisons and jails. Statistics alone cannot do justice to the widespread abuses and violations of human rights that pervade the prison system from top to bottom. It is a system in which hundreds of thousands of men are raped each year; in which racist and neo-Nazi gangs run drugs, gambling and prostitution rings from inside their prison cells, buying and selling weak and vulnerable fellow inmates as sex slaves, while the authorities turn a blind eye. It is a system in which thousands of inmates are subjected to virtual sensory deprivation and social isolation for years on end and often driven crazy, if they were not seriously mentally ill to begin with. It is a system in which large numbers of women are sexually abused and hundreds of thousands of mentally ill individuals get little or no treatment. It is also a world in which corrections officers risk daily assaults, poor health, broken marriages and premature deaths.

Nor can statistics measure the human and social effects of mass incarceration on those left behind—deeply troubled children, wrecked families and broken communities. They cannot gauge the effect on race relations; they cannot encompass the indirect costs of a system that has become an incubator and reservoir of infectious diseases like HIV, hepatitis C and drug-resistant tuberculosis.

This book addresses these omissions by looking beyond the numbers and giving a voice to some of the men and women in the U.S. prison system. Why is this important? First, because try as we might, we cannot separate ourselves from those who are behind bars. The vast majority of inmates—around 95 percent—eventually are released to return to the community. Society is profoundly influenced by the abuses they suffer or perpetrate, the skills they pick up—whether legitimate or criminal—the diseases they contract and the treatment they receive or do not receive.

The Centers for Disease Control highlighted this in a 2001 report:

> Conventional wisdom holds that prisons and jails are walled off and separate from the community. More and more, however, people are recognizing that this is not true. Many ties connect the community with prisons and jails. For one, inmates are constantly moving back and forth between corrections and the community.

Problems or risky behaviors begun in prison or jail return with inmates to the community after release.[21]

A second reason the issue should compel attention is that building and maintaining such a massive prison system does not come cost free. In California over the 1990s, the number of prison guards increased by 10,000, while the state university system had to lay off 10,000 employees. In the mid-1990s, California was spending $6,000 a year for each student in its admired state university system and $34,000 a year for each inmate in its prisons.[22] Ultimately, the bill comes back to the taxpayers. The dollars devoted to prisons come at the expense of other social goals. By 2003, states all across the nation were finding this out the hard way as they struggled to close yawning budget deficits.

But beyond the debate over dollars, in a deep sense our prison system says something about who we are as a people. The late Supreme Court Justice William Brennan wrote:

> Prisoners are persons whom most of us would rather not think about. Banished from everyday sight, they exist in a shadow world that only dimly enters our awareness. They are members of a "total institution" that controls their daily existence in a way that few of us can imagine. Prison is a complex of physical arrangements and of measures, all wholly governmental, all wholly performed by agents of government, which determine the total existence of certain human beings (except perhaps in the realm of the spirit, and inevitably there as well) from sundown to sundown, sleeping, walking, speaking, silent, working, playing, viewing, eating, voiding, reading, alone, with others…It is thus easy to think of prisoners as members of a separate netherworld, driven by its own demands, ordered by its own customs, ruled by those whose claim to power rests on raw necessity. Nothing can change the fact, however, that the society that these prisoners inhabit is our own. Prisons may exist on the margins of that society, but no act of will can sever them from the body politic.[23]

In discussing the U.S. prison system, the first thing we should ask is, how did we get to where we are? How did the system grow so massive? It was not an accident. It was the result of deliberate policy, pursued by Democrats as well as Republicans, an expression of national political will. While gutting much of its social safety net by slashing welfare programs, subsidized housing for the poor and treatment for the mentally ill, the United States turned incarceration into the *de facto* final destination for those unable to find a place for one reason or another in our education-based, high-tech, winner-take-all economy.

Clearly, every society is going to have its winners and losers, its outcasts and misfits—not just criminals, but also the homeless, the very poor, the abused, those addicted to drugs and alcohol and the mentally ill. The question is, how does society treat them? Many valiant people put their hearts and souls into efforts to help. But treatment and welfare programs are vastly underfunded and swamped and shrinking. The vacuum is filled by the criminal justice system.

For most of the 20th century until around 1970, the U.S. prison population had remained remarkably stable at around 0.1 percent of all Americans. In 1972 there were only some 326,000 Americans behind bars, yielding a rate of around 160 per 10,000 in the population,[24] a little higher but not drastically out of line with other Western democracies. Now, according to the latest Justice Department figures, the U.S. incarceration rate stands at 726 per 100,000[25]—by far the highest in the world (see table).

Some National Incarceration Rates
(per 100,000 of the population) [26]

USA	726
Russia	628
Thailand	401
South Africa	400
Iran	229
Mexico	156
United Kingdom	138
France	90
Sweden	60
Japan	40

The prison population started to climb at a moment in U.S. history when the Civil Rights movement had faltered. Poverty and hopelessness overtook many of America's inner cities, breeding addiction, crime and violence. As race riots shook American cities in the summer of 1968, Republican presidential candidate Richard Nixon seized the issue. "We need a new respect for the law in this country—a new determination that when a man disobeys the law, he pays the penalty for his crime," he declared. In view of President Nixon's later history, this comment takes on a certain retroactive irony.

Nixon coined the phrase "War on Drugs," which he intended as a stark contrast to President Lyndon Johnson's "War on Poverty." Over time, as the country became more and more conservative, the war on drugs gradually supplanted the war on poverty, sucking up millions of lives and billions of dollars, but yielding little or no progress. The war on drugs became the single biggest factor behind the explosion in America's prison population.

In 1973, by which time Nixon was deeply embroiled in the Watergate scandal, New York Governor Nelson Rockefeller took the war on drugs to a new level. He pushed through what were then the nation's harshest sentences for drugs crimes, including 15-year prison terms for possessing small amounts of narcotics. Soon other states and the federal government were following New York's example.

By the mid-1980s, the nation was transfixed by what seemed an unstoppable crime wave. A crack cocaine epidemic spawned a devastating wave of murders in U.S. cities as rival drug gangs fought vicious turf battles. Rarely did a local TV news report fail to open without an account of a gruesome murder. In 1986 *Time* magazine declared crack cocaine the top issue of the year. CBS produced an acclaimed special, *48 Hours on Crack Street*, that garnered the highest ratings for any news show for 5 years. As America looked for answers, first lady Nancy Reagan urged young people to "Just Say No." In September 1986 alone, the *New York Times* ran 169 articles about drugs. Not surprisingly, the proportion of Americans who identified drugs as the nation's number one problem climbed from 3 percent to 13 percent in 1986 and hit 65 percent by late 1989.[27]

Psychologists Craig Haney and Philip Zimbardo commented, "The counterrevolution in crime and punishment began slowly and imperceptibly at first and then pushed forward with a consistency of direction and effect that could not be overlooked. It moved so forcefully and seemingly inexorably in the 1980s that it resembled nothing so much as a runaway punishment train, driven by political steam and fueled by media-induced fears of crime."[28]

Inflamed by the media, politicians competed for the title of who could be toughest on crime. The elder George Bush won the 1988 presidential election by painting his Democratic opponent, Massachusetts Governor Michael Dukakis, as dangerously wishy-washy. Bush seized on the case of Willie Horton, a convicted murderer who raped a white woman and tortured her husband after he was allowed to walk out of a Massachusetts prison on a weekend pass approved by Dukakis. The image of Horton, bearded, brooding, scowling and black, defined for many Americans their idea of what a criminal looked like.

In 1992 Bill Clinton was determined not to fall into the same trap as Dukakis. He interrupted his campaign to return home to Arkansas for the execution of Ray Rector, who had murdered two men, then turned the gun on himself. Rector was left lobotomized by his botched suicide. He appeared unable to remember his crime or understand his fate. On the night of his execution, he saved the pecan pie from his last meal—for later.

In the 1980s and 1990s, Congress and state legislatures passed literally hundreds of crime bills. Perhaps the single most important was the Anti-Drug Abuse Act of 1986, brainchild of Tip O'Neill, the powerful Democratic Speaker of the House of Representatives. In June of that year Len Bias, a celebrated University of Maryland basketball star, died of heart failure triggered by taking cocaine. Two days earlier, Bias had been drafted by the Boston Celtics, then the dominant team in professional basketball. In death, Bias immediately became a symbol for the drugs scourge.

O'Neill, a classic Irish-American politician from Boston, was famous for saying that all politics is local. Responding to a city plunged into grief, he realized his party had a golden political opportunity. O'Neill pushed Congress to rush an antidrug bill through without committee hearings before the November midterm elections so the Democrats could take credit.

The act imposed tough mandatory minimum sentences for drugs offenses. For instance, anyone caught selling 100 grams of heroin, 100 kilos of marijuana or 10 grams of methamphetamine would be punished by at least five years in prison without parole. When it came to cocaine, the act contained an especially controversial provision. Anyone convicted of selling five grams of crack cocaine, mainly used by African Americans, or 500 grams of powder cocaine, mainly consumed by whites, received a 5-year minimum sentence. Why was crack treated 100 times more severely than powder, even though pharmacologically they are the same drug? Supporters of the law said it was because crack was uniquely addictive and centrally implicated in the crime wave that was turning inner cities into virtual war zones. Critics blasted the law as blatantly racist.

In 1988, Congress revisited the issue and made the law even tougher. It designated crack cocaine the only drug for which a first offense of simple possession could trigger a federal mandatory minimum sentence.[29] Congress left the 100-to-1 crack-to-powder punishment ratio unchanged. Repeated attempts to repeal or modify the provision all failed.

From 1980 to 2001 the annual number of drugs-related arrests tripled to reach 1,586,900—4,348 arrests a day, or one every 20 seconds.[30] Around 20 percent were for selling or manufacturing drugs; 80 percent were for possession.

A report in May 2005 by The Sentencing Project illustrated the way the "war on drugs" was being fought. It found the number of arrests for marijuana offenses had risen from 327,000 in 1990 to 697,000 in 2002. Eighty-eight percent of these arrests were for possession alone. "The war on drugs has become a war on marijuana," co-author Ryan King said. The annual cost of fighting this war on marijuana—$4 billion.[31]

And mandatory sentencing laws meant not only that more Americans were going to prison for nonviolent crimes but that they were staying behind bars for much longer. The average sentence imposed by U.S. District Courts for drugs offenses rose from 54.5 months in 1980 to 75.5 months in 2000. For assault, the figure was 33 months. For fraud, it was 23.5 months.[32]

The distortions created by mandatory sentencing were dramatically illustrated by the case of Weldon Angelos, a 25-year-old who, in November

2004, received a 55-year prison sentence for selling two small bags of marijuana to a police informant. Judge Paul G. Cassell of the United States District Court in Salt Lake City said he pronounced the sentence reluctantly but his hands were tied by the mandatory minimum law. He had to give Angelos the 55 years sentence because the young man had a gun in his pocket during the drug transaction. Judge Cassell called the sentence "injust, cruel and even irrational," the more so because only two hours earlier he had sentenced another man to only 22 years after he was convicted of beating an elderly woman to death with a log.[33] There is no logic and no justice behind such disparities.

While Congress passed more and more tough laws, the states were doing their part as well. From 1993 to 1995, almost half the states enacted some form of "three strikes and you're out" legislation. California, which led the way, was soon sending away felons like Gary A. Ewing, who got 25 to life without parole for stealing three golf clubs from a pro store, and Leandro Andrade, who got 50 years without parole for stealing nine children's videos worth around $150 from Kmart. They included *Cinderella*, *Snow White* and *Free Willie 2*.[34] The whale went free, but Andrade did not. In 2003, the Supreme Court upheld his punishment as constitutional.[35]

The laws enacted by Congress and the states fell most heavily on the poor and especially on minorities, even though the evidence suggests that African Americans, whites and Hispanics use drugs in roughly equal proportions. In 2001 a national government survey concluded, "Rates of current illicit drug use among the major racial/ethic groups in 2001 were 7.2 percent for whites, 6.4 percent for Hispanics and 7.4 percent for blacks."[36] Since African Americans account for about an eighth of the population, one would expect them to account for a similar proportion of drugs-related arrests, all other things being equal. But they actually made up 35 percent of those arrested, 55 percent of those convicted and 74 percent of those jailed for drugs possession.[37] In Illinois, an African American man was 57 times more likely than a white man to be incarcerated for drugs.[38]

"We have created an American *gulag*," said national drugs czar Barry McCaffrey in a 1996 speech. "We have 1.6 million people behind bars, and probably two-thirds of those in the federal system are there for drugs-related crimes."[39]

With 2 million people behind bars, it is worth asking what America gets for its money. Crime rates certainly fell dramatically throughout the 1990s. However, there is a fierce debate about the extent to which mass incarceration contributed to this or whether other factors—demographic, social or economic—played a larger role. Wherever one comes down on this, it is hard to argue that the imprisonment of hundreds of thousands of people for nonviolent drugs possession offenses was cost effective. In the early 1970s, when the war on drugs began, it cost around $110 million a year. President George W. Bush's fiscal year 2003 budget proposed $19.2 billion to fight drugs.[40] And the drugs trade goes on unabated.

Joseph McNamara, a former police chief who spent 35 years on the front lines of the drugs war, reached a grim conclusion. "Jailing people because they put certain chemicals into their bloodstream is a gross misuse of police and criminal law. Jailing drug users does not lessen drug use, and incarceration usually destroys the person's life and does immense harm to that person's family and neighborhood," he said.[41]

In the 1980s, police started heavily targeting African American neighborhoods while largely ignoring middle-class whites who indulged their drug habits in the privacy of their suburban homes rather than on street corners. One 1997 study in Massachusetts found African Americans were 39 times more likely than whites to be incarcerated for a drugs-related offense.[42] Another in Baltimore found that in 1980, 18 white juveniles and 86 black juveniles were arrested for selling drugs. By 1990, the number of whites arrested fell to 13; the number of African Americans jumped to 1,304.[43]

Soon, prisoners were flooding into the penal system in unprecedented numbers. Existing facilities were quickly overwhelmed, and states had to embark on a massive prison-building program. After 1985, the California prison system added more prisoners each year than the system had added in the average *decade* between 1950 and 1980.[44] But California was dwarfed by Texas, which went from a relatively small system in the 1960s with around 14,000 inmates in 12 penal farms that largely paid for themselves to a $2.5 billion a year behemoth running 144 facilities with around 150,000 inmates.[45]

As went Texas and California, so went the nation. From 1985 to 1995, state and federal authorities were putting up new prisons at an average rate of one a week.[46] In 1995 alone, 150 new prisons were built in the United States and 171 existing prisons were expanded. The following year, contractors broke ground for 26 new federal penitentiaries and 96 state prisons.[47] New York went from 21 to 71 prisons within 25 years, while its inmate population grew from 12,500 to over 70,000.[48] It cost New York around $100,000 to build each new prison cell and around $30,000 a year to keep someone locked inside it.[49]

As sentences became longer, conditions became harsher. The aim of incarceration once had been a combination of deterrence, punishment and rehabilitation. Now it came down to punishment, pure and simple. While few went as far as Sheriff Arpaio or Sheriff Hege, states and counties rushed to abolish inmate privileges like coffee, orange juice, exercise equipment, air conditioning, TVs and radios. Some prisons imposed grooming standards. Men were told they could no longer grow dreadlocks, ponytails, beards or handlebar mustaches. Women were deprived of lipstick, mascara and earrings.[50] Prison chiefs cited security and hygiene concerns. "It's an escape risk to let prisoners grow big beards and change their appearance. You want to make sure the picture you have of the person on file is the way that person looks. Plus it's unhealthy to live like that in a crowded environment," said Ron Angelone, who ran Virginia's prison system from 1994 to 2002.

States cut education and vocational training for inmates. Some made troublesome or ill-disciplined inmates eat unpalatable food, like the Maryland prison loaf, a foul-smelling mixture of dehydrated potato flakes, grated imitation cheese, powdered milk, raisins, carrots, tomato paste, wheat bread, beans and spinach molded into a loaf and baked for an hour.[51]

Few states invested much effort in drug or alcohol treatment even though inmates were highly likely to be substance abusers. In one Department of Justice study in 1999, three-quarters of prisoners said they had been abusing drugs or alcohol in the time leading up to their arrest. Only 15 percent received drug treatment in prison.[52]

Inmates were also likely to be physically or mentally ill, or both. Figures on disease rates in prison can be misleading, since not every prison system tests every inmate for every disease. For example, 39 states test inmates for HIV only if they are involved in a fight that causes bleeding.[53] Still, the Centers for Disease Control estimates that the AIDS rate inside prisons and jails is five times higher than in the general population.[54] A study on inmate health commissioned by Congress found that 17 percent of all Americans living with AIDS in 1996 passed through a correctional facility that year.[55]

There was increasing evidence that inmates, newly-released from prison, were spreading HIV into the community. Dr. Peter Leone, HIV treatment program director for the North Carolina Department of Health and Human Services, believes this is one reason for a spike in infection rates among African American women that has begun showing up in the statistics in recent years. Dr. David Wohl, an infectious disease specialist at the University of North Carolina said: "Many inmates who have been locked up awhile want two things when they come out. One of them is a Big Mac. The other is sex. If you're going to get them with sex messages, you have to be quick.[56]

The risk of spreading a disease like tuberculosis is particularly high in overcrowded prisons with their poor ventilation systems. One deadly outbreak of multidrug-resistant tuberculosis in the early 1990s was traced to New York prisons. It cost the state and federal health authorities an estimated $1 billion to stamp out.[57] Most prisons and jails test inmates for tuberculosis, but many jails release them before the results come through.

Most prison systems do not test for hepatitis C, a potentially fatal disease common among drug abusers that attacks the liver and is spread through contact with human blood. If they did, they would have to offer costly treatment, in some cases liver transplants, which would quickly bankrupt the system. Take the case of Horacio Alberto Reyes-Camarena, a convicted murderer facing a death sentence in Oregon for killing an 18-year-old woman. In 2003 the cash-strapped state was spending $120,000 a year for Reyes-Camarena to have kidney dialysis while he went through a lengthy appeals process. To save money, state officials proposed placing him on a transplant waiting list.[58] He was ultimately turned down by a medical review panel as an unsuitable candidate for the operation.[59] The CDC estimates that up to 332,000 prisoners have hepatitis C, a rate 9 to 10 times higher than in the general population.

Anyone who has ever spent much time in a U.S. prison or jail soon becomes aware that a high number of inmates have serious mental illnesses. They are present at every level of the system, from county jails and small-town lockups all the way through to death rows. They are the ones who continually holler, the ones who smear feces on the walls and who refuse to follow orders or look after their personal hygiene. They may mutilate themselves, attack guards or attempt suicide. In the past 30 years, while the nation constructed more and more prisons, it also closed most of its mental hospitals. The Los Angeles County Jail became the world's largest mental hospital with approximately 3,300 seriously ill inmates on any given night.[60]

"Jails and prisons have become the final destination for the mentally ill in America—it's the most pressing issue facing psychiatry today," said Steven Lamberti, a psychiatrist at the University of Rochester.

In 2000, the BJS estimated that around 16 percent of inmates in state prisons were mentally ill—191,000 individuals.[61] Adding the federal prison system and county jails dramatically raises that number, probably to at least 300,000. With such numbers, an unbiased outsider could be forgiven for concluding that being mentally ill has itself become a crime in the United States.

In recent years, women have been the fastest growing sector of the prison system. For most of the 20th century, the United States had incarcerated only around 5,000 to 10,000 women. The number held in state prisons passed the 100,000 mark in 2003. By mid-2004, the BJS found over 190,000 women held in prisons and jails, more than double the 1990 figure.[62] Notes criminologist Meda Chesney-Lind, "The war against drugs was a largely unannounced war on women."[63]

Statistically, African American women were two-and-a-half times more likely than Hispanics and five times more likely than whites to end up behind bars.[64] Even more alarmingly, around 65 percent of women in state prisons had children under 18;[65] around 5 percent were pregnant when they entered.[66] A few women in a small number of prisons are allowed to keep their babies with them for a limited time after they give birth. Most have to give them up immediately, and some may lose them to foster care and adoption.

Children are some of the saddest invisible casualties of the U.S. prison binge. The BJS, in 2000, estimated that 721,500 of America's prisoners, excluding jail inmates, were parents of at least one child, while at least 1.5 million children had a parent in prison.[67] One in every 14 black children has a parent in prison on any given day, but of course, over the duration of an entire childhood, the figure is much higher.[68] Children whose parents are incarcerated experience a broad range of problems, including rage, guilt, low self-esteem and depression. They are more likely to live in poverty, more likely to suffer abuse at the hands of caregivers, more likely to fail at school, more likely to take drugs and more likely to end up in juvenile jail. Half of all juveniles in custody have a parent or close relative in prison.[69]

Another fast-growing segment of the prison population, especially since the 9/11 attack on the World Trade Center, are noncitizens. They include illegal immigrants, permanent residents and asylum seekers. Many have committed no crime. Some come to the United States to escape torture in other countries. They are immediately imprisoned and may be held for months or years until their cases are decided. Because foreign nationals do not automatically have the right to legal representation, they are even more powerless than their American counterparts. Their ranks include around 5,000 children detained every year by immigration authorities—kids like Alfredo Lopez Sanchez, a 16-year-old Mayan boy from Guatemala, who came to this country to escape an abusive father.

Sanchez was held in four locations, including a Florida adult jail and a juvenile detention center in Pennsylvania. For five weeks he was locked alone in a room of a Comfort Suites Hotel in Miami with guards outside the door. When I went to Miami to meet him, Sanchez possessed one blue T-shirt, one pair of sweat pants and one set of underwear, which he washed in the sink with hand soap every night. "Each day the maid comes in and changes the sheets. The bed gets clean clothes but I don't," he said. After 19 months in detention, a judge eventually ordered him released and granted him legal residency.

By the late 1990s, the growth in the prison population seemed to be stabilizing. But it jumped again by 2.6 percent in 2002, by another 2.1 percent in 2003 and by 2.3 percent in the first half of 2004. There is little chance that it will fall significantly in the foreseeable future. On the contrary, it shows every sign of being a permanent feature of U.S. society. Meanwhile, as the prison population ages, the financial burden on states and the federal government is rising. States that abolished parole or passed three-strikes laws are beginning to discover the costs of locking up inmates until they grow old and frail. Many have been forced to established geriatric units and hospices behind bars. Treating those with cancer, Alzheimer's disease or the other infirmities of old age does not come cheap.

In North Carolina in 2003, legislators looked for ways to raise an extra $1.5 billion to close a budget deficit while finding hundreds of millions for new prisons to meet the still-growing demand for more inmate beds. "Prisons are the silent killer in the budget," said Rep. Greg Thompson, the state's Republican chairman of the House Appropriations Committee.[70]

In 2003, Robert Presley, Secretary of California's Correctional Agency, made some gloomy predictions.[71] He noted that after several years of decline, crime rates were rising again, and his state's prison population had resumed its growth. Maximum security inmates were the fastest-growing segment as well as the most expensive to house. Just paying for prisoners' health was costing the state almost $1 billion a year. Despite the building boom of the previous 20 years, prisons were at an average of 191 percent of capacity. Severe overcrowding increased the spread of disease and violent incidents. An average of nine employees was assaulted in prison every day; meanwhile, overtime for corrections officers had increased sharply because of chronic staff shortages.

With almost 50,000 on the payroll, the California Department of Corrections was already one of the state's largest employers with an annual budget of $5.5 billion.[72] That was all very fine during the boom days of the 1990s when the state had more money than it knew how to spend. But by 2003, California was drowning in a sea of red ink. Struggling for ways to deal with a massive deficit of $38 billion, then-Governor Gray Davis proposed cutting almost every budget item *except* prisons, for which he suggested raising spending by $115 million to $5.5 billion.[73]

Governor Arnold Schwarzenegger, who replaced Davis in October 2003, formed a 40-member independent review board headed by former Gov. George Deukmejian. In June 2004, the board came up with 200 recommendations to overhaul what it called a "dysfunctional and abusive" system. The introduction to that report read:

"California's $6 billion correctional system suffers from a multitude of problems—out of control costs; a recidivism rate exceeding that of any other state; reported abuse of inmates by correctional officers; an employee disciplinary system that fails to punish wrongdoers; and the failure of correctional institutions to provide wards and inmates with mandated health care and other services."[74]

The recommendations included changing the name of the agency in charge of prisons to "The Department of Corrections and Rehabilitation" and changing the correctional culture by, among other things, ending the prison guards' "code of silence." However, just four months later, Schwarzenegger vetoed two bills that would have allowed clergy and the media the automatic right to enter prisons in order to interview inmates and report on conditions behind bars. [75]

The new governor did persuade the powerful California prison guards union to delay a schedule pay raise, saving some $108 million for fiscal year 2005.[76] In exchange, Schwarzenegger abandoned a proposed overhaul of the parole system that would have kept more people out of prison by putting some violators in community-based drug treatment and halfway houses and subject others to electronic monitoring.[77]

Prisons in California and other states have consistently tried to reduce costs by trimming "frills." Texas lawmakers proposed cutting the calories for inmates, giving them powdered milk and soy burgers.[78] California prepared to scale down basic literacy programs for inmates and close a treatment program for addicts and a mental health program.[79] In June 2003, at Lancaster maximum security prison north of Los Angeles, inmates were put on a 24-hour lockdown to reduce overtime pay to guards. All 4,000 inmates were denied exercise and kept in their cells around the clock.[80] Any prison warden knows that kind of regime is just not sustainable. Punishing inmates for no reason is the best way to stoke prison unrest.

Even efforts by some states to speed up the release of nonviolent offenders were highly unlikely to reduce the total prison population. One reason: a large number come straight back. By 2000, over 650,000 prisoners a year were being released on parole or after completing their terms.[81] A large number remained addicted to drugs and alcohol. Those who sincerely wanted to go straight faced crushing obstacles to rebuilding their lives. Many jobs and housing options were permanently closed to them; many social benefits were permanently denied. Little surprise that a BJS study found that over two-thirds of those released were rearrested within three years, either for parole violations or for new crimes.[82]

While states struggled, thousands of businesses got fat off supplying prisons. As early as 1994, the *Wall Street Journal* proclaimed the birth of a "prison-industrial complex."[83] The law enforcement technology industry, which produces high-tech items like the latest stab-proof vests, helmets, stun guns, shields, batons and chemical agents, is worth over $1 billion a year.[84]

With 2.3 million people engaged in catching criminals and putting and keeping them behind bars, accounting for a monthly payroll of $8.1 billion,[85] the "corrections industry" had become one of the largest sectors of the U.S. economy, employing more people than the combined worldwide workforces of General Motors, Ford and Wal-Mart, the three biggest corporate employers in the country.[86] If a nation was defined by what it produced, the United States had become a prison nation.

3

ENTERING THE GATES

"The Constitution does not mandate comfortable prisons ...
but neither does it permit inhumane ones."
Supreme Court Justice David Souter[1] ∎

In the summer of 1971, four young professors conducted one of the most famous psychological studies ever devised—the Stanford Prison Experiment. The researchers, Philip Zimbardo, Craig Haney, W. Curtis Banks and David Jaffe, transformed a section in the basement of Stanford University's psychology department into a mock prison. They removed the doors of laboratories and replaced them with bars, turning them into cells, while a corridor served as the exercise area. A small closet on one side of the corridor became "The Hole" for solitary confinement.

The scientists selected 24 healthy, intelligent, middle-class males from among 70 who had responded to a local newspaper ad that offered $15 a day for volunteers willing to take part in a psychological study. The volunteers were divided into two groups by the flip of a coin. Half were randomly assigned to be guards and half to be inmates. The experiment began with the surprise "arrest" of those designated as inmates. The bewildered volunteers were brought in squad cars with sirens blaring to the Palo Alto police department, where they were booked, read their rights and fingerprinted. Then they were taken to the mock jail where they were searched, stripped naked, deloused, issued prison uniforms and taken to their cells.

What transpired over the following days shocked the researchers. On the second day, the prisoners protested their treatment. The guards quickly crushed the rebellion, stripped the prisoners naked, removed the beds from their cells and forced the ringleaders into solitary confinement. They then began to harass and intimidate the prisoners. One of the experimenters, Phil Zimbardo, described what transpired.[2] "Every aspect of the prisoners' behavior fell under the total and arbitrary control of the guards. Even going to the toilet became a privilege which a guard could grant or deny at his whim. Indeed, after the nightly 10:00 p.m. lights 'lockup,' prisoners were often forced to urinate or defecate in a bucket that was left in their cells. On occasion, the guards would not allow prisoners to empty these buckets, and soon the prison began to smell of urine and feces—further adding to the degrading quality of the environment."

Many of these "guards" had seemed to be gentle, caring young men who described themselves as pacifists or Vietnam War doves. They were given no specific training or instructions on how to behave. They made up the rules as they went along. But as the days passed, their cruelty increased. They forced prisoners to clean toilet bowls with their bare hands, had them do push-ups and jumping jacks until they were past the point of exhaustion and made them chant demeaning slogans. Not all the guards were equally cruel. Some were tough but fair. There were also some the scientists called "good guys" who did little favors for prisoners and never punished them. However, around a third of the guards became extremely spiteful and hostile and appeared to enjoy thinking up new ways to humiliate the prisoners. They seemed to relish the power they had suddenly been granted and set the tone for the rest of the guards, who were unable to challenge or resist them. One, whom the others nicknamed John Wayne, was particularly sadistic.

Christina Maslach, who was Zimbardo's girlfriend and later his wife, met "John Wayne" when she visited the experiment. First she saw him in ordinary clothes on his way to report for an eight-hour guard shift. She said that out of uniform, he was a "charming, funny, smart young man." In uniform, he was transformed. He began talking in a Southern accent. "He moved differently and the way he talked was different, not just in the accent, but in the way he interacted with the prisoners. It was like Jekyll and Hyde," she recalled.[3] By the end of the experiment, the guards were intensifying their abuse of the prisoners in the middle of the night when they thought the researchers were not watching. They did not know their every action was being captured on film.

It was Maslach who persuaded Zimbardo to call a halt to the experiment after six days instead of the planned two weeks. She strongly objected when she saw prisoners being marched to the toilet with bags over their heads, their legs chained together, hands on each other's shoulders. "It's terrible what you're doing to these boys," she said.

Her words were a reality check to the researchers, who had themselves become deeply involved in their roles as prison wardens.

Why is the Stanford experiment still relevant? Obviously, not because most or even a sizeable minority of guards in real American prisons behave anything like the young men in the study. Most just want to get through their shifts without harm and go home to their families. But prisons are tough, harshly coercive environments. Violence constantly bubbles beneath the surface, creating tension and fear. The experiment showed, in the words of the researchers, the "extraordinary power of institutional environments to influence those who passed through them."[4] Lance Corcoran, a former California correctional officer who is executive director of the California Correctional and Peace Officers Association, put it this way: "We are surrounded by everything in society that is not acceptable—profanity, obscenity, discrimination, hatred, prejudice. It affects you." In such stressful circumstances, the potential for abuse is always there. If there are insufficient institutional and societal checks on mistreatment, it will occur.

What occurred in Abu Ghraib prison in Iraq in 2003 and 2004 is a perfect illustration. Although controversy still swirls around the extent to which the abuse there was a result of official policy, dictated or condoned by senior government and military officials, there is no doubt that a small group of extremely sadistic guards was able to set the tone. Other, weaker, characters joined in the abuse; still others who knew that it was wrong chose to stay silent. Only when one brave military policeman came forward was the scandal revealed. And on his return home, Specialist Joseph Darby, the whistleblower, had to be placed under protection when he and his family received death threats from fellow Americans.

Society clearly has an overwhelming interest in protecting itself from dangerous criminals, and nothing should be done to compromise that task. But it also has an interest in ensuring that human rights and standards of decency are observed behind bars to the maximum possible extent. The abuses an inmate suffers in prison are easily recycled to the outside world after he is released.

How, then, does society ensure that prisons remain safe and humane places for inmates, corrections officers and civilian employees alike?

The only way is through the constant vigilance of federal, state and local authorities, backed by the power of the judiciary, monitored by the media and supported by public opinion. Unfortunately, in the United States today, none of these protective mechanisms seems fully up to the task.

Over the past generation, the vast majority of elected officials have been far more concerned with waging a "war on crime" than with what happens to criminals once convicted. Long-time Philadelphia Judge Lois Forer termed this mentality "the rage to punish." Craig Haney, one of the Stanford experiment researchers, said this uncontrolled fury had been indulged so completely that it threatened to override any competing concern for humane justice. "For the first time in the 200-year history of imprisonment in the United States, there appear to be no limits on the amount of prison pain the public is willing to inflict in the name of crime control," he wrote.[5] "We have entered the 'mean season' of corrections in which penal philosophy amounts to little more than devising 'creative' strategies to make offenders suffer."[6]

Neither should we put too much store in the ability of the courts to act as public watchdogs in limiting and punishing prison abuses. To be sure, courts have convicted and punished many individuals for acts of prison brutality, neglect or incompetence. Individual lawyers have devoted their careers to representing victims of mistreatment and have sometimes achieved notable victories. A handful of judges and Department of Justice investigators have forced counties and states to raise standards and fix egregious faults. But legal oversight unsupported by public opinion and government action is an inefficient as well as costly way of checking abuse. It deals with symptoms and not causes. It sometimes punishes particularly gruesome injustices already committed but does little to change the culture that spawned them. It usually focuses on the actions of individuals, and it is not always possible to narrow down abuses to single individuals when the whole system is implicated.

Courts also operate within the prevailing mood of public opinion. Juries all over the country have awarded literally billions of dollars in civil judgments to compensate victims of prison abuse and their families. But it remains extraordinarily difficult to secure criminal convictions in such cases, especially when trials often take place in small, rural communities where so many prisons nowadays are sited. In recent years, juries in Florida, California, Colorado, Virginia and elsewhere have declined to convict corrections officers in high-profile cases in which prisoners suffered grievous injury and in some cases death. Usually, prosecutors in such cases must rely on the testimony of convicted criminals, some of whom may be deeply unsavory characters. By contrast, the defendants present themselves as upstanding members of the community. In such cases, a juror's sympathies are clear.

As for the media, investigative reporters have done commendable work in uncovering prison scandals all around the country. This book builds on some of their efforts as well as on the tireless labors of groups like Human Rights Watch, Amnesty International and the American Civil Liberties Union. But their access to prisons is severely limited. To give one example, in early 2005, the Atlanta-based Southern Center for Human Rights launched a lawsuit alleging abuse of elderly and sick prisoners at the Hamilton Aged and Infirm Correctional Facility in Hamilton, Alabama.[7] The suit alleged that the facility was severely overcrowded, that inmates lacked access to adequate medical help, that the prison was filthy and unhygienic and that some prisoners lay in their own feces for days on end. In response, the Alabama Department of Corrections said health services at Hamilton were well above federally-mandated standards.

When I asked to visit Hamilton, the Alabama Department of Corrections turned down my request. There was no way to verify the various claims involved or to report to the American public on what was actually happening there.

I have written extensively on conditions in so-called "supermax prisons" but I have never been inside one, despite many requests to visit. I can and do correspond with supermax inmates and their families, interview staff and former staff, and examine voluminous legal documents. But I cannot see for myself.

Even when prison authorities permit a journalistic visit behind bars, they decide where the reporter can go and who he can speak to. On my own prison visits, I was accompanied by officials at all times. When I asked to speak to a particular inmate, the official made him or her sign a personal release form. Sometimes, the official allowed me to speak to inmates in semi-private; sometimes not. In any case, inmates have to weigh their words very carefully when they speak to reporters. They know the reporter is only going to be there for a couple of hours. They may be there for many years.

Despite these limitations, prison stories do get written. But that work is swamped by the constant, sensationalist coverage of crimes that floods the airwaves, day in, day out. Crime rates fell dramatically in the 1990s. Crime reporting continued to rise. Crime affects everyone—or can be made to seem as though it does. What goes on in prisons seems distant and removed, as if it is happening in another country, almost on another planet.

Clearly, prisons differ widely. Most states operate a security classification system of up to six categories. Category I or II institutions house inmates convicted of nonviolent crimes as well as those who have shown over time that they are willing and able to follow prison rules and not make trouble. Inmates typically work or take vocational courses during the day and often develop constructive and even friendly relations with correctional officers. These institutions often work fairly well. Corrections officers like working in prisons where inmates have lots to keep them busy. "I want as many programs available as possible. The fewer programs, the more violence and the more recidivism. Prisons are volatile places. If you treat men like men, they generally behave like men. If they are treated like animals, they respond like animals," said Lance Corcoran of the California corrections officers' union. Warden Burl Cain, of Angola State Prison in Louisiana, has four rules for a good prison: "Good food, good medicine, good playing, good praying."

However, in times of massive budget deficits, prison administrators have found it increasingly difficult to justify education or vocational programs for inmates when school spending is being cut in the community. People ask, why spend money on "them" when my children are being deprived? Many states have cut prison programs or eliminated them completely. That reduces prison to the core function of keeping inmates locked up and isolated. Any idea of rehabilitation is lost.

The higher a prison's security classification, the more dangerous and disruptive its inmates and the more violent and repressive the atmosphere will be. The worst prisons are our nation's "superghettos"—places where all the ills and dysfunctions of society are distilled, refined, purified and magnified under one roof. The worst evils that afflict our culture thrive in these prisons—drugs trafficking, prostitution, assault, murder, intimidation, substance abuse, rape, extortion, gambling, bribery, corruption, mental illness and disease.

American prisons have always been tough. In 1842, Charles Dickens visited the Eastern State Penitentiary in Philadelphia, where inmates were held in solitary confinement to contemplate their misdeeds. The Quakers who built the prison believed that extended solitude would make criminals penitent and regretful, hence the word *penitentiary*. Inmates had to wear special masks that prevented them from communicating with one another during rare trips outside their cells. The penitentiary was world famous. A decade before Dickens' visit, the French government sent Alexis de Tocqueville to study it. Sixteen years later, in 1858, 10,000 tourists bought tickets from the warden's office and took a tour.[8] Dickens was shocked and appalled by what he saw. He wrote, "The system here is rigid, strict and hopeless solitary confinement. I believe it, in its effects, to be cruel and wrong...I believe that very few men are capable of estimating the immense amount of torture and agony which this dreadful punishment, prolonged for years, inflicts upon the sufferers."[9]

What would Dickens have thought about today's so-called "supermax" prisons, where inmates are held in solitary for years with little or no human contact? Has anything really changed? Perhaps the biggest difference is that nobody nowadays harbors the illusion that prolonged isolation will make the inmates penitent. It is much more likely to drive them mad.

Prisons have always held a powerful fascination for Americans. One Internet film guide lists 170 productions with prison themes, starting with *The Big House* (1930) and *I Am a Fugitive from a Chain Gang* (1932).[10] Some notable recent entries include *The Shawshank Redemption (1994)* and *The Green Mile (1999)*. Chain gangs are a recurrent theme in many prison films, notably *Cool Hand Luke* (1967), in which Paul Newman plays a rebellious prisoner who keeps escaping from a chain gang. Each time he is recaptured, he suffers severe punishment at the hand of the sadistic warden who tells him, "What we've got here is a failure to communicate."

Chain gangs seemed to be part of the distant past until Sheriff Arpaio and some of his colleagues revived them, albeit in a modified form. However, the idea of prisoners doing hard labor in the fields and breaking their backs on the roads persisted in some Southern states well into the 1970s. Lon Bennett Glenn, a corrections officer who served for more than 30 years in the Texas prison system, recalled how things were run when he was a rookie in 1966: "The inmate workforce was awakened at 3 a.m. for breakfast. The last inmate was served at 5:45 a.m. No inmates were allowed to eat after that time. The field force turned out for work at 7 a.m., winter and summer. In 1966–69, when a taxpaying citizen of Brazoria County, Texas, drove by the Clemens Unit on Highway 36, he didn't have to look hard to see his tax dollars at work. All he had to do was look for the cloud of dust the inmate line force created as it worked."[11]

In those days, Texas prisons were still largely segregated. The field force was divided into a white line, a black line and a Mexican line, and interaction between them was restricted. Desegregation was only fully enforced in the 1980s, just as the Texas prison population was exploding and the federal courts were intervening to force reforms. In this time of flux, with prisoners and wardens uncertain of the new rules, a power vacuum developed that was quickly filled by the growth of violent, race-based prison gangs. Against this background of racial gang warfare, a new kind of ethnic separation arose. Today, anyone entering a Texas prison, or indeed almost any American prison in the higher security classifications, is confronted with a cruel reality. Official segregation has ended. De facto, unofficial segregation is stronger than ever.

Without question, prisons are the most racially segregated as well as the most racist places in America. Prisoners cluster for protection with their own ethnic group and immerse themselves in what they imagine to be their own culture. Whites listen to country music or rock and roll; blacks play rhythm and blues, rap or Motown. Latinos listen to salsa. There is little or no mixing. In this world, the predominant emotions are fear and anger. There is only one virtue—strength. All slights, all insults, real or imagined, must be avenged. Anyone who complains to the authorities is a snitch, and the penalty for snitching is death. To survive, a prisoner unable to physically protect himself must have some skill or asset he can sell for protection or he must become part of a group. Sometimes, what he is forced to sell is his own body.

Racial separation starts the moment a new inmate, or *fish*, enters the prison gates. Former inmate Jimmy Lerner recalled his arrival in a Nevada prison with a group of other new inmates. "The moment we entered the bullpen all the black convicts took seats on one side and Kansas (a prisoner) and his all-white choir claimed the other bench at the bottom of the steel staircase."[12] Sergeant Grafter, a correctional officer, then addressed the group: "You are convicts. Your job here is to lie, cheat, steal, extort, get tattoos, take drugs, sell drugs, shank, sock, fuck and suck each other. Just don't let us catch you. That's our job."

The sergeant also had some blunt health advice for the newcomers. "This prison has a combined HIV and hepatitis C infection rate of 60 percent. If you choose to say yes, and use drugs, and you will—that's your job—then snort them, smoke them, or swallow them, but don't shoot them."

Race permeates every aspect of prison life, and prison authorities take great care to keep ethnic groups apart to avoid bloodshed. In some prisons, they place different groups in separate cell blocks and have them exercise, eat and shower at separate times. Whenever members of rival groups cross paths, there is a danger of violence. However, in 2002, a California judge ruled that the longtime practice of locking down groups of inmates in their cells for extended periods based on their race or ethnicity alone was unconstitutional. A prisoner at the Pelican Bay State Prison had sued the state for locking him in his cell for five weeks, after a riot in which one inmate was killed and 32 were wounded. Aaron Escarala said he had taken no part in the violence and had been punished simply because he was a Latino from southern California.

"Prisoners have a right to live in a prison environment in which they are not discriminated against on the basis of ethnicity," wrote Del Norte County Superior Court Judge Robert Weir. "Racism among inmates flourishes in the prison setting and is far more pronounced in prisons than in society generally. The Court is mindful of the complexity of the matter, the drastic and possible lethal consequences of mistakes."[13]

In February 2005, the Supreme Court ruled five to four that California's policy of assigning inmates to racially segregated cells was unconstitutional unless the state could show it had no race-neutral way to prevent interracial violence. "We reject the notion that separate can ever be equal," Justice Sandra Day O'Connor wrote for the majority. "When government officers are permitted to use race as a proxy for gang membership and violence without demonstrating a compelling government interest and proving that their means are narrowly tailored, society as a whole suffers." [14]

A prison subculture divided by race has also become a world dominated by prison gangs. A new offender entering prison is quickly greeted by race-based groups like the Aryan Brotherhood, the Bloods, the Crips, the Mexican Mafia, Nuestra Familia and the Black Guerilla Family. Some are tightly organized crime syndicates, some are more ideological. All are brutal and ruthless. For many inmates, it is a matter of survival either to join one of these groups or to pay them for protection.

The origins of these gangs are murky. Some began in the inner cities and spread to prisons; some began in prisons and spread to the inner cities. The Mexican Mafia, also known as *La Eme*, is said to have been born in 1956 or 1957 at the Deuel Vocational Institute, a California youth facility. A group of 13 Mexican inmates from the barrios of East Los Angeles formed the gang to protect one another from other inmates.[15] Authorities tried to split gang members up by sending them to different institutions but only succeeded in spreading membership through the entire prison system and from there back to the streets. Over time, enmity developed between these young urban Hispanics and others from northern California, many of whom came from a more rural background. They too began organizing, calling their gang *La Nuestra Familia* (NF). NF members called themselves *Nortenos*, or northerners, and wore red. Eme members were *Surenos*, or southerners, and wore blue. In 1968, open war broke out between the two groups in San Quentin Prison, after some Eme members assaulted two NF members in a disagreement over a pair of shoes. The war has claimed scores of lives and still rages with undiminished ferocity.

Over the years, other Hispanic gangs have emerged. *Neta* mainly consists of Puerto Ricans. The Latin Kings started as a street gang in Chicago in the 1940s and has established a presence in East Coast prisons. The Texas Syndicate began in California's Folsom Prison and has the reputation of being especially violent. It recruits from Latin American countries, including Colombia, Cuba and Mexico. And there are others as well, too numerous to list. In 2002, a federal court sentenced seven members of a gang called the *Barrio Azteca* to 15 years, on top of their existing prison terms, for racketeering. The Department of Justice described the group as an "extremely violent gang operating in the El Paso/Cuidad Juarez area as well as in federal correctional facilities, the state prison system and local jails. Their enterprise included extortion, assault, murder, attempted murder, money laundering and narcotics trafficking."[16]

Among African American gangs, the Black Guerrilla Family (BGF) stands out. It was founded in 1966 at San Quentin Prison by George L. Jackson, a former Black Panther member. The gang proclaimed an overtly political program of eradicating racism, maintaining dignity in prison and fomenting opposition to the U.S. government.[17] It soon degenerated into a violent drugs cartel. Naturally, long-established black street gangs like the Crips and their traditional enemies, the Bloods, also have a major prison presence. Crips usually align with the BGF when they enter prison and continue to wage endless war against Bloods.

The predominant white prison gang, the Aryan Brotherhood (AB), got its start in San Quentin in the mid-1960s. Despite its white supremacist name and the fact that some members sport swastika tattoos and other Nazi symbols, its leaders do not concern themselves overmuch with extremist ideology. They are primarily an organized crime group interested in drugs trafficking, protection rackets, prostitution and extortion both inside and outside prisons. In 2002, the federal government unsealed a 110-page indictment against 40 alleged AB members and associates, including four women and one former prison guard, for 16 murders, 16 attempted murders and numerous other acts of violence. It was the culmination of a six-year investigation by the Bureau of Alcohol, Tobacco and Firearms (ATF). The 110-page Grand Jury indictment provided a valuable insight into the workings not only of the Brotherhood but of other prison gangs as well.[18]

"The Aryan Brotherhood is a powerful gang that controls drug distribution and other illegal activity within portions of the California and federal prison systems and has worked to expand its influence over illegal activity conducted outside of prison," the indictment said. "The Aryan Brotherhood enforces its rules and promotes discipline among its members and associates by murdering, attempting to murder, conspiring to murder, assaulting, and threatening those who violate the enterprise's rules or pose a threat to the enterprise.... Inmates and others who do not follow the orders of the Aryan Brotherhood are subject to being murdered, as is anyone who uses violence against an Aryan Brotherhood member. Inmates who cooperate with law enforcement authorities are also subject to being murdered."

Prospective AB recruits must be sponsored by another member and serve a probation period during which their obedience is tested. Usually they must "blood in" to confirm membership—that is, carry out a hit or significant act of violence. As in other gangs, they must swear an oath of lifelong loyalty. Other white prisoners are forced to pay "taxes" to the Aryan Brotherhood, while gang members released from prison try to muscle white drugs dealers and other criminals to pay protection.

According to the indictment, the AB was run by Barry Byron Mills and Tyler Davis Birmingham, both inmates of the Administrative Maximum Security (ADX) prison in Florence, Colorado, also known as the "Alcatraz of the Rockies," where the Federal Bureau of Prisons sends its most dangerous and notorious criminals. Other ADX inmates include Theodore Kaczynski, the "Unabomber"; Richard Reid, the "Shoe Bomber"; and Terry Nichols, convicted in December 1997 of conspiracy in the Oklahoma City bombing.

Prison gangs are as tightly organized as major corporations. In 1980, members of the Aryan Brotherhood's federal prison faction formed a three-man "Federal Commission." Thirteen years later, the commission created a "council" with authority over day-to-day operations in federal prisons. The gang's California prison branch devised a similar structure. The gang communicates across the prison system using codes and hidden messages as well as a network of AB members and associates. Corrupt prison guards also help operations. The indictment alleged that Joseph Principe, at that time a correctional officer at the Florence ADX, several times arranged for AB leaders to recreate in the prison yard together so they could plan gang activities and make decisions.

The indictment also illustrated exactly how a gang murder goes down. In its stilted legal language, this is how it described the process that led to the 1995 murder of Charles Leger, a gang associate who had incurred the wrath of the leadership.[19] It begins with clause 221 of the indictment.

221) In or about August 1995, defendant DAVID MICHAEL SAHAKIAN sent a note to defendant MICHAEL PATRICK McELHINEY saying that he wanted to have Aryan Brotherhood associate Charles Leger murdered.

222) In or about August 1995, defendant MICHAEL PATRICK McELHINEY selected Gregory Storey to murder Charles Leger.

223) In or about August 1995, defendant MICHAEL PATRICK McELHINEY sent a note to defendant DAVID MICHAEL SAHAKIAN agreeing that Charles Leger should be murdered.

224) In or about August 1995, defendant DAVID MICHAEL SAHAKIAN ordered Gregory Storey to murder Charles Leger.

225) In or about August 1995, defendant DAVID MICHAEL SAHAKIAN provided Gregory Storey with a knife to be used to murder Charles Leger.

226) On or about August 25, 1995, Gregory Storey murdered Charles Leger by stabbing him to death.

227) In or about 1996 and 1997, defendants MICHAEL PATRICK McELHINEY and DAVID MICHAEL SAHAKIAN ordered a number of other inmates to testify falsely that Gregory Storey killed Charles Leger in self-defense.

By mid-2005, half of the defendants—those not charged with capital offenses—had accepted plea bargains. The other 20 were still awaiting trial.[20] In one bizarre episode, jailed New York Mafia kingpin, John Gotti, the "Dapper Don," offered to pay AB members to kill a fellow prisoner, Walter Johnson. Gotti had insulted Johnson when the two crossed paths at the federal prison in Marion, Illinois, on July 17, 1996. The next day, Johnson managed to get Gotti on his own and beat him bloody. Gotti asked the Aryan Brotherhood to have Johnson murdered, and the order went out to all AB members to kill him whenever the opportunity arose. However, AB gang members could never get close enough to kill him. Johnson was transferred a couple of times and released in May 2001. The story has a grisly postscript. Less than a month after he was freed, Johnson shot and killed Marlon Morales, a 32-year-old transit officer who asked to check Johnson's ticket while he was riding the Washington Metro. Johnson was arrested in Philadelphia the next day and sent to a Washington, D.C., jail pending trial. In 2003, a fellow inmate armed with a broken broom handle fashioned into a shank stabbed him at least 40 times.[21] Johnson survived the attack and by 2004 had recovered enough to stand trial. He was convicted on seven charges, including murder, and received life in prison without the possibility of parole.[22] Still, questions remained. No one was arrested for the attack on Johnson while he was in jail. Did AB members finally make the hit? Gotti died of throat cancer in a prison hospital in June 2002, but Johnson's lawyers told the court they believed the contract was still in effect.[23]

Prison gangs have an incredibly complex network of alliances as they conduct their wars, making life even more complicated for correctional officials. The Aryan Brotherhood has a working relationship with the Mexican Mafia and the Dirty White Boys, an Anglo offshoot of the Texas Syndicate. It also uses Nazi Low Riders, a mixed White-Hispanic gang, to do some of its dirty work. The Black Guerrilla Family has an active working relationship with La Nuestra Familia but wages war against the Aryan Brotherhood and the Mexican Mafia. Don Novey, the former head of the California correctional officers' union, said, "An officer going on to their duty site has to deal with the interactions between the Black Guerrilla Family, the Crips, the Mexican Mafia, the Nuestra Familia, the Aryan Brotherhood, the Hell's Angels and the wheeling and dealing among the gang leaders as it applies to drugs and sex."[24]

Law enforcement agencies have expended great efforts to combat gang influence in prisons. In many states, any inmate identified as a hard-core gang member is dispatched to a top security prison and held in administrative segregation. In California, gang activists are sent to Pelican Bay, a prison in a remote corner of the state, 363 miles north of San Francisco. There, they are put in the Special Security Housing Unit (SHU), known as "the Shoe," where they remain isolated in windowless cells and are denied access to prison work programs and group exercise. California officials and corrections officers are convinced that this strategy has reduced violence throughout the system. Lance Corcoran of the correctional officers' association said, "We've been very successful in cutting down inmate-on-inmate violence. If you're identified as a gang member, it's 'bye bye' for you because you are going to do indefinite time in the Shoe."

Statistics only partially back him up. In the mid-1980s, attacks on inmates and staff were claiming over 20 lives a year in California. The year after Pelican Bay was opened in 1989, the number of fatal attacks dropped to 11, and in subsequent years it has never topped 16, even as the prison population has continued to rise. In 2001, there were 13 fatalities: four inmates were stabbed to death, four beaten to death and five strangled. No correctional staff were killed. However, looking at nonfatal attacks, a different pattern emerges. The number of inmate-on-inmate assaults has continued to climb, from 4,982 in 1992 to 11,514 in 2001. Almost two thousand of these nonfatal assaults involved use of a weapon. In 2001, there were also 2,768 inmate assaults on staff, of which 1,092 involved a weapon.[25] One problem is that for every gang leader removed to Pelican Bay, another quickly emerges to take his place. The supply from the streets is unending.

And gang leaders remain dangerous, even in the dark recesses of the Pelican Bay SHU. In 1999, Gerald Rubalcaba, an indicted Nuestra Familia gang leader who was already serving a life sentence at Pelican Bay, ordered the killing of an ex-gang member, Robert "Brown" Viramontes, who had "betrayed" the gang by trying to build a new life free of crime. How did such a closely guarded criminal manage to communicate with his associates? He used the U.S. Postal Service. Viramontes was killed while working in his garden in a San Jose suburb on April 19, 1999. The plot only came to light after the four murderers turned against each other.[26]

Gang leaders can also communicate with their underlings simply by picking up the telephone. A 1999 report by the Justice Department concluded that "a significant number of federal inmates use prison telephones to commit serious crimes while incarcerated—including murder, drug trafficking and fraud."[27] The report found that only 3.5 percent of the tens of thousands of calls made each day from federal prisons were monitored. Many calls were conducted in foreign languages, yet none of the prisons in the study had any staff members fluent in French, Russian, or Chinese. Some did not even have staff that could speak Spanish, even though a large number of inmates were Spanish speakers. In one case, a Baltimore drugs dealer called Anthony Jones was incarcerated at a prison in Allenwood, Pennsylvania, for illegal possession of a firearm. While at Allenwood, Jones found out that a grand jury was investigating his drug activities. He used the prison telephones to order his associates on the outside to murder two witnesses he suspected had testified against him. One was killed and the other shot several times. Jones was convicted of murder and attempted murder in May 1998 and sentenced to life without parole.

The issue of telephones presents a dilemma. There is a strong interest in allowing inmates to maintain as much contact with their families as possible. Studies have shown that a prisoner who stays in touch with his family and remains connected to his community has a much better chance of staying straight after release. However, many prison authorities have chosen instead to use telephones as a way of milking profits from a particularly defenseless section of society—the families of people behind bars. Most states have concluded sweetheart deals with one or two telephone companies, allowing them to charge prisoners outrageous rates in exchange for a share of the take. The prisons win, the big telephone companies win, the inmates and especially their families lose. In many state prison systems, what on the outside would be a 10-cent call costs $9. Inmates are only allowed to make collect calls. In many states the recipient is liable for a surcharge of $2.50 or $3.50 as soon as the connection is made and the conversation costs 36 cents a minute or more. The call automatically terminates after 15 or 20 minutes. For the conversation to continue, the inmate must call collect again, incurring another surcharge.

For the prisons, this has become quite a bonanza. The state of Nevada in 1999 made $20.5 million from inmate calls, Florida made $13.8 million and Georgia made $10 to $12 million.[28] Of course, cost is no barrier for gang leaders who have plenty of money. The burden falls squarely on poor families that can least afford it. For some families, telephone calls to a loved one behind bars can run into thousands of dollars a year.

While some prison chiefs and law enforcement agencies try to combat gang activities, the dirty little secret is that many correctional officials find it more convenient to turn a blind eye. In some prisons, it becomes an unspoken deal. The guards control the perimeter, but gangs run virtually every other aspect of prison life. Wardens and officers allow the gangs to terrorize vulnerable inmates and to go about their illegal businesses so long as peace is maintained. When inmates complain of being beaten or raped by gang members, they are often ignored. Prison chiefs have a particular dislike for so-called "jailhouse lawyers"—inmates who have gained enough knowledge of the legal system to be able to file numerous lawsuits on their own behalf and for others. Prison activists allege that authorities commonly retaliate against such inmates and others whom they view as a nuisance by leaving them at the mercy of gang members or by placing them in situations where they are certain to face physical or sexual abuse.[29]

In some cases, fraternization between gang members and prison staff goes far beyond silent cooperation. Christine Achenbach was executive assistant to the warden of the Florence ADX, essentially fourth in command at the nation's most secure federal prison. In 2002, she and Kellee Kissinger, a manager at the prison, were convicted of having sex with inmates. Achenbach performed oral sex on Ollie Perriman, a convicted cocaine dealer. She allegedly gave him money and illegally brought him out of his cell so that they could spend time together in her office. She also had a steamy relationship with Marvin Linnear, a leader of the Crips gang in the prison. According to court documents, she allegedly tipped gang members off when the authorities were planning drugs shakedowns and told them the location of hidden cameras. Achenbach wrote passionate love letters to Linnear. In one, she wrote, "I cannot sleep. Thoughts of you seem to have consumed my mind, heart and soul."[30] Her activities only came to light when her lovers started fighting over her sexual favors. Achenbach's friend, Kissinger, who herself admitted having affairs with two other prisoners, testified against her colleague in exchange for a sentence of four years' probation and a $2,400 fine. Achenbach was sentenced to five years of probation and four months of home detention.[31]

Former Texas warden Lon Bennett Glenn said sexual liaisons between prisoners and guards were fairly common in his experience but were generally hushed up. Those caught were quietly allowed to leave the state's employ with no further steps taken against them. "On more occasions than I care to count, male employees have been caught giving oral sex to convicts, sometimes several convicts," he said.[32]

Sexual fraternization was just one of several problems at the Florence ADX, where eight inmates were murdered in the first six years after the prison opened in 1995. One, Joey Jesus Estrella, was flung into a cell with two cousins, William and Rudy Sablan. Estrella owed other inmates money and had asked to be placed in segregation for protection, but his request was ignored. Within hours, the word spread through the prison population that Estrella was trying to weasel out of his debts. From that moment, under the prisoners' code, his life became forfeit. He begged a guard to transfer him to another cell away from the cousins. The guard allegedly giggled. Then the two cousins strangled Estrella with a head-phone cord, cut his throat with a plastic razor and sliced him open, removing some of his organs and placing them on the table.[33]

In another case in Florence, an inmate named Frank Melendez, who was suspected of snitching, lay strangled in his cell for four days before guards discovered his body. All that time, prison records showed him reporting for meals, taking showers and exercising in the yard. Officers counted him as present at least 20 times. Finally, his cellmate, Mirssa Araiza-Reyes, told an officer he had killed Melendez and pointed out the body. "I took care of that snitch for you," he boasted.[34] Araiza-Reyes got eight years for voluntary manslaughter.[35]

In 2003, former prison guards at Florence took the stand to testify how they had essentially formed their own gang called "The Cowboys" to dish out punishment to inmates. The jury eventually convicted three of the seven guards and acquitted four others. Three other guards had previously pleaded guilty.[36]

Ron McAndrew, who served as warden at three Florida prisons during a 23-year career in corrections, said all the large prisons in the state were plagued by "goon squads" of officers who terrorized inmates and staff alike. "The horrifying part is there are not enough professionals who are willing to go after the goons," he said. [37]

While a few officers cross the line by brutalizing inmates, others are willing to do them favors in exchange for money. Glenn, the former Texas warden, said his state had never kept official statistics on the number of employees fired or allowed to resign for smuggling money or narcotics to convicts. "But if I had a dime for every one I saw during my career, I could have retired five years earlier…It doesn't take long for weak, criminally-minded employees to figure out they can make much more money smuggling drugs to convicts than by being loyal, by-the-books correctional officers," he said.[38]

If prison staff provide one way for drugs to enter prisons, there are many others. The main ones are through prison visitors and packages mailed to inmates. In California, prisoners have the right to receive one 30-pound package every three months. Staff members search every package but admit that it is easy to miss things. Packages often contain boxes of snack foods stuffed with drugs. One California official told me he had seen heroin rolled into little balls and then hidden at the bottom of a box of Coco Pops cereal. The box was then resealed so that there was no sign it was ever opened. "It's like looking for a needle in a hay-stack," he said. In the federal prison system, some institutions have to go through 3,000 pieces of mail every day and double that amount on Mondays. The sheer volume swamps them.[39]

Former Virginia Corrections Chief Ron Angelone said civilian staff and volunteers working inside prisons also presented a problem. "We've had chaplains, social workers, nurses, librarians who for whatever reason felt they were willing to take the chance and break the law to assist an inmate," he said.

When it comes to visits, the classic method of smuggling drugs is for an inmate's wife or girlfriend to stash them in a small balloon or condom, which she hides in her mouth. At the end of a visit, the stash is transferred mouth-to-mouth during a passionate goodbye kiss. The prisoner swallows the balloon and fishes it out of his stool later. But there are many other methods. Visitors may simply hide drugs in intimate places on their bodies. Family members can usually buy canned drinks from vending machines in the visiting room, and it's easy to hide small packages of drugs inside them. The inmate takes a swig from a can of Coke and swallows the package. Visitors have hidden drugs in babies' diapers. In one case mentioned in the Aryan Brotherhood indictment, a lawyer for one of the gang leaders hid drugs in his shoes. A hollowed out heel can contain a large quantity of heroin. Visitors can arrange to wear the same style and size shoes as an inmate and switch during the visit. Heroin can be ironed into the middle of a file of legal papers. The corners of other pages may be soaked in LSD.

A report by the Inspector General of the Justice Department released in January 2003 found that illegal drugs were present in practically every one of the nation's 102 federal prisons, regardless of security designation. In fact, the higher the security level, the more inmates tested positive in random drugs tests. The report concluded that inmate visitors, staff, and the mail were the three primary ways drugs got in, but staff smuggling was particularly worrisome. "While the number of staff who smuggle drugs into Bureau of Prisons institutions is small, they can do more damage to the safety and security of the institutions than visitors who smuggle drugs. When staff smuggle drugs, the amounts are often larger, they reach more inmates, and more money is involved," the report said. It criticized the Bureau of Prisons for failing to take commonsense steps implemented by most state systems, such as searching staff when they enter, conducting random drugs tests and limiting the amount of personal property workers are allowed to bring onto the premises.[40]

Even with these extra precautions, drugs are still common in state prisons. When a group of female prisoners from Hawaii was sent to Oklahoma in 2001 because of overcrowding at home, they quickly discovered that inmates had access to large quantities of heroin, crack, crystal methamphetamine and marijuana. "There were drug dealers in this prison, a whole bunch of them. They'd have it regularly; they'd get shipments in," one prisoner told the *Honolulu Advertiser*. One former prison staff member, Sid Stell, told the newspaper that inmates openly smoked dope in the prison dormitories. "We did urinalysis on inmates on a regular basis and they were clicking positive, like, most of the time," he said.[41]

Many prisoners enter prison as alcoholics, creating a hot market for home-brewed hooch. "Cell block wine" or "pruno" can be made out of a wide variety of products—fruit, vegetables, cafeteria punch, sugar, flavored gelatin, honey, hard candies, even tomato ketchup—anything with sugar that can ferment into alcohol. In winter, the institutional home brewer stores his product near a water heater to speed up fermentation. California corrections officer Donald Bauman told me he had found 20-gallon trash cans full of pruno during random searches of a prison facility that was devoted to treating inmates for addiction. To put a crimp on illegal alcohol production, some institutions have started giving prisoners artificial sweeteners instead of sugar and stopped putting fresh fruit into boxed lunches served to inmates.

Gambling is common in prisons, especially sports betting. According to criminologists Jeffery Ian Ross and Stephen C. Richards, it may actually be responsible for more institutional violence than drugs or gangs. There is an increased risk of beatings and killings after the World Series, the NBA playoffs and the Super Bowl.[42]

Of course, there are some prisoners who manage to kick their habits in prison. Many do so with the help of religious organizations such as the Prison Fellowship Ministry founded by former Watergate figure Chuck Colson. President George W. Bush has enthusiastically endorsed Colson's belief that offenders do not simply need rehabilitation; they need "regeneration of a sinful heart." For Colson, "Jesus Christ alone has the authority and power to make broken lives new."[43] In 2001, Colson's group mobilized 50,000 volunteers and held an average of 165 in-prison seminars, 5,534 Bible studies and 546 special in-prison programs every month, reaching 150,000 prisoners. Seminars last up to three days and include worship, instructional teaching, small group interaction and lectures on various aspects of prison life. In 1997, as Governor of Texas, Bush allowed Colson to launch an intensive two-year prison program known as the Inner Change Freedom Initiative. The organization took over an entire wing of a state prison to run an around-the-clock curriculum for 200 carefully selected inmates. Participants spent the final 18 months of their sentences attending evangelical prayer meetings, studying the Bible and preparing for release. The program, which has since spread to Kansas and Iowa, continues for six months after release, when volunteers mentor the former inmates and help them with employment and other needs. A University of Pennsylvania study found that two years after their release, over 17 percent of graduates from the Texas program had been rearrested; however, this rate was half of that of regular released prisoners.[44]

Even without that kind of intensity, religion can be a positive force in the lives of prisoners. In Maryland, I took part in a prayer service organized by the Lutheran Community of St. Dymas. In the Jessup medium security prison, I met Stephen Johnson, serving 50 years for killing his own 18-month-old child while under the influence of drugs. "I am more free now in here than I ever was before. I had the American dream—wife, family, job—but I was blinkered," he said. "I can't go home but I can maintain my focus, stay on an even keel and try to be a better person."

James Trut, halfway through a seven-year stretch for drugs trafficking, told me, "I wasn't doing any good in here. There's a lot of drugs and fighting. I was doing heroin. Then I started coming to services about two months ago. I've been clean a month and a half." Bobby McDonald, in the middle of a 30-year sentence for second degree murder, sounded almost ecstatic about his religious conversion. "I came to know the Lord through this experience. I wake up in the morning and refresh myself with the Lord. I start the day with prayer, pray through the day and end the day with prayer. There's lots to be thankful for. I have food and a warm bed, which is more than a lot of people have a few miles away from here in Baltimore," he said.

It was easy to feel the power of the message the Rev. Charles Frederick delivered to the prisoners. "No matter where we have been, there is forgiveness of our sins. Just because you live in this place doesn't mean you do not get forgiveness. Some of you understand that though you are incarcerated, you have also been set free to worship and to feel God's grace," he said.

Former Texas warden Glenn had a more cynical view of religion in prison. "The prison environment is corrupting, especially to those professing to be of strong religious persuasion. Over the past 30 years, I've seen two priests and several lay ministers terminated for smuggling various items to convicts. I've lost count of the number of 'religious volunteers' who have been banned from the prisons for smuggling or being romantically involved with convicts," he said.[45]

Along with mainstream religions, prison systems have been forced by courts to accommodate a variety of other beliefs, including Native American religions, Wicca and other Pagan sects. In 2001, the state of

Wisconsin hired the appropriately named Rev. Jamyi Witch to become the nation's first full-time, salaried, Wiccan state prison chaplain. The appointment of a witch named Witch to minister to prisoners caused some political consternation. Other states routinely allow Wiccan volunteers to conduct services and rites behind bars. Paul Huban, chaplain at the Idaho Correctional Center, said there were 30 Wiccans at that prison, making Wicca the third most popular religion there. In the Nebraska prison system in 1999, there were 1,738 Protestants, 757 Catholics, 96 Muslims, 11 Buddhists, 85 followers of Native American religions, 47 who practiced a form of Norse paganism known as Asatru, eight who worshipped an ancient Egyptian goddess, Maat, and two Wiccans.[46]

Fred Britten, warden of the Tecumseh State Correctional Institution, Nebraska's newest prison, said authorities had set aside an area for outside worship. Showing off the new facility to reporters, he said, "This outdoor worship area is for Native American Sweat Lodge cleansing ceremonies. It's also for prisoners of the Asatru faith who worship Norse gods. Prisoners may have more religious diversity than anyplace else in Nebraska. If it's a recognized religion and there are a small number of inmates that want to practice that, then we're obliged to work with that religious request."[47]

Prison authorities regard some of these religions with well-founded suspicion. Some prisoners join to enjoy the privileges of outdoor meetings and access to sweat lodges. Some join so they can meet in private and plan criminal activity. Some members of Asatru, for example, may be devoted to worshipping the sun and other fairly harmless Teutonic or Norse mythological beliefs. Others have a sinister racist agenda, according to Mark Pitcavage, fact-finding director for the Anti-Defamation League. "This is a very difficult area for prison officials because there are also genuine converts. It's hard to prove that a particular prisoner doesn't really believe in a particular religion. It's clear that a great many prisoners are 'converting' to racist Asatru, which is the chief prison rival to Christian Identity, as a way of getting special privileges," he said.[48]

Christian Identity is a neo-Nazi, anti-black, anti-Semitic group that has been actively sending materials to inmates. With plenty of time on their hands, some prisoners are desperate for reading matter and welcome anything they can get their hands on, including extremist publications that tell them they are not criminals but victims of a nefarious Zionist conspiracy.

Islam is possibly growing even faster than Christianity in prisons. After the September 11 attacks, some politicians started to pay attention to what Muslim prison chaplains were telling their flocks. They did not like what they heard. Many clerics followed a particularly strict form of Islam known as Wahhabism and were openly preaching an extreme anti-American message. New York Senator Charles Schumer said one Wahhabi cleric, Warith Deen Umar, had risen to become Administrative Chaplain of the entire New York Department of Correctional Services.[49]

"A strict believer in Wahhabi Islam, Umar was responsible for the hiring and firing of all chaplains in the New York prison system, exercising complete control over personnel matters. But last year, Mr. Umar was banned from ever again entering a New York State prison after he incited prisoners against America, specifically preaching to inmates that the 9/11 hijackers should be remembered as martyrs," he said.

Schumer said Wahhabi clerics were also active in the U.S. Federal Bureau of Prisons through two organizations linked to terrorism. "These organizations have succeeded in ensuring that militant Wahhabism is the only form of Islam that is preached to the 12,000 Muslims in federal prisons. The imams flood the prisons with anti-American, pro-bin Laden videos, literature and sermon tapes. They destroy literature sent to prisons by more moderate Shia and Sunni organizations and prevent imams that follow these traditions from speaking to prisoners. In addition, non-Wahhabi Muslim prisoners who seek to practice their religion often receive death threats from Wahhabi prisoners who have been instructed by Wahhabi imams," Schumer told a Senate subcommittee in June 2003.

If one prisoner wants to kill another, there are many ways to do it. Perhaps the most publicized recent prison murder happened on August 23, 2003, when John Geoghan, a former priest and convicted child molester, was strangled and stomped to death by fellow inmate Joseph Druce in a Massachusetts prison. Druce, a convicted murderer serving a life sentence and a member of the neo-Nazi Aryan Nation, followed Geoghan into his cell, jammed the electronic door with a book, bound his hands with a T shirt and strangled him with a sock he had been stretching for some time. He then repeatedly jumped on the body and beat the defrocked priest with his fists. There was only one guard on duty at the time, and he could not open the cell door until several other officers arrived to force it open.[50] Child molesters are particularly vulnerable in prison, and it later emerged that guards had been taunting Geoghan, that his food was contaminated and excrement was placed on his bed.[51]

Corrections officers say inmates are infinitely inventive when it comes to making weapons. They construct homemade knives, or shanks, out of plastic cups, milk cartons, earphone jacks and hair brushes. Prisoners can roll up a magazine so tight that it becomes a dangerous weapon. Something as innocuous on the outside as dental floss is lethal behind bars. Anything made of metal or wood—a piece of prison fence, a light fixture, a fragment purloined from the prison kitchen or infirmary—is ideal. Prisoners spend many hours patiently rubbing or scraping such objects against a cement wall or floor until they are sharp. They can rub their weapon in feces and snap it off inside the body of their victim. They can also throw feces or urine or blood at a correctional officer or spit in his coffee when he is not paying attention, and the officer never knows what germs he has been exposed to.

No wonder so many corrections officers succumb to stress. Ted Conover, an investigative reporter who spent a year working as a corrections officer at Sing Sing, memorably said, "What's the first three things you get when you become a CO? A car, a gun, a divorce." Prison guards have the highest rates of divorce, heart disease and drugs and alcohol addiction and the shortest life spans of any New York state civil servants.[52]

According to Lance Corcoran, many officers are ashamed to seek help until it is too late. "Officers don't meet with counselors. There's a lot of macho, even among our female members. We average six suicides a year. Some take comfort in a bottle. Some do drugs. We're in denial. It's not something people want to talk about or face up to. There's burnout, but people are afraid to leave the job and give up the benefits," he said. "The toughest thing is this: when a fireman goes to a fire, he can put out the fire. He sees results. When a police officer makes a bust, he sees a result. Even you, when you write an article you see a result. But in our case, there is no end product. The faces may change but they keep coming and coming and it's the same, day after day after day."

In such a stressful and corrosively racist atmosphere, it is not surprising that some officers also practice racism. In 2000, the state of Washington paid $250,000 to settle a lawsuit by African American prison guards who accused the Department of Corrections of condoning racist behavior at the Callam Bay Corrections Center. According to the Southern Poverty Law Center, the guards said they were denied promotions, threatened and subjected to racial epithets by white colleagues. Some white guards took to calling Martin Luther King Jr. Day "Happy Nigger Day" and bragged about their association with groups like the Ku Klux Klan.[53]

In Florida, 46 black officers complained of being subjected to racial slurs and harassment by colleagues. One officer, Roy Hughes, said that when he entered his commanding officer's office he noticed a "hunting license" on the wall, reading, "OPEN SEASON ON PORCH MONKEYS." Others reported encounters with white officers sporting Klan tattoos. One black officer found his office ransacked and "KKK" daubed on his bulletin board.[54] The state investigated but found no evidence of widespread discrimination.[55]

A far bigger problem is racism directed against prisoners. Many of the new prisons constructed in the 1980s and 1990s are located in remote, overwhelmingly white rural districts. White officers find themselves guarding hundreds of black and Hispanic prisoners from inner cities hundreds of miles away. At least when officers and inmates are members of the same community, they can have a common language. Each knows where the other is coming from. In these new rural prisons there is a total disconnect, aggravated by mutual fear and distrust.

In 1999, around 500 prisoners from Connecticut were sent to Virginia to ease overcrowding in their home state. They were housed at Wallens Ridge State Prison, a Category VI supermax sited in a remote southwestern part of the state near the Kentucky border. According to a report by the Connecticut Commission of Human Rights and Opportunities, they were immediately faced with racial slurs and harassment. Guards routinely used words like "spic," "nigger," "porch monkey" and "boy" when addressing them. Black and Hispanic prisoners were allegedly subject to more cell searches and pat-downs than were whites, and guards fired rubber bullets at them for walking too fast or not walking in a straight line. In one instance, black and Hispanic inmates were ordered to crawl on all fours toward a corrections officer in the recreation yard. One officer asked an inmate, "You ever been shot by a White man, you ever been stunned by a White man?" Another said, "Yo, black boy, you in the wrong place. This is White man's country." The Virginia Department of Corrections denied that racism took place, but the Connecticut report noted that several white inmates had corroborated the allegations.[56]

In August 1999, New Mexico sent 108 prisoners to Wallens Ridge after a prison riot in which an officer was killed. Most were nonviolent offenders who took no part in the riot, but officers at Wallens Ridge were primed for their arrival. Verbal abuse and intimidation started the moment they arrived. Moses Rodriguez recalled guards shouting as he got off the bus, "You fucking Mexicans, you're in the United States now. You're in no place you've ever seen before." The inmates were taken into the cell block one at a time and every one of them was allegedly beaten. "They twisted our arms, they were punching us and kicking us. A lot of people got shot with stun guns," Rodriguez said.

Calvin Jackson was also there that night. "I had to spread my legs as far as the shackles would go. Then one of the guards stood on the chains. They were taunting us, 'How does that feel, waterboy? Guess what, waterboy, you're not going to leave here. We're going to hang you.' At the foot of the stairs, two guards lifted me and I suffered a ruptured rotator cuff. I asked for medical treatment and got nothing," he said. Conditions did not improve over time. The prisoners were held in solitary confinement. "They (guards) would come by the cells and beat on the doors to keep us awake. They would say how they liked to shoot at beer cans, coke cans, Mexicans and Africans," Jackson said.

Guards at Wallens Ridge punished any sign of resistance or disobedience by firing electroshock weapons. Their arsenal included the Ultron II, a handheld device that delivers 50,000 volts of electricity; the Taser, which fires electric darts connected to wires; and the ICE shield that is activated to deliver a powerful electric shock whenever a prisoner touches it. Connecticut prisoners were shocked for offenses such as verbally abusing a guard, kicking a cell door, not coughing loudly enough during a body cavity search or walking too slowly.[57]

Prison activists have complained for years that these weapons, which have never been rigorously tested for safety, represent a lethal threat to prisoners with heart problems and other chronic health conditions. They say guards use them to punish prisoners rather than solely for self-defense.

"In my experience, all too often in American corrections, such weaponry is used as a 'first strike' response, before other less painful and injurious tactics are exhausted or thoughtfully considered," said Steven J. Martin, a former correctional officer and consultant on the use of force to the Department of Justice and several state departments of corrections. [58]

The other favorite punishment at Wallens Ridge was the use of so-called "five-point restraints," which the Virginia Department of Corrections refers to as "humane restraints." The prisoner is bound to a steel bed by straps at his ankles and wrists and another across his chest so that he is totally immobilized. In Wallens Ridge, sometimes the inmates were strapped face down. The standard punishment time in restraints was 48 hours and sometimes even longer. Prison records showed five-point restraints were used against Connecticut prisoners at least 79 times from November 28, 1999, to April 24, 2001. Prisoners were normally only allowed to use the bathroom every eight hours, and many of them soiled themselves and were left lying in their own waste for hours.[59]

According to Judith Stanley, director of accreditation at the National Commission on Correctional Health Care, when a prisoner is restrained for clinical reasons, he must never be held for more than 12 hours, and inmates must be released for at least 10 minutes every two hours to exercise their limbs and prevent the risk of blood clots. A nurse should check on the inmate's condition every 15 minutes. In no circumstances should a prisoner be restrained face down. Wallens Ridge was in violation of all these standards. The NCCHC accredits several state prison systems as meeting its standards for health care, but Virginia is not among them. William Rold, an attorney who has advised several state prison systems on health issues, told me that medical staff who approved the extended use of restraints for periods of more than a few hours were violating their professional ethical standards.

The effects of such prolonged restraint include numbness, stiffness, loss of circulation to the limbs and bruising and cuts to the ankles, wrists and torso. Prisoners tied down for such an extended time may run the risk of nerve damage, blood clots and circulatory damage.

On June 29, 2000, these procedures all went horribly wrong. A 50-year-old prisoner called Lawrence Frazier, who suffered from diabetes, called an officer from his cell and reported that his blood sugar was getting low and he was starting to feel sick. At breakfast, officers noticed he was staggering as he picked up his meal tray. According to the Serious Incident Report filed by the officer on duty, a nurse went to check on Frazier and observed he was having seizures. The report continues: "Officer D. responded with Officers K., M. and Y.[60] Officer D. entered the cell with the officers and maintained control of Frazier who was on his bunk. Restraints were placed on inmate Frazier. Nurse J. attempted to check him. At this point, inmate Frazier was thrashing about in his cell violently. Nurse J. was unable to properly check Frazier and informed Officer D. that inmate Frazier needed to go to the infirmary. Inmate Frazier was then placed on a gurney. He was then escorted directly to the Medical Unit, Treatment Room #1."

In the treatment room, a doctor determined that Frazier's blood sugar was low, and a nurse gave him some glucose. At this point, according to the report, Frazier became "physically and verbally disruptive" and began thrashing about wildly. The doctor ordered him transferred to a cell in the infirmary but told the officer in charge he felt Frazier's behavior, specifically the way he was thrashing around, was "behavioral" rather than caused by his sickness.

The report goes on: "Inmate Frazier became increasingly combative; he thrashed about and repeatedly attempted to get up from the gurney against security staff's direction. Officer H. and Officer F. repeatedly instructed inmate Frazier to calm down and informed him he was being moved into a cell for medical treatment. Inmate Frazier would not respond. He was singing and shouting. He increased his combativeness and thrashing about. At least three times, inmate Frazier attempted to sit up and get off the gurney. Each time, Officer F. warned inmate Frazier to stop. Each time, Frazier disregarded the orders and continued his attempts. Officer F. applied the Ultron II (electric stun gun) each time for 2–3 seconds to Frazier's left side. At this time, inmate Frazier ceased attempting to get off the gurney." After consulting with the officer in charge and the doctor, the decision was made to place Frazier in five-point restraints. Shortly after this, he died.[61]

The Virginia medical examiner's officer concluded that Frazier died of "cardiac arrhythmia due to stress while being restrained following stunning with an Ultron II device." The Virginia Department of Corrections suspended use of the gun "until issues regarding use of the device" were clarified.[62] The Connecticut Department of Corrections settled a lawsuit with Frazier's family for $1.1 million.[63]

4

THE VULNERABLE

"The vilest deeds like poison weeds,
Bloom well in prison-air."
Oscar Wilde[1] ■

O n July 31, 2002, Linda Bruntmyer sat in a room at the U.S. Capitol and told members of the Senate Judiciary Committee what happened to her son, Rodney Hulin.

"When Rodney was sixteen, he and his brother set a dumpster on fire in an alley in our neighborhood. The authorities decided to make an example of Rodney. Even though only about $500 in damage was caused by the fire, they sentenced him to eight years in an adult prison," Bruntmyer said.[2]

On November, 13, 1995, Hulin arrived at the Clemens Unit, a prison in Brazoria County, Texas. Rodney was a small guy, only around five feet two and weighing 125 pounds. He was completely defenseless. Predictably, he was raped within a week. A medical examination found tears in his rectum but the prison authorities denied his pleas not to be returned to the general prison population. He wrote to the prison warden: "I have been sexually and physically assaulted several times by several inmates. I am afraid to go to sleep, to shower, and just about everything else. I am afraid that when I am doing these things, I might die at any minute. Please sir, help me." When Rodney's mother called the warden to find out what was happening to her son, he said Rodney needed to grow up. "This happens every day, learn to deal with it. It's no big deal."

Choking back tears, Bruntmyer finished her story: "On the night of January 26, 1996, my son hanged himself in his cell. He was seventeen and afraid, and ashamed, and hopeless. He laid in a coma for the next four months before he died."

Rodney wrote a suicide note to his family the night he hanged himself and passed it to another inmate, Scott Gibson, who was in an adjoining cell. Gibson was alarmed and called a guard, but the officer refused to read the note. In his letter, Rodney wrote: "I have found forgiveness for those who have hurt me in my life, which has been a very short one, only 17 years. Since I was placed in prison, 7/31/95, I have found myself to be more mentally and emotionally destroyed than I have ever been. I'm very sorry to end my life this way. But if I don't do this, someone will. I'm saying I'd rather die of my own free will than be killed. I love you Mom and Dad."[3] The state of Texas settled a civil suit brought by Hulin's parents out of court, paying the family a "substantial settlement."[4]

If the kind of abuse Rodney Hulin suffered was an isolated incident, it would be shocking enough. Tragically, studies suggest that it happens to thousands of men every single day in U.S. prisons and jails across the country, hundreds of thousands of times a year. Women are also raped in large numbers in U.S. prisons, usually by corrections officers. Their plight is discussed in a later chapter.

Nobody knows how many men are raped in prison. Before 2005, the government had never collected statistics.[5] Most victims feel too embarrassed and humiliated even to tell friends and loved ones and too terrified to tell prison authorities. "They are deeply ashamed and believe that somehow it was their fault and that they are no longer men. Quite often, victims turn to drugs and alcohol. Many say they feel numb, like they are apart from the world. Others act out their own sexual victimization on other people, or they may just shut down sexually. They honestly believe they have a sign on their forehead saying, 'I am a victim; use me, abuse me,'" said therapist Steven Braveman of Monterey, California, who has treated several prison rape victims.

Under the macho rules that govern prison life, sexual predators consider it perfectly manly to rape a fellow inmate as long as they are the ones doing the penetrating or receiving oral gratification. Convicts call such men "pitchers" or "topdogs" or "booty bandits"; their victims are called "catchers," "punks," and "June bugs." And prison rape is usually not a one-time event as it often is on the outside—it repeats itself day and night, sometimes for years.

Congressman Frank Wolf, a Virginia Republican who has spoken out about the problem, said rape victims suffer deep torment. "Severe psychosis is the most common outcome of prisoner rape. Sexual assault can often break a prisoner's spirit. In the advanced stages of rape trauma syndrome, a survivor's mood often swings between deep depression and rage. Prisoner rape may be the quickest, most cost-effective way of producing a sociopath."[6]

Apart from the shame, there is an even more compelling reason that most victims do not report rape. Under the prison "code of silence," any prisoner fingered as a "snitch" can measure his life expectancy in hours rather than days. Rapists often warn their victims to keep their mouths shut if they want to live. It is no surprise, therefore, that the number of officially reported incidents is laughably low. When victims do report the abuse, the authorities often ignore their complaints or tell them to shape up and "act like a man." Victims have no recourse to the courts until they have exhausted the prison's administrative complaints procedures—a process that usually takes months, during which they may be raped again and again.

In 2003, landmark bipartisan congressional legislation passed both houses of Congress unanimously and was signed by President Bush. The Prison Rape Elimination Act, backed by an unusual left-right coalition, required the U.S. Department of Justice to collect statistics and conduct research on the extent and harmful effects of prison rape and to establish a confidential reporting system for victims. It provided $60 million a year for an annual Justice Department survey of 10 percent of the nation's 8,700 correctional institutions. States and prisons that continue to have high assault rates could lose federal funding if problems persist. Prison activists hailed the legislation as a major step forward.[7] Still, it faced considerable obstacles in implementation. The act created the National Prison Rape Commission and nine commissioners were appointed after a delay of several months. But there were problems finding an executive director for the commission. The commission emphasized corrections qualifications in its job description and only advertised the opening for two weeks. Once hired, the first executive director then faced a three-month delay in receiving a Department of Justice security clearance. Then, citing personal reasons, he resigned before any progress was made. By the middle of 2005, there was still no replacement. Two public hearings were scheduled and then canceled at the last minute but hearings finally did take place in Washington DC and San Francisco in the summer of 2005 and the commission heard many moving stories from rape victims as well as other testimony.[8]

Plans for the statistical study, which was a crucial part of the act, also moved slowly. In a briefing paper published at the end of June 2004, the Bureau of Justice outlined some of the problems inherent in collecting reliable statistics on such a sensitive subject.[9]

There was the need to ensure respondent confidentiality and ease inmates' fears of reprisals. The data collectors also had to overcome a general reluctance to report past incidents. On the other side of the fence, prison wardens and officers had concerns about their legal liability and the reliability of self-reporting. The Arizona prison guards union ran an article in its newsletter warning its members they might find themselves convicted for not preventing sexual assaults that were impossible to prevent.[10]

At one BJS workshop, some corrections officials pressed for the inclusion of new survey questions asking inmates whether they had ever made false reports about sexual abuse. They eventually withdrew their suggestion.[11] To address concerns about accuracy and confidentiality, the BJS developed a new computer-assisted method of collecting data, under which inmates would respond to questions delivered via earphones using a touch screen. The first nationwide survey was expected to begin in Summer 2006. In July 2005, the BJS issued a preliminary report on sexual violence officially reported to prison and jail authorities the previous year cataloging 8,210 incidents. The Bureau said that figure probably represented the tip of the iceberg.

Scientific studies that had been conducted before the major BJS study had suggested that prison rape in the United States is a devastating human rights abuse of massive proportions. One of the most comprehensive studies surveyed male inmates in seven Midwestern male prisons in the 1990s. It found that 21 percent of inmates reported they had been pressured to have sex against their will and one in ten had been raped. Two-thirds of the victims had been violated repeatedly, some more than 100 times in a year.[12]

Stephen Donaldson, who was gang raped in a Washington, D.C., prison in 1973 and later became president of Stop Prisoner Rape Incorporated, analyzed all the available surveys and studies in 1995. He estimated that around 530,000 male inmates of prisons and jails were sexually harassed each year and 242,000 were raped.[13] Donaldson contracted AIDS as a result of his experience and died in 1996 at age 49.

According to Robert Dumond, a mental health counselor who extensively researched the issue, prison rape is a major public health problem. "The mental health consequences are catastrophic. Male and female victims often experience Post Traumatic Stress Disorder, anxiety, depression and exacerbating of preexisting psychiatric disorders, and most victims are at risk of committing suicide as a means of avoiding the ongoing trauma.... The public health consequences are equally overwhelming. In addition to the devastating physical consequences of the assaults themselves, victims may contract HIV/AIDS, other sexually transmitted diseases and other communicable diseases such as tuberculosis and hepatitis B and C, which are rampant in U.S. correctional institutions."[14]

Despite mountains of scientific and anecdotal evidence, many correctional authorities still deny that the problem exists and insist that most sex behind bars is consensual. "I don't think we get a lot of complaints. No matter what we do to stop sexual activity in prison, it does occur because you have a community of consenting adults. They can clearly decide for themselves what is appropriate and what is right," said Larry Traylor, a spokesman for the Virginia Department of Corrections.

Human Rights Watch wrote to state prison authorities in 1997 asking about the extent of the problem. Most states said there was no problem. New Mexico said it had "no recorded incidents over the past few years." Colorado, Kansas, Kentucky, Missouri, Pennsylvania, New Jersey, Oregon, South Dakota and Wisconsin all said they had fewer than ten reported cases a year.[15] Texas investigated 123 cases in 1997 and 103 in 1998.[16]

Then there was the considerable problem of inmates being raped by guards. The case of Garrett Cunningham was fairly typical. This is his story, in his own words, as related to the Commission on Safety and Abuse in America's Prisons.[17]

"In 2000, I was housed at the Luther Unit in Navasota, Texas. While at the Luther Unit, I worked in the prison's laundry under the supervision of corrections officer Michael Chaney. After just a few weeks of working with Officer Chaney, he began to touch me in a sexual manner during pat searches. At first, I thought it was an accident, but as it continued every day I soon realized his inappropriate touching was intentional. He also stared at me when I showered and made sexual comments. I was afraid to tell anyone about my problems with Officer Chaney, but in March 2000, I finally went to the unit's psychologist and told him about the touching and crude comments. He asked me if I thought it was an accident and I told him that it could not be because it happened all the time. He advised me to stay away from Officer Chaney."

"The prison psychologist's advice did nothing to prevent the continuing sexual harassment, so a month later I decided to go to the prison's administration for help. I approached the assistant warden and his second-in-command officer and told them about Chaney's sexual comments and sexual touching during pat searches. They told me that I was exaggerating and that Chaney was just doing his job. I eventually confronted Chaney and told him to stop touching me. He only got angry and continued to harass me. I tried again to get help from prison administrators but I was told to keep my mouth shut."

"Officer Chaney eventually raped me in September 2000. On that day, I had just finished my job at the prison's laundry and began walking to the back of the room in order to take a shower. Suddenly, Chaney shoved me, knocking me off balance. I screamed and struggled to get him off me, but he was too big. Officer Chaney weighed about 300 pounds. I am 5 feet 6 inches tall and weigh 145 pounds. While I struggled, Chaney handcuffed both my hands. He then pulled down my boxers and forcefully penetrated me. When I screamed from the terrible pain, Chaney told me to shut up. I tried to get away, but I could barely move under his weight. After it was over, I was dazed. He took me to the showers in handcuffs, turned on the water and put me under it. I was crying under the shower and I saw blood running down my legs."

"When he took the handcuffs off me, he threatened me. He said if I ever reported him he would have other officers write false assault cases against me and I would be forced to serve my entire sentence, or be shipped to a rougher unit where I would be raped all the time by prison gang members. He also warned me not to say anything to the officials I had complained to before, because they were his friends and they would always help him out."

"I wrote the Internal Affairs Department two times about Chaney's inappropriate touching. They never addressed my concerns and failed to take precautions to protect me. I was too scared to file a written complaint against Chaney because I feared retaliation from prison officials. Instead, I requested a private meeting with an Internal Affairs investigator. I received no response to my request and Chaney was never punished for assaulting me."

"Officer Chaney went on to sexually harass and assault other prisoners. One year later, Nathan Essary began working under Chaney's supervision in the same laundry where I had previously been assigned. On several occasions, Nathan was forced to perform sex acts on Chaney. Fortunately for Nathan, he was able to collect Chaney's semen during two of the attacks and DNA testing positively linked the samples to Chaney. Chaney finally resigned from the Luther Unit in January 2002 when he was indicted for his crimes against Nathan Essary. Last month, he pleaded guilty to sexual contact with an incarcerated person. He will serve no time in prison."

A shocking April 2005 report from the Department of Justice inspector general[18] quoted Kathleen Hawk Sawyer, a former director of the Federal Bureau of Prisons, as saying that although only a small percentage of staff members committed sexual assaults against inmates, sexual abuse of prisoners was "the biggest problem she faced as Director." The report said guards usually took advantage of vulnerable or psychologically weak inmates, including those who had previously been sexually abused or who had mental health issues. But the crime of sexually abusing an inmate of a federal prison was only a misdemeanor punishable by a maximum of one year in prison, and many federal prosecutors were not interested in prosecuting such cases at all, the report said. Worse, laws covering sexual abuse of inmates did not apply in facilities run by outside contractors, such as private prison corporations. In those institutions, staff could molest inmates with no fear of punishment.

Even when prosecuted, the punishments for sexual abuse of inmates were "not significant," the report said. Most offenders received probation. "Prison staff who sexually abuse inmates often do not believe they will be caught, and if they are caught do not believe they will be punished. Moreover, staff can generally conceal their sexual abuse because they are familiar with the prison and its operations, they control the prison environment and they can arrange discreet encounters with inmates," the report said.

Many prison guards deny that rape is a problem. Brian Dawe, a former corrections officer in Massachusetts, said the problem was blown out of proportion by the media. "There are enough willing participants in prison. There are a lot of homosexuals and bisexuals, and even heterosexual inmates don't generally regard it as homosexuality when it's in prison," he said.

Many men decide not to fight their abusers; they know they are going to be raped anyway. The only question is whether they are going to be beaten to a pulp first. Some may find a prison "daddy" and live as his "wife," making his bed, doing other domestic chores in the cell and providing sexual services in exchange for protection. "That still makes it rape," said psychiatrist Terry Kupers. "It may appear to be sex between consenting adults but many men only 'consent' to being penetrated out of fear that refusal will lead to more beatings and rape," he said.

To the extent that the issue is publicly discussed, it is often the subject of jokes, like the one about not picking up the soap in the prison shower. In 2002, a soft drinks company ran a TV ad for 7-Up in which a company spokesman was seen handing out cans of soda to prisoners. When he accidentally drops a can, he jokes that there is no way he is going to bend down to pick it up. Later in the ad, a cell door slams, trapping the spokesman on a bed with another man who has his arm around him. The company pulled the ad after a month in the face of protests.[19]

According to Dumond, certain categories of male prisoners are especially vulnerable. They include the young and inexperienced; the physically weak and small; inmates suffering from mental illness; inmates who are not affiliated with gangs; inmates who have violated the code of silence; and homosexuals or transsexuals.

Roderick Johnson, a nonviolent drugs offender who is gay, fell into the last category. In a legal complaint against the Texas Department of Criminal Justice filed in early 2002, Johnson alleged that he was turned into a sex slave at the Allred Unit prison in Iowa Park, Texas. "Gang members routinely bought and sold Mr. Johnson as a chattel, raped and degraded him on a virtually daily basis, and threatened him with death if he resisted. Prison officials at Allred were well aware of his plight, but refused to conduct any meaningful investigation of his complaint and refused his repeated pleas to be housed in safekeeping. They made clear by word and deeds that they took sadistic pleasure in his victimization," the complaint alleged.[20]

Prison gangs gave Johnson the name "Coco" and referred to him as "she." First, he was "owned" by a member of the Gangster Disciples, who sold his services to other inmates and shared him with fellow gang members; later he was "sold" to the Bloods. His abusers forced him to have oral sex with them, to gratify them manually and to submit to anal intercourse. Four times, Johnson went before prison authorities for "life endangerment hearings." Prison officers refused to move him into segregation or transfer him to another prison. They told him to fight, or find himself a boyfriend who could fight for him.

At a deposition on December 5, 2002, Johnson faced questioning from Deven Desai, a lawyer representing the Texas Attorney General. He explained how he became the property of another inmate, a member of the Gangster Disciples gang.

Q: How soon after you got there did all this stuff start?

A: It started within days of me being there. Any time a homosexual come into any wing, it's going to be like, you know, throwing a steak in there with a bunch of wild dogs. All of them are going to try and attack that same steak at the same time. What happened was he basically was in a bidding war with other inmates that was on that section as to who I was going to be with while I was over on that section.

Q: Okay. And how do you know he was in a bidding war with these other inmates?

A: Common sense. Everybody's like: She's going to be with me. I'll have her. This is going to be mine. In prison, like I was saying, the gangs control the living space. You actually control the security of this facility, but the prisoners themselves have their own law and code of conduct.

Johnson later explained how he got his prison name, Coco: "If you are homosexual, you are considered a female among these men and you will take on the name of a female. You do not have a right to have your own name used. Because like I said...if I have the name Roderick in prison, I'm considered a man because I use a man's name. If I have the name Coco, I'm considered female because that's a female name. And if you're considered female in the general population, then you are considered someone that's available for sexual exploitation because you don't make any rules."

Q: Were the other inmates who raped you also in the Gangster Disciple gang?

A: No, sir. Most of them were Crips. Some of them were Bloods, Mandingo Warriors.

Q: Okay. And when you say "own" you, the Gangster Disciple gang was the first to officially own you, how did they own you?

A: Own you means that they speak for you. When it's considered speaking for you, that means that if you and I have a problem, you don't talk to me. You don't come to me with that problem. You need to go to S^{21} and you need to address whatever problem that you're having with me or whatever business you feel like you want to have with me, you need to address him. And then he'll take care of the business between me and him or whatever business it would be between me and you.

Q: So do you know who the leader of the Disciples was?

A: They call him Gangster and he was on 7 Building.

Q: Now the other inmates that raped you, did they rape you in their cell, your cell?

A: Most of that took place in the showers and stairwells. And on certain occasions, I was told to go in the cells. But that had to be approved through S first.

Desai asked Johnson about his allegations of how prison officers treated his complaints:

Q: At this hearing, you say that Officer B laughed at you and told you to remove the makeup and L told you: "If you want to be a ho, you'll be treated like a ho."
A: Yes, sir.
Q: And to get a man, right?
A: Yes, sir.
Q: And then B said: "Preferably a black one since it's the Bloods you're having problems with."
A: Yes, sir.
Q: And R said: "You ain't nothing but a dirty tramp and learn to fight."
A: Fight or accept the fucking, yes, sir.

In recent years, in response to legal orders to clean up their act, Texas corrections officers have undergone training on how to recognize and deal with sexual abuse among the prison population. How useful has it been? Judge from this exchange later in the legal discovery proceedings, when Johnson's lawyer, Margaret Winter, questioned Richard Wathen, assistant warden at the Allred Unit.

Q: Have you ever been instructed that sexual harassment is a part of a continuum of sexually assaulting behavior?
A: No ma'am.
Q: Are you aware that sexual predators attempt to wear down a target's defenses through continued verbal harassment?
A: No ma'am.
Q: Have you received any training on the subject of offender on offender sexual victimization?
A: Yes ma'am.
Q: When did you receive that training?
A: I can't give you specific dates.
Q: Has it been within the last two years?
A: Yes ma'am.

Q: Has it been within the last year?

A: Yes ma'am.

Q: Has it been within the last six months?

A: Yes ma'am.

Q: And was there a specific part of that training that related to offender on offender sexual victimization?

A: Yes ma'am.

Q: There were materials that were delivered to you on that subject?

A: Yes ma'am.

Q: You studied the materials?

A: Yes ma'am.

Q: Do you remember what those materials were called or what it looked like?

A: No ma'am.

The key to protecting prisoners who are experiencing abuse is to take their complaints seriously and get them away from their abusers. However, 80 to 85 percent of requests by prisoners for protective transfers in Texas are denied, according to prison logs quoted by the ACLU.[22] The issue of Johnson's request for a transfer came up later in the Richard Wathen deposition.

Q: Is there any circumstance you can think of in which you wouldn't grant safekeeping to an inmate who says, "I'm being threatened and I'll be hurt unless I engage in sex?" Why wouldn't you grant safekeeping? Can you think of a reason why you would not?

A: Yes. His claims were not verified.

Q: What does verified mean?

A: Proven.

Q: But what does proven mean? What level of proof do you need?

A: Until I'm convinced.

Q: Do you agree that an inmate's own account of his sexual victimization should be given credence unless there's good reason to the contrary?

A: No. Not necessarily.

If the victim is a homosexual, he may face deeply entrenched prejudice and homophobia. How are we to interpret this exchange between Deven Desai, representing the state of Texas, and Roderick Johnson?

Q: How do you as a Christian man balance your homosexuality with your Christianity?"

A: From my personal opinion, I really don't feel that I'm any different from anyone else that serves God, you know…I mean, everybody has their own ways. Even yourself, you have something that you do wrong that God wouldn't approve of. So I feel like that I'm just as equal as you. I still have the same chance. As long as I do what's right by others, try to respect and honor others and do things that's favorable in God, I don't think that there is an imbalance.

On December 19, 2003, Johnson was released to a halfway house in Austin. When I spoke to him a few days later, Johnson was exhibiting classic signs of Post Traumatic Stress Disorder, suffering from nightmares, flashbacks and bouts of depression and anxiety. He was taking medication and attending counseling. Meanwhile, the state of Texas succeeded in tying up his lawsuit with procedural motions for almost two years. The state argued that Johnson had failed to pursue all the internal remedies open to him and that top prison officials had no way of knowing he was being raped and therefore were not responsible. In September 2004, the Fifth Circuit Court of Appeals ruled unanimously against the state and in favor of Johnson, allowing his civil suit to go forward.[23]

Rape in Texas prisons was a central issue in *Ruiz* v. *Estelle*, one of the most famous penal cases ever to be heard in the United States, which went on for 30 years and only finally ended in June, 2002. It began in 1972 when David Ruiz, an inmate serving life imprisonment for armed robbery, filed a handwritten federal suit claiming that Texas prison conditions violated the Eighth Amendment of the U.S. Constitution against "cruel and unusual punishment." After a trial lasting almost six months, Justice William Wayne Justice agreed and placed the whole prison system under the control of his court. Justice wrote in his 1981 judgment, "It is impossible for a written opinion to convey the pernicious conditions and the pain and degradation which ordinary inmates suffer within the Texas Department of Corrections walls—the gruesome experiences of youthful first offenders forcibly raped; the cruel and justifiable fears of inmates, wondering when they will be called upon to defend the next violent assault…."[24]

In 1999, Justice held another trial to rule on the state's request to end his court's supervision of the prison system. He found some improvements but said there was still shocking abuse. With regard to rape, he wrote, "The evidence before this court revealed a prison underworld in which rapes, beatings and servitude are the currency of power. Inmates who refuse to join race-based gangs may be physically or sexually assaulted.... Many inmates credibly testified to the existence of violence, rape and extortion in the prison system and about their own suffering from such abysmal conditions."[25]

Rape is also a serious problem in U.S. jails, where the population is more transient. New people are constantly being checked in and processed, and inmates are often in motion, on their way to and from court hearings or moving in groups for showers, exercise or work. Guards cannot be watching all of them all the time, but sexual predators are constantly on the lookout for "fresh meat." Robert, a young man who found himself in jail in Nevada, was an example.

"I was arrested for possession of marijuana and taken to Clark County Detention Center in Las Vegas. I had been there for eight days when I was rushed in the shower. Two men held me down and the third raped me. The whole thing took five minutes and I've been carrying it around with me ever since," he said. Robert did not want his full name used.

"I told a guard about it. He was sympathetic but he told me, 'Those guys are going to prison and you're going to the same hole they are. If you complain, you'll be marked as a snitch.'"

Jails can be overcrowded, chaotic places, and defenseless inmates can easily find themselves sharing a cell with violent sexual predators. That's what allegedly happened in June 2003 to a University of Florida student sentenced to 72 hours in jail on a marijuana charge. The 19-year-old was placed in a seven by eight-foot cell with a man awaiting trial for sexual battery. Shortly after midnight when all was quiet, the man held a ballpoint pen to the student's throat and raped him. The victim did not directly report the attack, but his family members became concerned when he hinted that something had happened in a phone call the next morning. "It's truly a shame that this had to happen to someone who had no expectation other than spending 72 hours in the county jail," said Major Robert Chapman, the director of the jail in Alachua County.[26]

If rape merely went on with prison authorities standing by passively, that would be outrageous enough. But there is substantial evidence that many corrections officers turn a blind eye. Some in authority use rape or the threat of rape as a management tool in running their institutions. They believe that allowing some of the most violent prisoners to have their way with weaker inmates stops them from making trouble. "It keeps the really mean prisoners quiet. The nonviolent ones are the ones who get raped and sold as sex slaves," said Jeanette West, whose 19-year-old son was raped in prison in Illinois. Rape can also be used to punish troublemakers or pay back prisoners who have threatened a guard. Many prison rapists have nothing to lose from their action. Their sentences are already so long that any further punishments are meaningless to them.

"Prison rape to a large degree is made more serious by the deliberate indifference of most prison officials. Oftentimes these officials will purposefully turn their backs on unspeakable acts in order to maintain 'peace,'" said Jack Cowley, a retired Oklahoma prison warden. "Thus managing a 1,000-man prison designed for 500 becomes much easier. Survival of both staff and inmates is best insured."[27]

Rape has become such an integral part of prison life that it is hard to suggest ways of dealing with it without a wholesale cultural change within the system. Until corrections officers, prison wardens, legislators and the public start caring about what happens behind bars, not much is going to change. Short of that, there are some measures that might help. Keeping accurate statistics, as mandated in the congressional legislation passed in 2003, might help draw some public attention to the extent of the problem. Identifying potentially vulnerable inmates as they enter the system and making sure they are not housed alongside violent predators would certainly help. Taking their complaints seriously and addressing them swiftly would also be a step forward. Above all, indicting and punishing corrections authorities who allow rape to flourish would send a strong signal. But that is easier said than done. Even when the judicial authorities pursue cases, it can be extremely difficult to gain judgments against corrections officers, no matter how strong the evidence. If the abuse happens in one of America's many rural prisons, the trial is likely to take place in the local community where the prison is a major employer and guards are neighbors and friends.

Take the case of Wayne Robertson, a brawny muscle-bound convict who served time in Corcoran State Prison, in California's Central Valley, where he was known as the "Booty Bandit" for his propensity for raping cellmates—at least a dozen. Robertson had a specific role in prison society—he specialized in bringing cocky young street toughs down to size.[28] Enter Eddie Dillard, a skinny little man of 130 pounds, who had assaulted a female correctional officer at another prison. In March 1993, guards shoved Dillard into Robertson's cell to "teach him how to do his time." Dillard begged officers not to put him in a cell with Robertson, but his pleas were ignored. He was locked in for three days before the cell door opened and he was able to escape. Robertson admitted to a grand jury that he had repeatedly sodomized Dillard by force and threatened to kill him if he put up a fight. But he said to call it rape didn't seem fair. "Rape is a vile act," he insisted.[29]

In 1999, four Corcoran corrections officers came to trial in King County Superior Court, only 20 miles from the prison, charged with aiding and abetting the rape. From the start, prosecutors faced an uphill task. They could not find officers willing to testify about Robertson's fearsome reputation, and the case was made even more difficult when the judge dismissed six of the seven charges, saying a four-year statute of limitation had expired. On the seventh, she ruled that the prosecution would have to prove the four officers knew for a fact that Dillard was going to be raped, not just that it was probable. The prison officers' union paid the guards' legal expenses and then launched a TV and radio advertising campaign in the highly conservative county. The ads showed images of tattooed convicts looking menacing and evil and harried guards walking "the toughest beat in the state." During jury selection, 500 residents were called for service; more than a third said they either worked at a local prison or had a relative who did. The defense managed to dismiss every prospective black juror, leaving a white and Hispanic panel to judge the white officers.

On November 8, 1999, the jury rendered its verdict. All four officers were acquitted.[30]

5

THE SANITY
OF THE SYSTEM

*"Madness is rare in individuals—
but in groups, parties, nations and ages it is the rule."*
Friedrich Nietzsche[1] ■

D eer Lodge, Montana, according to the local Chamber of Commerce, is "where the real west lives." Among its attractions are scenic drives, snowy peaks, crystal clear mountain lakes and Old Montana Prison Museum, site of the first lockup in the Montana Territory. Built in the 1880s, the prison now welcomes visitors. "Through guided and self-guided tours you can experience how many of Montana's famous outlaws did time. Hear and read about the prison riots that took place in 1908 and 1959. See 'Turkey Pete's' cell, just as it was when he died."[2]

Turkey Pete was a convict whose real name was Paul Eitner. Convicted of murder and sentenced to life in 1918, Eitner spent 49 years in Cell No. 1. He earned his nickname after he was put in charge of the prison turkey flock. Whether or not he was mentally ill at the start of his sentence, there is no doubt that as the years passed, Eitner completely lost touch with reality and started to believe he was running the prison. Guards and fellow inmates alike humored him and went along with his fantasy life, even after Eitner decided to "buy" the prison and run it from his cell. Inmates were allowed to print "Eitner checks" in the prison print shop, and Eitner used the currency to "pay" all prison expenses, including the guards' salaries. He finally died in 1967, aged 89.[3]

Deer Lodge is still a prison community. The present-day Montana State Prison (MSP)—home to some 1,300 offenders, including six who have been sentenced to death—is a short, three-mile drive out of town. In 1999, a new prisoner arrived. His name was Mark Edward Walker. The treatment he received was a lot less benign than that accorded to Turkey Pete.

Mark Walker has had a lot to contend with in life. He is hypoglycemic, which means he suffers from low blood sugar, which can lead to exhaustion, temper outbursts, irritability, difficulty sleeping, depression and other symptoms. Walker is legally blind and has no peripheral vision. He also has nystagmus, a condition that causes both of his eyes to twitch constantly and forces him to turn his head to the side when speaking to other people. He thinks and speaks so fast that others often have difficulty following him. Additionally, Walker has been diagnosed with bipolar disorder, or manic depression.

In December 1994, Walker was charged with felony forgery, arson and two counts of criminal mischief. He had set fire to a tarpaulin covering a motorcycle in his parent's garage and also admitted forging his brother's signature on several checks.[4] Walker received a suspended five-year sentence but violated the terms of his probation. When the state ordered him imprisoned, Walker absconded to Colorado, where he was arrested in December 1997. In prison in Colorado, he was diagnosed as mentally ill and put on a drug regimen, which included Lithium, a medicine often used to treat bipolar disorder. Staff in the Colorado prison reported that Walker generally behaved well and he did not receive any major disciplinary write-ups. Doctors there succeeded in managing his various ailments. On November 6, 1998, Walker was ordered to be sent back to the Montana State Prison. What happened next was described by Justice James C. Nelson, a member of the Supreme Court of Montana, in a judgment issued on April 29, 2002.[5]

"On February 5, 1999, Walker's first day at MSP, the intake officer described him as quiet, timid and cooperative. On February 10, 1999, Walker notified MSP staff psychiatrist, Dr. David Schaefer, that he was experiencing stomach pains due to the Lithium. He requested that a snack be provided to accompany his medication and alleviate the nausea associated with taking his Lithium. Shortly after these requests, Walker stopped taking his Lithium. Thereafter, his behavior showed a progressive decline," Justice Nelson wrote. "For the next six months, Walker averaged eleven severe disciplinary infractions a month. According to various correctional officers, Walker had transformed from a timid and quiet inmate into an excited, belligerent, hostile, disruptive and suicidal inmate."

He screamed all night long and pounded continuously on the metal sink in his cell. A corrections officer notified the prison medical staff of his behavior three or four times, but no one did anything. In the meantime, Walker was spitting on officers; covering his cell walls with ketchup, mustard and mayonnaise; throwing his food tray out of his food slot and onto the floor; covering his cell window to prevent officers from seeing in; and purposely flooding his cell.

Justice Nelson wrote, "Walker's behavior culminated in three suicide attempts. On October 7, 1999, Walker was evaluated by medical staff for swallowing a staple. The psychiatrist noted in his report following that incident that Walker was at chronic risk for self-harm. On October 8, 1999, Walker tried to hang himself with a sheet. And, on October 12, 1999, he tried to hang himself with his prison overalls. Both the guards and the inmates quickly tired of Walker's behavior. Hence, Walker was put on a series of Behavior Management Plans (BMPs)."

A BMP is a prison disciplinary tool based on a carrot-and-stick principle. If an inmate's behavior improves, his conditions are lightened. However, if he will not or cannot behave, they get worse and worse until he is condemned to the nearest thing to hell the prison system can devise. Walker was placed in a bare, windowless cell. It contained a cement bed, a cement table, a stainless steel sink, a stainless steel toilet and a stainless steel plate that served as a mirror. There was a single light fixture in the ceiling, but the guards controlled the lighting. The light remained on 12 to 16 hours a day. He got no recreation time out of his cell.

There was no hot food. He was fed exclusively on individually wrapped slices of meat or cheese with bread. At meal times, the guards would order Walker to the back of his cell and tell him to face the wall. They would then place the food on a slot in the door. Sometimes officers would unwrap the food before placing it on the slot. Toilet cleaning tools and other cleaning supplies were passed through this same slot. Walker refused to eat the unwrapped food that passed through the filthy slot.

Justice Nelson wrote, "On October 12, 1999, Walker tried to hang himself with his coveralls, hence he was sent to the infirmary for several days. On October 18, 1999, Walker was returned to his cell in A-block. He was stripped of all of his clothing and put in his cell naked. He was not permitted to have bedding or a pillow, and the water to his sink and toilet were turned off. The guards controlled the water and turned it on at regular intervals. Walker was given a 'space' or 'suicide' blanket consisting of two wool blankets sewn inside a canvas cover. Walker remained in his cell, naked, with only his suicide blanket for four days."

He got his mattress back on October 22 and a pillow the following day, but he did not have his clothes returned until October 29. He had been naked for 11 days.

Justice Nelson: "On February 26, 2000, MSP officials started Walker's fifth BMP because Walker claimed to have taken some pills in another suicide attempt. All of Walker's clothing and bedding were taken away. Walker was again forced to sleep naked on a concrete bunk with nothing but a suicide blanket for warmth for over a week. On March 4, 2000, Walker's mattress was returned to him. On March 5, 2000, he received his pillow. On March 6, 2000, after nine days of being naked in his cell, MSP officials returned his coveralls."

Prison psychiatrist Dr. David Schaefer had evaluated Walker on March 11, 1999, but did not review his medical records or conduct psychological testing. Dr. Schaeffer discontinued Walker's Lithium prescription and concluded he did not have a serious mental illness, but rather an "antisocial personality with narcissistic traits." On October 7, 1999, Dr. Schaefer evaluated Walker again after Walker swallowed a staple. Dr. Schaefer reported that Walker was at chronic risk for self-harm, but hopefully, he "will fall short of killing himself." Again, he prescribed no medication.

Dr. Andrew Schoening, a prison psychologist who worked alongside Dr. Schaefer, also saw Walker but concluded his behavior was not the result of mental illness, but "just poor judgment." Two independent psychologists hired by Walker's attorneys reached very different conclusions. Dr. William Stratford noted that prison authorities in Colorado had correctly diagnosed and treated him, but those in Montana had utterly failed to do so. He called Walker's treatment "negligent and scandalous." Dr. Terry Kupers, an expert on mental illness in prison who has reviewed conditions in many different states and has written a book on the subject,[6] concluded that the prison diagnosis that Walker was not mentally ill was "preposterous." Dr. Kupers testified that Walker's treatment was "counter-therapeutic, punitive and cruel." He stated, "If it's a security program, I think it's just cruel and inhumane. If it's a treatment, it is ethically wrong and far below the standard in terms of all of the fields of mental health." Kupers noted that even a sane person thrown into that kind of extreme isolation would soon begin to suffer massive anxiety, acute confusion, paranoia, problems with concentration and memory and aggressive or self-destructive behavior.

At trial, several other prisoners testified about general conditions in the cell block. There was often blood, feces, vomit and other types of debris in the cells they were forced to inhabit. One inmate described how he was once placed in a cell with human waste rubbed all over the walls and vomit in the corner. He claimed corrections staff ignored his complaints and told him to "live with it."

The court, by six votes to one, found that Montana's treatment of Walker had violated the Eighth Amendment ban on cruel and unusual punishment. Justice Nelson summed up, "When the rights of even the most disrespected among us are ignored, all of society is diminished. Accordingly, we hold that…BMPs and the living conditions on A-block constitute an affront to the inviolable right of human dignity possessed by the inmate and that such punishment constitutes cruel and unusual punishment when it exacerbates the inmate's mental health condition." Chief Justice Karla M. Gray was the sole dissenter. She argued that the case was moot because Walker had completed his sentence by the time it was decided.

Montana's Department of Corrections was not chastened by the Supreme Court decision. Far from it. On May 1, 2003, it issued a statement lambasting the Court.[7] "The Court's willingness to micro-manage the state's prisons represents judicial activism at its worst," the department said. "The Supreme Court second-guessed the Department of Corrections' own doctors and chose to believe Walker's 'hired guns' who had far less familiarity with the inmate and his manipulative behavior…. The whole state should be shocked and dismayed at the Court's eagerness to trample on the executive branch's ability to run its prisons."

Walker's case may be extreme; unfortunately it is far from unique. Almost unbelievable acts of cruelty have been and are being perpetrated against mentally ill prisoners all over the United States. Many live in filth and degradation. Dr. Craig Haney, one of the authors of the Stanford Prison Experiment who has spent 30 years studying corrections, visited a number of prisons in Texas as an expert witness in the 1999 *Ruiz* case. Even he was unprepared for what he encountered when he entered some of the state's high-security cell blocks. "In a number of instances, there were people who had urinated in their cells and the urination was on the floor," Haney testified. "There were many people who were incoherent when I attempted to talk to them, babbling, sometimes shrieking, other people who appeared to be full of fury and rage and were, in some instances, banging their hands on the side of the wall and yelling and screaming; other people who appeared to be simply disheveled, withdrawn and out of contact with the circumstances or surroundings. Some of them would be huddled in the back corner of the cell and appeared incommunicative when I attempted to speak with them. Again, these were not subtle diagnostic issues. These were people who appeared to be in profound states of distress and pain."[8]

Asked what stood out most in his mind, Haney said, "The bedlam which ensued each time I walked out into one of those units, the number of people who were screaming, who were begging for help, for attention, the number of people who appeared to be disturbed, the existence, again, of people who were smeared with feces, the intensity of the noise as people began to shout and ask, 'Please come over here. Please talk to me. Please help me.' It was shattering. And as I discussed this atmosphere with the people who worked here, I was told that this was an everyday occurrence, that there was nothing at all unusual about what I was seeing."[9]

The mentally ill are some of the most tragic cases inhabiting the U.S. prison system. They are particularly poorly equipped to survive in the brutal prison world. As psychiatrist Terry Kupers has written, many find it almost impossible to hide their fear and weakness. Antipsychotic medications may slow their reaction times, which makes them more vulnerable to being attacked and raped, which in turn exacerbates their mental state. They are slow to react to guards' orders and constantly get written up for disciplinary infractions or are subject to brutal cell extractions.[10] If they act out, they are punished with greater and greater severity, just as Walker was punished. If they try to commit suicide, they are punished for that too, if they manage to botch the attempt.

Lance Corcoran, who spent 13 years as a guard, said most corrections officers heartily disliked dealing with the mentally ill. "They are unpredictable, very difficult to manage and expensive. The public would rather they just disappear. We try to have respect and understanding that some folk are not necessarily in control of their actions at all times because of mental illness. You always knew when guys on my tier were off their medication because their behavior changed drastically," he told me.

It is not surprising that some prison guards forced to work with such individuals in frightening and appalling conditions quickly lose patience and take out their frustrations on the prisoners. If an out-of-control inmate tries to attack a corrections officer, retaliation is swift and certain and is applied with overwhelming, sometimes deadly force. Prisons function on the strict application of rules and orders. "Go here, stand there, turn around, bend over, leave your cell, go back in your cell, eat now, wash now, sleep now." People with mental illnesses are often incapable of following such a regimen. In any case, even with the best will in the world, prison is hardly a place where any meaningful treatment can be offered. For many who have the tough, day-to-day task of running these institutions, the best option is to heavily medicate them until they are released, which over 90 percent of them eventually are. Convicts describe the characteristic gait of the overmedicated inmate as the "Thorazine shuffle."

If we were talking about a relatively small number of people and a small number of abuses, the problem of the mentally ill behind bars would be tragic but perhaps understandable. We are not. Ted Conover, who spent a year working as a guard at Sing Sing, wrote, "You don't have to work the galleries long to realize that a large proportion of inmates were mentally ill. The symptoms ranged from the fairly mild—talking to oneself, neglecting to bathe—to the severe: men who didn't know where they were, men who set fire to their own cells, men so depressed they slashed their wrists or tried to hang themselves."[11]

In 1999, the Bureau of Justice Statistics released the first comprehensive report on mental illness in prisons and jails. The bottom line: "An estimated 283,000 mentally ill offenders were held in the nation's state and federal prisons and local jails at midyear 1998." That came out at around 16 percent of the total prison population. An additional 547,800 mentally ill people were on probation.[12] Breaking down the numbers, the BJS report found a higher rate of mental illness among women than men. Almost 40 percent of white female state prisoners aged 24 or younger were identified as mentally ill. The number of mentally ill behind bars was at least double the rate in the general population. More than 60 percent had been charged with rules violations in prison.

Prison guards usually have little or no training in how to deal with the mentally ill, so one could perhaps understand their frustrations. That is not the case with psychiatrists employed by state prison systems. Evidence in the *Ruiz* case in Texas suggested that some prison psychiatrists simply refused to believe that inmates were sick, no matter how disturbed their behavior. They had apparently identified themselves so closely with the prison authorities that they no longer regarded themselves as acting primarily as physicians for their patients.

Many states have great difficulty in attracting psychiatrists, psychologists and psychiatric social workers to work in prisons, especially those sited in remote rural areas. In California in the late 1990s, the state prison system was paying mental health professionals 7 to 40 percent less than their counterparts made in private practice. A prison clinical psychiatrist earned up to $4,575 a month in prison. His private counterpart made an average of $6,250. In 1995, U.S. District Court judge Lawrence K. Karlton called the state's treatment of mentally ill inmates "cruel and unusual" and ordered a drastic improvement. But the Department of Corrections found it almost impossible to hire and retain qualified staff.[13]

Clearly, prison psychiatrists are tremendously overworked and practice their profession in unpleasant conditions with patients who may be violent and abusive. Equally clearly, some of the mental health professionals who choose to work in the prison system seem to have forgotten why they entered the profession in the first place. Their actions suggest that they have become so burned out that they have lost the ability to see their patients as fellow human beings worthy of compassion.

In his 1999 *Ruiz* judgment, Judge William Wayne Justice cited the case of one inmate who had a history of smearing himself with feces, complaining of hallucinations and claiming to be the Messiah. A prison psychiatrist, a Dr. Taylor, determined the inmate was malingering and wrote, "I feel certain that we will have some grandiose display of abnormal behavior, perhaps reaching a magnitude of once again smearing feces. I would be interested to observe if the patient consumes his feces or whether he just smears his feces."[14]

Then there was Adan Garza, who entered the Texas prison system with a well-documented history of suicide attempts, self-mutilations, hallucinations and hospitalizations. The prison psychiatrist, Dr. Tchokoev, thought he was play-acting, took him off his medication and prescribed heavy field work. Garza returned to his cell, where he cut himself and then attempted to hang himself. He did not quite succeed in ending his life. Years later, he remained in a vegetative state.

Or take the case of Timothy Perry in Connecticut. At 21, Perry was a very disturbed young man with a long history of mental illness. In January 1999, he was admitted to the Cedarcrest Regional Hospital in Newington, a facility run by the state. Doctors there diagnosed him as suffering from a long list of mental problems—schizophrenia, schizoaffective disorder, impulse control disorder, borderline personality disorder with antisocial features, major depression and oppositional defiant disorder.[15] He had difficulty controlling his temper and would often act aggressively. At the end of March, Perry struck one of his doctors. Instead of sending him to a high-security mental hospital, the staff had him arrested and transferred to prison.[16] After he had been at Hartford Correctional Center for 12 days, Perry again became severely agitated and disturbed. He was pacing around the dayroom, yelling and banging on the windows and standing on tables and chairs. When asked to return to his cell, he charged at one of the officers. Some of what happened subsequently was captured on videotape. Seven corrections officers piled on Perry, took him to the ground and handcuffed his wrists behind his back. They forced him face down on a mattress, shackled him with leg irons and choked him. He was not actively resisting but was gurgling and perhaps trying to spit, so a guard took a towel and held it over his mouth and face. A report by the Connecticut Office of Protection and Advocacy for Persons with Disabilities stated, "Throughout the entire tape, Mr. Perry is not seen to resist or even to move. Yet, at one point, the officer filming the event clearly remarks that, 'Inmate Perry is still resisting.'"[17] Although he was unconscious and may already have been dead, a prison nurse injected him with a powerful sedative. She failed to take his vital signs or check him for injuries. Finally, the officers turned Perry on his back, cut or tore off the rest of his clothes and left him strapped down alone in a cell. Two hours later, another nurse noticed his feet were blotchy and discolored. She tried to take his pulse and discovered he was cold and stiff. He had been dead for some time. A shift commander at the prison later allowed some of the guards involved in the incident to erase part of the incriminating videotape. In 2002, the state of Connecticut paid Perry's family $2.9 million to settle the case out of court, the highest settlement in state history for an unmarried person. Most of the guards received reprimands; a couple received short suspensions. The nurse was transferred to another state agency but was not disciplined or punished.

One might think that a $2.9 million payout would prompt the Connecticut Department of Corrections to review procedures for subduing prisoners. One would be wrong. Seven months later, another prisoner died at another Connecticut prison, the Garner Correctional Institute, in a virtual carbon copy of the Perry incident. The victim this time was Bryant Wiseman, 28, who suffered from paranoid schizophrenia. For some reason, although Wiseman's records indicated clearly that he was apt to become violent if he were allowed to stop taking his medications, a prison doctor stopped prescribing them. Wiseman soon got into a fight with another inmate. Officers and staff rushed to subdue him, piled on top of him, handcuffed his wrists behind his back, put him in leg irons, savagely beat him, asphyxiated him, caused him to vomit, rendered him unconscious and comatose, and ultimately killed him.[18] Again, the incident was videotaped. Even when it became clear that Bryant was in serious trouble, medical staff allegedly failed to properly check his vital signs or perform CPR.

Antonio Ponvert, the lawyer who represented the Wiseman and Perry families, believes fear is the major factor that drives corrections officers to commit acts of such brutality against mentally ill inmates. "The prison system is incredibly high stress, tense and dangerous. The first instinct of a guard when faced with any kind of threat is to lash out and put it down before he gets hurt or to rush to help his buddy who is under attack. That leads to excessive force, which in turn leads to cover-ups, which in turn provides me with more than enough cases to pursue," he said.

But fear cannot explain what happened to Vaughn Dortch, a mentally ill inmate of California's Pelican Bay prison, in 1993. His fate was described in a 1995 judgment by Thelton E. Henderson, Chief Judge in the U.S. District Court for the Northern District of California.[19] Dortch suffered second- and third-degree burns over one-third of his body when he was given a bath in scalding water in the prison infirmary. The week before the incident, Dortch had bitten an officer. He also created a nuisance by smearing himself and his cell with his own feces. Corrections officers were clearly fed up of dealing with Dortch and decided to teach him a lesson. A nurse called Barbara Kuroda testified that she saw how Dortch, his hands cuffed behind his back, was forced into the boiling hot bathtub. She heard one officer say he would clean Dortch up with a hard bristle brush wrapped in a towel. Judge Henderson wrote, "Kuroda's unrebutted testimony is that she overheard the officer say about Dortch, who is African-American, that it 'looks like we're going to have a white boy before this is through' and that 'his skin is so dirty and so rotten, it's all fallen off.'"

Concerned by this remark, Kuroda walked over toward the tub. She testified that Dortch's skin had peeled off from just below the buttocks and was hanging in large clumps around his legs, which had turned white with some redness. "Even then, in a shocking show of indifference, the officers made no effort to seek any medical assistance or advice," Judge Henderson wrote. Dortch later sued the state and won a settlement of $997,000.[20]

The story of how and why U.S. prisons and jails were turned into de facto insane asylums began in the early 1960s. At that time, hundreds of thousands of people suffering from serious mental illnesses were kept in large state mental hospitals, where treatment was impersonal and sometimes abusive and cruel. The 1962 publication of Ken Kesey's *One Flew Over the Cuckoo's Nest*, with its vivid portrayal of the sadistic Nurse Ratched, added strength to a growing "de-institutionalization" movement. The first psychotropic drugs were becoming available at this time, giving hope that most of the mentally ill could live and receive treatment in the community instead of being warehoused in mental institutions. In 1963, President Kennedy signed into law the Community Mental Health Centers Act. The law envisaged that patients would receive care and follow-up services in a network of outpatient clinics and residential programs. Over the next few years, patients were released into the community en masse, but most of the money to fund the clinics never materialized. Congress failed to fund them. A presidential commission on mental health in July 2003 described a system that was "fragmented and in disarray...leading to unnecessary and costly disability, homelessness, school failure and incarceration."[21] To save money, states started closing mental hospitals without making provision for patients. Many mentally ill individuals were not only thrown on the streets but also lost their Social Security benefits and quickly fell into poverty.

We see these people every day on our city streets—unkempt men and women pushing supermarket carts piled high with belongings, muttering to themselves, pestering passersby. They live by panhandling or petty crime; some sell their bodies if they are able. Sooner or later, many are inevitably drawn into the criminal justice system, especially since cities started cracking down on "quality-of-life offenses" like drinking alcohol or urinating in public or jumping subway turnstiles. According to the Sentencing Project, a Washington think-tank that studies prison issues, around 700,000 of the 10 million adults booked into local jails each year have active symptoms of serious mental illness. Most are also substance abusers.[22] Many churn through the system for years, stuck in a perpetual revolving door that leads from the streets to jail and back again, with occasional forays to the hospital emergency room, until they commit a crime serious enough to send them away to prison.

The numbers are striking. In 1955, there were 559,000 patients in state mental hospitals. Now there are around 72,000, even though the nation's population has grown by nearly two thirds.[23] Washington, D.C., has lost 92 percent of its public mental hospital beds since 1955; Maryland has lost 86 percent and Virginia 82 percent.[24] In Florida, the number of mentally ill people in jails and prisons outnumbers the number of patients in state mental hospitals by nearly five to one.[25] What we see here is a dual process. Over the past 40 years, the number of prison beds has skyrocketed, while the number of psychiatric beds has plummeted. During the 1990s, 40 state mental hospitals closed, while more than 400 new prisons were opened.[26] It is hard to write this without suspending disbelief; nevertheless it is a fact that the three largest mental institutions in the world are the Los Angeles County Jail, Rikers

Island in New York and Cook County Jail in Chicago.[27] "The jails have become first-care facility for many homeless people. For veterans. For people who literally belong in hospitals and clinics dealing with issues that affect their mental health," said Los Angeles County Sheriff Lee Baca.[28]

Conditions in the Los Angeles County Jail prompted a Department of Justice investigation, which in 1997 reported a variety of abuses and concluded that the county violated inmates' constitutional right to mental health care. The investigation found that inmates were locked up in cramped, dingy cells where some languished for days or weeks without medication, while others were overmedicated.[29] In December 2002, the county settled a federal lawsuit by agreeing to improve standards and procedures for dealing with the mentally ill at the jail.[30] The county agreed to maintain around-the-clock mental health screening of all inmates as they were booked in to check whether they had a mental illness or had attempted suicide or had suicidal tendencies. Those in need of emergency mental health services were to receive them without delay.

Jails are on the front lines, since they are usually the first point of contact the mentally ill person has with the incarceration system. Their first task, therefore, is to identify those in need of mental services on intake, with particular attention to those at risk of committing suicide. Unfortunately, too often they fail to do so. A Justice Department investigation in 2002 into the Santa Fe Adult Detention Center concluded that staff there totally failed to provide adequate mental health services to inmates. In one case, an inmate told medical staff on intake that he had recently suffered a significant personal loss and felt he had nothing to live for. "He reported that he had been diagnosed with Post Traumatic Stress Disorder and that he was taking an antidepressant for this condition. He also stated that he felt he needed to see a psychologist. Despite these indicators, the screening nurse concluded that the inmate needed only a routine mental health referral, as opposed to an immediate mental health evaluation and determination whether mental health services were necessary," the report said. The inmate committed suicide two weeks later.[31]

The Justice Department investigators also found there was not a single staff member at the jail licensed to diagnose psychiatric illness or prescribe medication. One inmate arrived at the jail with a documented history of prior treatment for bipolar disorder and depression. For some reason, a jail counselor decided to take her off her medication. Naturally, her condition worsened dramatically. She began banging on the metal part of her bed, destroying her mattress with a razor blade and flooding her cell with water. "Both the counselor's notes and the inmate's sick call requests document that throughout this period, the inmate repeatedly requested a return to her previous medications, but the counselor denied her requests. The inmate's decline subsequently resulted in a suicide attempt....The counselor denied her repeated requests for medication without consulting with any practitioner trained and licensed to make such decisions. Thus, this inmate who had been treated by a psychiatrist with psychotropic medications for many months was forced to attempt to conform her behavior in a jail environment without any aid from medication. She experienced continued headaches, anxiety, depression and sleep disturbance and frequently found herself in segregation."[32]

Sheriffs are far from thrilled at the way their jails have been turned into dumping grounds for the mentally ill. "The problem continues to escalate. It is a major quality-of-life issue for severely mentally ill patients, because they are more likely to be beaten, victimized or commit suicide than those who are not sick. The handling and control of these inmates pose a serious safety threat to staff," said Thomas N. Faust, Sheriff of Arlington County, Virginia and Executive Director of the National Sheriffs' Association.[33]

Then there is the cost issue. The Los Angeles County Jail spends about $10 million a year on psychiatric medication.[34] In Maricopa County, Arizona, three psychiatrists were caring for an estimated 1,400 inmates with mental care needs.[35] Three psychiatrist slots were vacant, and there was also a chronic shortage of nurses. Leonard Sines, a nurse in the system, quit in June 2003, saying he felt his license was in jeopardy because of the poor standards of care offered. Patients were not given medication until they had seen a jail psychiatrist, even if they had verified treatment plans and medical records from the outside. The wait to see a psychiatrist was often three weeks or longer.

If caring for the mentally ill is becoming more difficult and expensive, failing to care for them often turns out to be even costlier. One survey found that 40 states had been sued for failing to provide adequate care to mentally ill inmates.[36] Many lawsuits arise after inmates commit suicide.

Take the case of Scotty Sisk, who died on July 6, 1999, in Shawnee County Jail in Kansas. Sisk, 23, a former college football star, got into trouble when he violated a court order to stay away from a former girl-friend and was sentenced to a year in jail. On the night that he died, he telephoned his parents and sounded despondent. His mother called the jail at around 9:15 that evening and told jailers she was worried her son was suicidal. Sisk was placed in a medical isolation unit and put on sui-cide watch. Guards were supposed to check on him every quarter of an hour. But two hours later, he pried a metal plate from the wall, tore strips from his blanket, tied them together to make a rope, leaned for-ward and choked himself.[37] "We were guaranteed that no harm would come to Scotty. However, three short hours later, Scotty was dead," his parents said. In the trial, it emerged that the sheriff had refused to invest in suicide prevention blankets that inmates could not rip into strips because they were "too expensive." The jury awarded $10 million to Sisk's parents, enough to buy quite a few blankets.

Suicide is a major problem for prisons and an even bigger one for jails. Studies have suggested that the suicide rate in prison is around double that of the general population. In jail, it is nine times higher.[38] Suicide ranks third, behind natural causes and AIDS, as the leading cause of death in prisons and is the number one cause in jail.[39] People entering jail after their arrest are often in a state of shock and psychologically vulnerable. However, the problem may be vastly underreported. Statis-tics are not systematically collected. Prisons may not classify drug over-doses as suicides. Some inmates find other ways to end their lives that are effectively suicide but are not recorded as such. Despondent prison-ers may take a walk into a prohibited area and get shot by a guard. This is known as death by gun tower.[40] They may pick a fight with a prison tough or gang member or renege on a gambling debt, knowing these are sure ways to court death. If a prisoner is taken to a hospital and pro-nounced dead there, he may not be listed as having died in custody.

Nobody regularly compiles statistics on jail suicides either, but evidence collected by newspapers is alarming. A *Detroit Free Press* series in August 2001 found that "at least 55 prisoners had died in metro-Detroit cells since January 1998—many from medical neglect, foreseeable suicides and other suspicious circumstances."[41] The Wayne County sheriff refused access to the records of three of the suicide victims until an advocacy group sued him. The *Louisville Courier Journal* in 2002 found that at least 17 people committed suicide in Kentucky jails during a 30-month period, most without having seen a mental health professional while in custody. At least two others died in restraints. One mentally ill inmate, Michael Labmeier, died after being hog-tied on January 29, 1999. The county settled a lawsuit by agreeing to pay $400,000 to his estate. The newspaper found that in one Kentucky jail, two inmates hanged themselves on the same light fixture on two separate occasions without anyone doing anything about it.[42]

The only systematic studies of suicides in the nation's jails were conducted in the late 1970s and mid-1980s. The more recent study found 453 jail suicides in 1985 and 403 in 1986, making suicide the leading cause of death in jails.[43] Other findings: 51 percent of suicides occurred within the first 24 hours of incarceration with 29 percent happening within the first three hours; 30 percent of suicides occurred during a six-hour period between midnight and six in the morning; 94 percent of suicides were by hanging; 48 percent of victims used their bedding; 89 percent of victims were not screened for potential suicide behavior when they were booked in.

Ron Angelone, head of the Virginia Department of Corrections from 1994 to 2002, told me prison suicides were virtually unavoidable. "You can't stop them. If a person wants to commit suicide, he or she will commit suicide," he said. But Lindsay Hayes, author of the most recent study and a leading authority on the subject, believes virtually all jail suicides could be prevented with proper training of personnel and inmate screening. Eight of ten suicides give advance warnings of their suicidal tendencies. Merely replacing sheets with coverings that cannot be torn into strips would reduce the problem and also reduce the huge payouts that often follow litigation. Teaching personnel proper first aid procedures would also save lives. Take the case of Tina Hatch, who died in Teton County Jail in Driggs, Idaho, on August 22, 2000. After staff found she had hanged herself, they did not immediately cut her down or remove the noose she had made out of a sheet. Instead, one officer checked for vital signs while another ran for a camera and photographed the victim. Neither attempted CPR. The sheet was only eventually removed several hours later during the autopsy.[44]

In the Santa Fe jail, staff routinely ignored suicide threats by inmates. One inmate held a note up to the door of his cell as an officer looked in. The officer did nothing, and the inmate was later found trying to hang himself with a sheet. In the booking area of the jail, where newly arrived inmates are housed, Justice Department investigators found there was no tool to cut down inmates trying to hang themselves, even after an inmate succeeded in hanging himself.[45]

Of course, good treatment presupposes goodwill on the part of staff that is not always forthcoming. The U.S. Department of Justice recorded the case of Matthew Mancl, who committed suicide in Pepin County Jail in Wisconsin on October 29, 1999. Two days before, a police sergeant overheard a jail deputy tell a colleague, "There's a problem in the jail. Mancl wants to kill himself. If the fucker wants to kill himself, make sure he's dead before you cut him down." The deputy was subsequently charged with obstruction of justice and admitted falsifying a jail log to reflect cell checks that had never taken place.[46]

Some politicians are looking for ways to reduce the number of mental cases in prisons and jails. Rep. Ted Strickland, an Ohio Democrat who once worked as a psychologist in a maximum security prison, has led the fight. "I have seen individuals who are living the rest of their lives behind bars because they committed crimes that probably would not have been committed had they received mental health treatment," Strickland said. "I have seen the effects of prison on the mentally ill and the effect of the mentally ill on the prison system. Individuals decompensate. Institutions destabilize. It is an obvious fact that prisons are neither designed nor intended to be therapeutic institutions."[47]

Strickland, backed by allies from both parties, was a moving spirit behind America's Law Enforcement and Mental Health Project Act, signed into law by President Clinton in November 2000. It provided funds to establish special "mental health courts" to divert nonviolent offenders away from prison and into treatment. Right now, people with mental illness receive no special deference from courts—they are treated just like any other defendant. Some may even be treated worse because criminal justice officials with little experience in dealing with mental illness see them as particularly dangerous.

Robert Dver, a deputy district attorney in Los Angeles County, said the mentally ill present a huge dilemma for prosecutors. "The easiest situation to deal with is when they are so sick they cannot take part in their own defense and are deemed incompetent. Then we can refer them to a mental hospital until they can cooperate in their own defense and understand what is going on. If they don't reach that level within three years, they become wards of the state," he said.

> The more common situation is less clear, and often we are faced with only bad alternatives. We don't have enough programs for the mentally ill. It's frustrating for the prosecutor because you know the appropriate option would be some kind of treatment facility but often we have to just treat them as another bad guy and send them to the joint. You can't just let them go. Every prosecutor has the same nightmare; nobody wants their name to wind up on the front page of the *Los Angeles Times* as the prosecutor who made a deal with some guy to go free and the guy then goes out and commits a terrible crime.

Los Angeles District Court Judge David Mintz sees plenty of mentally ill defendants before his bench. "I wish there were more alternatives available for the nonviolent offenders, such as dual diagnosis treatment facilities. Just sending them to drugs programs is often not appropriate. If you have a combination of mental illness and violent crime, there's not much you can do. You have to protect society," he said.

No matter how disturbed they are, the vast majority of mentally ill prisoners are eventually released. In Rikers Island, for years they were dumped in Queens by the Fifty-ninth Street Bridge in the middle of the night with a $3 subway card and $1.50 in cash. Rikers did not even bother laundering inmates' street clothes, even if they were soiled with urine or vomit when they were booked in. When they received their green fatigues, jail officials would stuff their street clothes into a bag. When they were released, the prisoners got their clothes back wrinkled and stinking.[48]

In 1999, seven Rikers inmates led by a man identified in court papers as Brad H. filed suit against the city to provide treatment services and follow-up for mentally ill inmates released from city jails. Brad H.'s own case was instructive. At age nine, he was dumped at a psychiatric center where he underwent shock therapy for several years until he turned 18 and was released. He spent the next 29 years, homeless and alcoholic, cycling in and out of jail a total of 26 times, always for nonviolent offenses. In 1988, he was released from a state prison with two weeks of medication in his pocket. He soon lost his eyeglasses and false teeth and spent the next nine months toothless and unable to see clearly, living in subway stations. Finally, he was arrested for jumping a turnstile and sent back to Rikers.[49]

In January 2003, the city settled the lawsuit. Inmates from Rikers are now released between five and six o'clock in the morning. An organization called the Fortune Society has opened a help center near the drop-off site. It offers coffee, a listening ear and referrals to health care services, education, job counseling and treatment for drugs and alcohol abuse.

Brad H. is one of a category of prisoners known to jail officials as "frequent fliers" because they keep coming back. A study conducted in 2000 by the Multnomah County Sheriff's Department in Portland, Oregon, found that fewer than 5 percent of the 45,000 people who passed through the county jail each year were consuming almost a quarter of its resources. One such frequent flier was Troy Lee Ford, a slight man in his mid-thirties who had been arrested 61 times in 5 years, almost always for nonviolent offenses, and had cost the county over $230,000. Ford, who was addicted to crack and was homeless, supported his habit by shoplifting, prostitution and serving as a go-between for dealers and addicts. Jail drugs treatment programs in Portland have been slashed to the bone. Ford's former probation officer told the *Willamette Week*, "Jail has no effect on Mr. Ford. He's addicted and they're not doing a thing for him. They are just warehousing him and then it's straight back out. It's a huge waste of money."[50]

Caring for the mentally ill in the community can be difficult and labor-intensive, but it pays big financial dividends as well as saving patients from a lifetime of pain. One pioneering program called Project Link, run by the University of Rochester, shows what can be done.

Participants are enrolled straight out of jail or referred by local hospitals. Participants each get a case worker who makes sure they take their medication and stay in touch with medical and social services providers. Some are given accommodation in group homes, where they get their medication every day from a trained custodian. They spend most of their time attending community programs.

Jerome Collier, who suffers from severe schizophrenia, had spent his whole adult life bouncing from the streets to jail or hospital. "I lived on the streets for 20 years. I didn't have nowhere to go. I did weed, cocaine, heroin, speed, acid, mescaline—I mixed it all up with my medication when I took it. I've been suicidal and homicidal. I've been in every emergency room in the county. I lost contact with my family, they were ashamed of me being their son. I did stealing—cars, breaking in houses, conning people out of their money, gambling. Once I broke into a house and set a fire. A fireman got hurt real bad trying to put it out," he told me when we met in 2002.

A study of past and present participants of Project Link found that in the year before joining the program, they spent an average of 109 days in jail and 105 days in the hospital. In their first year in the program, they averaged 40 days in jail and 14 in the hospital. The average cost of caring for them dropped from $62,500 a year to $14,500. "Few of our participants are going to be able to hold down regular jobs, but if they can stay out of jail and live in one place with a roof over their heads, and they are not harming themselves or others, that can be counted as an achievement," said psychiatrist Robert Weisman. "Our clients are often tough and obnoxious and don't follow directions or trust authority. We try to reach out to them with case workers from their own community."

Joining the program made Jerome Collier a busy man. "Every night I have Alcoholics Anonymous and Narcotics Anonymous. In the morning, I go to classes on anger management, smokers' class, exercise class, personal emotions class where I learn how to approach people, look them in the eye, don't lift my hands towards them," he said.

Another program in New York City called Critical Time Intervention takes a similar approach. Each participant gets a case worker for a critical nine-month period, during which they move into some form of subsidized group housing where they receive supervision and learn how to manage for themselves. The case managers try to ensure their clients stay on medication and off drugs, help them manage their money, solve crises that may occur and try to put them back in touch with their families.

The program is beginning to be copied around the nation, but like Project Link, it is labor-intensive and can handle only relatively small numbers. That's the hard way of dealing with the mentally ill, the one that involves treating them like people. Or there is the other way, the easy way, the way America has chosen, which consists of throwing them in jail and trying to forget they exist.

6

AN UNHEALTHY SITUATION

"A healthy body is a guest-chamber for the soul;
a sick body is a prison."
Francis Bacon ∎

On a cool summer day, a group of 30 newly arrived inmates filed into a room at California's San Quentin State Prison. The prisoners had just been processed, had given up their street clothes and were dressed in orange jumpsuits with "CDC prisoner" (California Department of Corrections) emblazoned on the back. Some looked cocky, as if they'd seen and heard it all before. Others seemed anxious and hesitant. John Romain, a veteran inmate, stepped to the front of the room.

"Welcome to San Quentin. What we're going to do here is try to educate you about HIV, AIDS and hepatitis," Romain said. For the next ten minutes, he laid out basic facts on how the diseases spread and warned the new inmates against sharing needles, tattooing, fighting, sharing razors and snorting drugs through shared straws. He told them they would be healthier if they refrained from sex.

"I take this seriously. Why? Because I'm HIV positive. I've been living with this for 16 years. It used to be that what you didn't know couldn't hurt you. But what you don't know now can kill you," Romain said.

"Since I've been in this institution, quite a few fellows have died of Hep C. It's a fact, people do drugs in prison. We're locked up but we shoot up anyway. But I'm telling you brothers, don't share needles. And don't do nothing that gets you near to another man's blood. Used to be, you was with your home boy and you want to be his blood brother, like for life. That ain't cool no more, because you don't know what he been doing and he don't know what you been doing. Find some other way to get good with your home boy."

In a question-and-answer period, prisoners wanted to know if they could become infected from a punching bag—highly unlikely—or from oral sex—possibly. In a final plea, Romain went over the basics again: "Don't share needles, don't do tattoos, don't share cotton balls, don't share water, don't share toothbrushes, don't share nothing with no one." Then the new arrivals were marched out of the room to begin their sentences.

The peer-counseling program at San Quentin, run by Centerforce Incorporated, a nonprofit organization headquartered in a ramshackle building just outside the prison gates, is a rarity in the prison system. Barry Zack, the program director, said it was difficult to persuade the authorities to allow his group to operate inside the prison walls. "Prison authorities do not like empowering prisoners, which is what we do by recruiting peer counselors. But using inmates to educate fellow prison-ers is much more effective than having outsiders come in to do it," he said. "Prisoners are much more likely to trust information they get from one of their own. Our counselors live in the cell blocks and are available to offer advice almost around the clock. Prisoners can approach them in the exercise yard or the dining room. It works." Still, he said, even with encouragement, only about 60 percent of new inmates asked to be tested for HIV and hepatitis. The rest preferred not to know.

Deadly diseases like HIV and hepatitis spread behind bars mainly through sharing needles. In a place where there is no legal source of clean needles, they become a valuable commodity to be used again and again for shooting drugs or tattooing.

Tattoos have long been part of prison life. Prison tattoo artists com-mand respect for their speed and artistry and their willingness to take risks, since most prisons officially ban such "body art" and punish practitioners if they catch them. A tattoo can denote gang membership and give an inmate an aura of toughness to intimidate would-be attack-ers. Nuestra Familia members often tattoo themselves with a sombrero and a bleeding dagger flanked by the letters *NF*. Aryan Brotherhood members decorate their bodies with images of hearts with daggers thrust through them and the letters *AB*. Also popular are spiders, swas-tikas and the figures 6-6-6, denoting the "mark of the beast" from the Book of Revelation. Two of the men who killed James Boyd, Jr., in Jas-per, Texas, in 1999 by chaining him to a pickup truck and dragging him along the ground had previously been in prison, where they covered their bodies with racist tattoos.

Prison tattoos can have personal rather than ideological symbolism. Some gang members tattoo tears on their faces, each one denoting a person they have killed or a family member or gang brother lost to violence. Others simply write the name of their sweetheart, or the date of their incarceration or other symbols with personal meaning. A bird signifies the freedom to fly. Crows and vultures are associated with death. What many inmates still don't realize, or choose to ignore, is that all prison tattoos are associated with death because of the risk of transmitting disease.

Inmates show considerable ingenuity in making tattoo guns. They can be improvised from melted down toothbrushes, sewing machine needles and motors stolen from portable tape players. The ink comes from ballpoint pens. One observer saw an inmate construct a gun from an electric shaver, the cutters replaced with a makeshift needle cut from a guitar string and the ink reservoir made out of an eyedropper. It was assembled with tape, string and glue, and the prisoner muffled the noise with a piece of foam rubber.[1]

Canadian prison authorities, grappling with the same problem, came up with an innovative and imaginative solution in 2004—they decided to open their own, clean, legal tattoo parlors in the nation's federal prisons. Under the plan, inmates would be trained to operate the tattoo parlors safely and hygienically. It was the latest Canadian "harm reduction initiative," following the successful introduction of methadone treatment clinics in all 53 Canadian federal prisons in 2003.[2] Could such ideas be copied in the U.S. prison system? Unfortunately, anyone who suggested them would probably be laughed out of court, or chased out of public life.

But the Canadian experiment did have the advantage of trying to deal with a real problem in a real way, instead of just mouthing off about the need to be tough on crime. In both Canada and the United States, the reality is that prisoners are unlikely to give up their tattoos any time soon. The threat of diseases like HIV or hepatitis that take years to incubate often seem unreal to a prisoner struggling to get through his term one day at a time. Yet the threat is real. According to the Bureau of Justice Statistics, at the end of 2000 around 2.2 percent of male state prison inmates and 0.8 percent of federal inmates were known to be infected with HIV—a total of 25,078.[3] That represented a rate around four times as high as in the general population. Among women, 3.6 percent of state prison inmates were HIV positive—some 2,243 individuals. But the

Bureau acknowledged the figures were incomplete. Only 19 states screen all incoming inmates for HIV, and only five have tested all inmates. Another 15 states test only inmates who belong to "high-risk" groups. Neither do the figures include jail inmates infected with HIV. A 2002 survey by the National Commission on Correctional Health Care estimated that figure at between 7,000 and 10,000 on any given day. The study calculated that during 1996, around 145,000 HIV-positive inmates were released from prisons or jails.[4]

New York is one of the five states that test all inmates, and it had the highest known population of HIV prisoners, with 8.5 percent of its population testing positive. Maryland, which was second with 4.3 percent, was spending up to $15,000 per inmate per year to treat the disease.[5] Prisons refuse to issue condoms to prisoners for fear of encouraging sex behind bars. Still, treatment of HIV in prison has improved dramatically in recent years, possibly because corrections departments realized that it is much cheaper to offer inmates drugs than to allow them to develop full-blown AIDS and then to have to treat them. As a result, AIDS-related deaths in prisons dropped dramatically, from a peak of 1,010 in 1995 to 174 in 2000.

If treatment of HIV represents at least a partial success story, the same cannot be said for hepatitis C, a blood-borne virus that attacks the liver. It spreads through contact with human blood, primarily by sharing contaminated needles, and can lead to life-threatening cirrhosis, liver cancer or liver failure. There is no vaccine. Anywhere from 12 to 35 percent of the prison population is infected, according to the Centers for Disease Control.[6] Most independent experts put the figure at or near the top end of that range or even higher. A 1994 survey of 5,000 incoming inmates by the California Department of Corrections found that 39.4 percent of males and 54.5 percent of females tested positive.[7] The National Commission on Correctional Health Care, in a comprehensive 2002 report to Congress on prisoners' health, estimated that up to 332,000 in prison and jail were infected with hepatitis C and another 36,000 were infected with hepatitis B.[8]

The real dimensions of the problem remain uncertain, since many states are reluctant to screen inmates: once they diagnose the disease, they have to treat it. Merely offering the test can involve expensive liver biopsies. Dr. Tony Swetz, director of inmate health for Maryland prisons, estimated that treating hepatitis C could cost between $12,000 and $20,000 per patient per year.[9] Because the disease can lay dormant for years before symptoms appear, many inmates are released without ever knowing they have it. In some advanced cases, the only treatment may be liver transplants. Phyllis Beck, director of hepatitis C awareness project in Oregon, said hundreds of inmates desperately needed treatment but only a handful were receiving it.

"We are seeing more and more inmates who are being released with cirrhosis or close to cirrhosis due to a lack of follow-up care after a positive diagnosis has been made," she said. Oregon started counseling prisoners about the disease in 2000. In the first year, around 10 percent of the state's 9,600 inmates requested a test. One-third tested positive.[10]

Dr. Scott Allen, medical director of the Rhode Island Department of Corrections, said data from biopsies taken in Virginia and Louisiana prisons showed the disease had been present in the prison system for decades and that many prisoners were progressing to advanced stages. He advised prison authorities to anticipate rising morbidity and mortality.[11]

A study by Abt Associates, a research and consultancy company in Cambridge, Massachusetts, concluded it would cost the state of Texas $40 million a year to diagnose and treat prisoners for hepatitis C.[12] Burl Cain, warden of Angola State Prison in Louisiana, told me in 2001 that his state had also run some preliminary figures and concluded it could cost $10 million to $20 million a year to treat the disease. "We shudder to think what it will do to our costs," he said.

But ignoring hepatitis does not come cost-free either. In October 2002, Washington State agreed to pay the family of Philip Montgomery $1 million to settle a wrongful death suit filed by his survivors. Montgomery had hepatitis C and died in prison from lack of treatment in September 1999. According to court depositions, prison health workers missed clear signs that Montgomery's liver was failing even after his eyes and skin turned yellow and his cellmate reported him writhing from intense stomach pain and slipping in and out of consciousness. On the night before he died, no doctor could be found to treat him, and a prison nurse failed to diagnose renal failure. By the time he was finally sent to the hospital, it was too late.[13]

In one shocking case, hundreds of Canadian hemophiliacs were infected with HIV or hepatitis by contaminated blood collected in a U.S. prison that was exported to their country. Some of this tainted blood was also sold to Europe and Japan. The blood was collected from prisoners in the Cummins penitentiary 70 miles southeast of Little Rock, Arkansas, and sold by the Arkansas Department of Corrections to companies that exported it to Canada and elsewhere. Long after effective tests for HIV and hepatitis became available, they were not always used at the prison. The U.S. Food and Drug Administration discovered that one testing laboratory was out of commission for two months, but blood collection continued. Prisoners were paid $7 a pint to donate blood, but several became sick because it was sometimes drawn using dirty needles. The program was only finally shut down in 1994.[14] The scandal spurred a major investigation in Canada, and eventually criminal charges were laid against the Canadian Red Cross, a U.S.-based pharmaceutical company and four physicians. Courts in Quebec and Ontario approved a $1.2 billion federal compensation package for victims. The Canadian Red Cross offered $60 million in compensation, and other lawsuits remain outstanding.[15] There can hardly be a better example of how disease within the U.S. prison system spread, not just throughout our society, but in this case infected innocent victims in friendly foreign nations.

Even leaving lawsuits aside, it would be a mistake to view tackling hepatitis C as a burden to be borne by prisons alone, since the ultimate cost of the epidemic will fall on society as a whole. More than 4 million Americans have been exposed to the disease. Up to 15 percent can expect to become seriously ill in the next 20 years. "If we aggressively treat people in prison, we could avert perhaps 30 percent of all the liver transplants that are going to be needed in the next ten or twenty years and save society billions of dollars," said Dr. Anne Degroot, of Brown University, who has treated AIDS and hepatitis patients in Connecticut prisons. In that sense, prisons offer society an opportunity to deal with a major problem before it explodes. Many health experts believe it is an opportunity that is being missed.

The same is true of other conditions as well, including sexually transmitted diseases and tuberculosis. In its 2002 report, the National Commission on Correctional Health Care made a powerful case for increasing prison health spending.[16] It noted that ex-offenders were already contributing to the spread of infectious disease in the community. "As these ex-offenders' diseases get worse, society may have to pay substantially more to treat them than if these conditions had been treated at an earlier stage—or prevented altogether—while these individuals were still incarcerated," it said. This is a powerful argument but there are few willing to listen. The truth is, spending more money to make convicts healthier is always going to be a tough sell when 43 million Americans, including perhaps 12 million children, have no health insurance and when retirees cannot afford the medications they need. Voters ask, with some justification, why their taxes should go for better health services in prisons when they themselves cannot afford the care they need.

Prison systems generally do a poor job of collecting accurate data on the physical and mental health of their prison populations. Several states were unable to provide any data at all for the 2002 study by the National Commission on Correctional Health Care. There are no national figures for incidence of asthma, hypertension and diabetes behind bars, and most states do not collect them. Still, it is clear from the information that does exist that prisons and jails are a serious incubator of disease. For example, up to 76,000 prison and jail inmates in 1997 tested positive in a blood test that suggested the possibility of syphilis. Another 60,000 were infected with gonorrhea or chlamydia. Despite the availability of an effective vaccine against hepatitis B, which leads to a variety of serious liver diseases if left untreated, few state prison systems had vaccination programs. As a result, in 1996 alone, an estimated 155,000 inmates infected with this highly preventable disease were released into the community.[17]

Most prisons and about 50 percent of jails screen intakes for latent tuberculosis infection and active TB disease. However, many inmates are released from jail before their skin tests can be read and are never followed up.[18] The 2002 Correctional Health study estimated the number of TB carriers released from prisons or jails in 1996 at 566,000. Around 1,400 people were released into the community with active, untreated TB disease.[19]

It is well known that prisoners around the world have consistently higher occurrences of tuberculosis than the general population. In the

United States, the rate is estimated at up to 11 times higher.[20] A 1993 study found that one year of jail time in New York City doubled the odds of developing the disease for an inmate who was not already infected.[21] Prisoners often share overcrowded, poorly ventilated spaces, and the frequent transfer of inmates within and between prisons and jails speeds the spread of the disease. One outbreak that originated in a New York State prison in the early 1990s spread to Florida, Nevada, Georgia and Colorado within two years. Significant TB outbreaks in prisons in California and South Carolina in recent years infected staff, visitors, external health workers and community contacts.[22] In California in 1995 and 1996, 32 inmates and parolees were infected in outbreaks that originated in special units for inmates with HIV. Because HIV so severely weakens the body's immune system, people infected with both HIV and tuberculosis have a 100 times greater risk of developing active TB disease. By the time the authorities got around to screening other inmates of the units, 190 had already been released. Health workers managed to track them down. Nine tested positive for tuberculosis. One inmate also infected his wife.[23] Fortunately this strain of tuberculosis was susceptible to drug treatment. Health experts live in fear that the next outbreak will involve the drug-resistant version of the disease.

Other diseases periodically break out in prisons and spread. In July 2002, an outbreak of Legionnaire's disease began in Vermont's Waterbury Prison and spread to a nearby office complex, infecting 23 people. A month later, several female inmates in Pennsylvania's Bucks County Prison contacted attorneys and complained they were not being treated for a skin condition. It turned out to be an antibiotic-resistant strain of staphylococcus aureus, which can be fatal if it spreads to the bloodstream. Testing in a local hospital found 376 people were infected. A federal judge ordered all 1,115 prisoners and staff to be tested; 34 tested positive.[24]

It is perhaps unfair to expect prisons to act as a front line in the nation's battle against infectious diseases when nobody is willing to give them the money to do so. But prisons still have the duty to care for the general health of their inmates, which in itself is a formidable challenge. This is a mainly poor, under-educated and uninsured population. New York state prisons reported the average age of people who died in custody of natural causes, excluding those who died of

AIDS, was 48.5—30 years less than for the general population.[25] A Massachusetts study published in 1997 found that an astounding 93 percent of the state's prison population did not have health insurance before they were incarcerated. After years of unhealthy living, many inmates have major medical needs. A survey of jail inmates in Hampden County, Massachusetts, found that 17 percent of males and 29 percent of females suffered from asthma; 11 percent of males and 15 percent of females had high blood pressure; and 29 percent of males and 41 percent of females reported bone or joint problems. Other health problems affecting prisoners disproportionately include cardiovascular disease, diabetes, skin conditions and poor dental care. In Hampden County, 35 percent of men and 39 percent of women had problems with their teeth and gums. Many had not visited a dentist in years.[26]

Prison wardens have often remarked to me that prisoners receive a much higher standard of health care behind bars than they ever did in the free world. But this is their right, not a favor the authorities grant them out of the goodness of their hearts. The Supreme Court ruled in 1976 that under the Constitution prisoners have the right to receive basic, decent, competent health care.[27] Many receive such care. Many do not. The really unlucky ones pay for poor care with their lives.

Probably the most searching examination of a state prison system's health record came in the 1999 *Ruiz* ruling that probed conditions in Texas prisons.[28] An expert witness, Dr. John Robertson, reviewed 35 of 40 reported cardiac deaths and 16 of 33 reported cancer deaths in Texas prisons in 1998. He concluded that 14 of the heart deaths and two of the cancer deaths either might have been or should have been prevented. In the cardiac cases, Dr. Robertson found medical staff repeatedly failed to recognize and evaluate serious signs of disease. In the cancer cases, he said two individuals experienced "significant delays in definitive diagnosis and treatment" that turned out to be fatal.[29]

Much of the problem stemmed from the prison system's heavy dependence on nurses or physician assistants to do the job of doctors. In his ruling, Judge William Wayne Justice gave a depressing series of case histories. "Inmate Arthur Heinz died at Garza West in 1998 after repeatedly returning to the infirmary with elevated blood pressure.

During half of his visits, he saw only a nurse. Medication was prescribed several times but no follow-up was scheduled. On his final visit, record was made of the possibility of previously unrecognized myocardial infarction, but it was not addressed or followed up. Inmate Heinz died of cardiac arrest five days later," the judge wrote.

Another inmate, Jason Wimberly, visited medical personnel five times within a day and a half with what Dr. Robertson said were obvious signs of appendicitis. Nurses failed to diagnose his symptoms until his fifth visit, by which time they had become life threatening. He was rushed to hospital with a perforated, gangrenous appendix. He was lucky. He lived. Gilberto Cristo did not. Cristo had a problem with his lungs. He received a number of X-rays, but doctors failed to spot a fast-growing cancer until it had spread throughout his body and was inoperable. Another inmate, unnamed in the judgment, was diagnosed as having a possibly life-threatening growth in his kidney and was scheduled for surgery within two to three weeks. For some reason, he was not sent for the procedure for six months, by which time the cancer was untreatable. He died.

How much of this was incompetence and how much the deliberate indifference of medical staff? The judge had no doubt that both were involved. He wrote, "Inmate Ophelia Rangel spent five days not eating and suffering from psychotic episodes and severe diarrhea, but she was not treated. She died....Michael Bias, who fell into a coma after a suicide attempt, was left to lie in one position, so that he developed infected pressure sores that led to a massive loss of skin, breakdown of muscle and kidney failure."

Layovonda Alexander, who was HIV positive, reported significant weight loss and was coughing up blood. Medical staff reported she was "refusing to work" and forced her to return to her prison job. She died. And the list goes on and on.

Texas is far from unique in providing inmates with substandard treatment. In Washington State, a prison system supervising 15,000 inmates employed only five full-time staff doctors in 2002. A state Health Department inspection found that all five of the state's largest prisons failed to meet standards for controlling infectious or communicable diseases. Staff at all five institutions kept illegible, incomplete or inaccurate patient records. Two prisons also stocked medications past their "use by" date; two had a critical shortage of nurses and two had failed to verify the professional licenses of clinicians. The state could not recruit enough workers to open a new infirmary it built at the Callam Bay Corrections Center. Another on McNeil Island remained closed three years after it was forced to shut down following a scathing Health Department report in 1999.[30]

In Alabama, where spending per inmate in the prison system is the lowest in the nation, even catching a cold can be deadly. Timothy Oliff had only a few months left on his marijuana possession prison term when he caught a cold and could not shake it. By the time health care workers in Elmore Correctional Facility sought emergency help, he was deathly sick, apparently with an advanced case of pneumonia. He died on February 26, 2003, three days after being taken to the hospital. He was 43.[31]

In February 2005, the Atlanta-based Southern Center for Human Rights launched a lawsuit on behalf of six inmates of the Hamilton Aged and Infirm Correctional Facility, a prison for the sick and disabled in Hamilton, Alabama. The suit charged that 300 inmates were forced to live in an unsanitary institution designed to hold only 67 and were often denied essential medical treatment, resulting in unnecessary suffering and premature death.

One of the plaintiffs, Terry Miller, suffered a car accident before being incarcerated and had a severe wound on the left side of his abdomen. The authorities refused to allow him to complete skin graft treatment and for three years only provided him with gauze for his wound, which constantly drained. Another, Jermaine Mitchell, suffered a stroke and was confined to a wheelchair. Due to lack of therapy, his muscles wasted away to the point where he lost almost all his hand strength and had difficulty sitting up.

Geriatric prisoners sometimes lay in their own urine and feces for two to three days without receiving assistance.

The infirmary had no emergency call buttons. When there was a medical emergency, prisoners pounded on the door leading to the nursing station. Often, correctional staff did not respond.

Inmates said the stench in the infirmary was unbearable, mold grew on the showers, the toilets often backed up and overflowed, and urine and feces were allowed to remain on the infirmary floor. Alabama Department of Corrections spokesman Brian Corbett said: "We feel the level of health care services at Hamilton rises well above minimal constitutional standards."[32]

One of the key problems at Hamilton was the lack of medical staff. A doctor visited once a month, and sometimes only once every two months. There was no dentist.

Recruiting medical staff for prisons is a problem nationwide. In New York, starting salaries for prison doctors were $18,000 to $36,000 below comparable medical salaries in the free world.[33] In Arizona, nurse vacancies in 2000 ran between 35 and 80 percent at the state's five biggest prisons, according to the Department of Corrections annual report for 2001. With an acute nursing shortage in many parts of the country, registered nurses are unlikely to be wooed into prison service unless they are offered pay and conditions that meet or exceed those in the private sector. The work is extremely tough and stressful. Correctional nurses have described how inmates jeer, wolf-whistle and ogle them whenever they set foot in a cell block. Some men make it their practice to expose themselves or openly masturbate whenever a woman enters. Professional burnout is a major problem, leading to high turnover and low retention rates.

A report by the California State Employees Association (CSEA) in 2003 found a 25 percent vacancy rate for nurses in state prisons. At many facilities, it was much higher. At Salinas Valley State Prison, 67.5 percent of nursing jobs were unfilled. At Folsom State Prison, the vacancy rate was 41 percent. "State nurses are fed up. They know they can double their salary in the private sector and they are doing it," said Karl Hennington, chairman of the CSEA bargaining unit that represents 3,380 state nurses.[34] More than 630 state-employed registered nurses quit during the year ending October 2002. Their departure left those who remained with longer hours and more patients to manage. It also forced the state to spend over $40 million a year to employ temporary replacements on short-term contracts. The temporary nurses were making an average of $59.36 an hour, while the state-employed RNs earned an average of $28.95 an hour.[35] Having temps in charge of treatment also makes for poor health care. There is no continuity of treatment or patient follow-up.

The danger is that those health professionals who remain in the prison system become so exhausted and burned out that they lose the sense of compassion so crucial to humane care. They cease seeing inmates as patients and begin to regard them as adversaries. A doctor in a federal prison told a Muslim inmate detained in the aftermath of 9/11, "If I was in charge, I would execute every one of you."[36]

Facing critical staffing problems, state prison systems cannot afford to be overly fussy about whom they hire. Often, they scrape the bottom of the barrel. In Wisconsin, at least six doctors and two nurses employed in prisons had their medical licenses limited or suspended by the state Medical Examining Board.[37] When lack of empathy combines with lack of competence, the results can be lethal. One New York prison employed a doctor who had had his medical license suspended for five years in 1987. He was limited to practicing in an "institutional setting" such as a prison after pleading guilty to five counts of professional misconduct, including one case of gross incompetence and gross negligence. A court-appointed monitor reviewed this physician's treatment of three prison patients who died under his care. One succumbed to a bacterial staph infection that went untreated for six months. In the weeks before he died, the inmate developed multiple lesions, and his kidney and liver functions were clearly deteriorating. Two days before he died, the desperate inmate told the doctor he had been vomiting blood. The doctor entered a note on the patient's file suggesting he did not believe him and took no action. Later, the patient told medical staff that he could no longer urinate. Again, the doctor did nothing. The inmate died the following day. The monitor wrote that the neglect of this patient during the final two days of his life was "terribly disturbing and contributed to his unnecessary death."[38]

Most states do not require prison doctors to be certified by professional boards. But there is a price for employing incompetent or uncaring staff. New York has paid out many hundreds of thousands of dollars in medical malpractice lawsuits. In 2001, the family of James Wooten was awarded $338,000 after a court blamed the state for his death from congestive heart failure at Cayuga prison. Carlton Goodwind won $150,000 for a burst appendix at Fishkill prison; Andre Davidson's mother and three children received $900,000 for his death from asthma at age 29 at Green Haven. Ibn Kenyatta won $1 million after staff at Fishkill prison failed to diagnose bladder and kidney problems until his kidneys had actually failed. They refused even to take his vital signs and referred him to a psychiatrist, saying his symptoms were all inside his head. He will never again urinate normally and must catheterize himself six times a day.[39]

In another New York case, inmate Paul Malcolm, 26, died at Auburn Correctional Facility after being exposed to pepper spray used against another inmate. Medical staff ignored his requests for an inhaler. After he died, authorities failed to inform his mother. Finally, worried that she hadn't heard from her son for several weeks and that none of her letters were being answered, she called the prison to find out he had been dead for five months. Officials told her they could not reach her, despite the fact that she had been living in the same place for seven years.[40]

A newspaper investigation into health care in Wisconsin prisons found similar neglect.[41] An inmate died of a ruptured appendix after complaining of the pain for two days. He was not taken to the hospital until it was too late. A 70-year-old complained of chest pain for three days and saw a prison doctor, who did not order an electrocardiogram or take other action. He died of a heart attack in his cell the next day. A 29-year-old woman died of asthma, gasping for air on the floor of a prison dining room. In Wisconsin, prison authorities kept details about the care given to inmates before they died a secret. The Department of Corrections refused to release final mortality review reports even to the families of the deceased. It also rejected a request from a state legislator to provide a list of inmates who had died in prison since 1990 along with their causes of death, and it fought efforts to establish an outside review panel.[42]

In an Alabama case, a judge ruled in 2002 that inmates were exposed to dangerous conditions while on prison work details. Around 300 inmates of the Elmore Correctional Center had to work at a recycling center inside the prison, where they often got stuck by needles contaminated by hepatitis and AIDS. In such cases, a person should begin preventive medication within 24 hours. At Elmore, it was delayed for several days or longer. Judge Tracy McCooey said she would begin fining the prison $100 a day unless they began offering prisoners prompt treatment.[43]

Sometimes, the level of incompetence in prison clinics reaches surreal levels. Take the story of David Padilla, an insulin-dependent diabetic with heart disease, incarcerated for drugs possession in the California Rehabilitation Center in Norco in 1996. From the day he arrived there, medical staff never checked his blood sugar, although they gave him regular insulin shots. On April 10, 1998, Padilla received his shot but awoke from a nap feeling ill and recognized he was going into insulin shock. He stumbled toward the exit of his dorm, where a guard told him to "quit fucking around" and refused to unlock the door. Padilla tripped and fell. The guard ran over and kicked him, yelling at him to get up. Only when he screamed in pain did the guard call for help. A staff fireman and three other prisoners, but no medical staff, responded. Ignoring all established medical procedures, they rolled him over and he heard a pop in his neck. When Padilla was finally taken to the prison clinic, Dr. Charn Toochinda ordered him flipped over again, causing further injury as well as excruciating pain. By the time he was taken to the hospital, he was paralyzed from the neck down and he will live the rest of his life as a quadriplegic. In May 2002, a California superior court jury awarded Padilla $2.5 million. The state did not appeal.[44]

Often, prisons and jails contract out medical services to private companies. The biggest is the Brentwood, Tennessee-based Prison Health Services (PHS), a subsidiary of America Services Group. Founded in 1978, PHS provides health care in more than 400 jails and prisons, covering 235,000 inmates in 35 states.[45] Its latest coup in the summer of 2003 was to win a contract to provide health care for 40,000 inmates in the Pennsylvania state prison system. The company has won praise from some health professionals for its work. It is committed to winning jail and prison accreditation from the National Commission on Correctional Health Care (NCCHC). Under its management, more than 130 prisons and jails have won NCCHC accreditation for the first time. The company also claimed to have saved its clients over $43 million in five years, while cutting inmates' grievances by 20 percent or more. It said it had reduced per-inmate medical expenses by up to 27 percent over three years and slashed annual growth in medical costs from almost 20 percent to four percent.

However, not everybody was cheering. In 2003, the company had more than 1,000 lawsuits pending against it, most of them alleging substandard care.[46] The allegation was that as a for-profit corporation, PHS put the bottom line above the patient and would do whatever it could to cut costs. The city of Philadelphia held hearings into company practices after the death of Jose Santiago, a diabetic who was held awaiting trial in 2000 and went into shock after health staffers denied him his medication. At a hearing, Donnie Moore, head of the local Guards Union, said correctional officers were often forced to do the job of health care workers because PHS failed to hire enough staff. He said he had seen five prisoners die because they did not receive medical attention.[47] Still, Philadelphia renewed its contract with the company in 2002 and again in 2003.

PHS also ran most of Maryland's prisons and Baltimore's notoriously unhealthy jails until 2005 when the state ended its contract with the company.[48] At the same time that the state was changing its health provider, the city of Baltimore was establishing a grand jury to look into the city jail's health care system in the face of numerous allegations of gross abuse and shortcomings.[49]

The saga of the Baltimore jail, and the fact that a judge felt the need to establish a grand jury, shows how hard it is to effect change, even after shocking and horrific conditions are exposed. In August 2002, the U.S. Department of Justice Civil Rights Division issued a scathing report about the jail, where around 2,500 people are held on any given day. Eighty percent of them, the report said, had not been convicted of anything and were incarcerated awaiting trial because they could not make bond.[50]

The violations spelled out in the report are too numerous to list here in full. They include:

- The smoke detectors, sprinkler system and fire alarms were inoperable and the facility contained excessive amounts of combustible materials.

- Inmates were not properly screened on entry for physical or mental illness. One inmate died of hypertension and cardiovascular disease on May 19, 2000, after a day and a half at the facility. His file revealed no medical screening or other attention during his time at the facility. Another inmate died on July 18, 2000 after 24 hours in custody. His pretrial services information printout indicated that he had a 10-year daily heroin addiction and high blood pressure and he was on medication for high blood pressure. Despite the fact that this information was available to the detention center, the inmate had no contact with a health professional during his stay at the facility. The jail also failed to provide adequate medical care for inmates with acute and emergent care needs. "Our review indicated that nurses sometimes practice outside the scope of their training and licensure," the report said. Additionally, "Our review of inmate deaths revealed several instances in which correctional officers failed to perform CPR, and waited for health care or emergency personnel to arrive instead. In an interview with a nurse by an investigator of a death that occurred at Central Booking on October 29, 2000, the nurse complained that she noted a pattern of correctional officers failing to initiate or assist in CPR."

- Treatment of patients with asthma at the facility was especially problematic. "Our medical consultant deems that two deaths at the facility attributed to asthma (one in August 1999 and one in December 2000) were preventable if the inmates' conditions had been properly treated," the report said.

- The jail failed to deliver adequate mental health care. "Specifically, BCDC does not provide adequate access to medication, access to care, and suicide prevention," the report said.

- Food service operations at BCDC did not meet sanitation requirements and put residents at risk of developing food borne illness. For example, trays of food were observed on top of garbage containers prior to service. Major pieces of food storage and service equipment were broken, including refrigerators, ice machines, and baking equipment.

- Dead roaches and droppings were prevalent. "We found evidence of roaches and rodents throughout the kitchen in the Men's Detention Center, including live roaches in the dishwashing equipment. We also found roach droppings, spiders, and gnats in residence areas throughout the facility."

- The facility lacked proper ventilation to prevent disease transmission and control odors. For example, a block of rooms in the Women's Detention Center where medically fragile inmates reside was too cold because of windows that allow wind in, and an inadequately balanced heating system. Other parts of the facility were far too hot.

- "We observed many inmates washing their clothes in the toilets in their cells. While facility staff claim that inmates have access to utility sinks or can send their wash to the laundry, inmates reported that they do not have time to wash their clothes in the sink and also shower and take care of other needs during their very limited out-of-cell time. They reported that they did not always get their clothes back if they sent them to the laundry."

There were more violations but the above examples should be sufficient to give a taste of what life was like in the Baltimore city jail. Again, the vast majority of inmates had not been convicted of a crime. They were basically there because they were too poor to afford bail.

In Alabama, a Birmingham company, NaphCare, took over as the state prison health provider in 2001. The first year it was in charge, inmate deaths rose from 61 the previous year to 87. The second year, they rose to 95. Under NaphCare, Alabama had around one doctor for every 3,000 inmates. An external audit conducted by Jacqueline Moore and Associates, a Chicago-based consultancy, found that chronically sick patients could go seven or eight months without seeing a doctor. Diabetes patients received blood sugar tests once a month instead of every day. In May 2003, the state terminated its contract with the health provider.[51]

Another private company, Physicians Network Associates (PNA), was in charge of health care at the Santa Fe County Adult Detention Center when experts from the U.S. Department of Justice paid two three-day visits in May 2002. A letter from Assistant U.S. Attorney General Ralph F. Boyd to Santa Fe County Commission Chairman Jack Sullivan on March 6, 2003, laid out an alarming description of the health care the 600 inmates were receiving, with some of the same faults as those observed in Baltimore, plus numerous additional ones.[52]

"The Detention Center, through PNA, provides inadequate medical services in the following areas: intake, screening and referral; acute care; emergent care; chronic and pre-natal care; and medication administration and management. As a result, inmates at the Detention Center with serious medical needs are at risk for harm," Boyd wrote.

The breakdowns started from the moment new inmates entered the facility. One in five never received a proper health screening for chronic or contagious disease. Even when staff identified individuals with serious medical needs, they failed to refer them for appropriate care. Not one inmate whose charts were examined by the experts was referred to the Health Services Unit for the attention they needed. Moreover, during screenings, jail officials did not protect patient confidentiality. Department of Justice observers were present while a female inmate went through her initial screening. During the interview, two male officers entered the room and listened in. One handcuffed the inmate while she was trying to answer intimate personal questions.

Only 37 percent of inmates received a full health appraisal within 14 days of their arrival. Only half received a TB skin test within 18 days. Even when inmates reported serious health problems, staff did not take prompt action. One inmate, who was transferred from another facility, told medical staff he had tested positive for glaucoma. A nurse made a note in his file but did not obtain his medical records from the previous institution. Nearly two months later, the inmate again complained about his condition. Nothing happened; he did not receive an eye examination. Four months later, during the inspectors' visit, a Department of Justice expert reviewed his file and brought the case to the attention of medical authorities at the jail, saying he was worried this patient's eyesight was at risk. Another month went by and nothing happened. After all this, when he was finally given an eye exam, it did not include a test to detect glaucoma. The inspector wrote, "As of our last review of his chart, it had been eight months since he originally reported this condition during the initial health screening, and his record still did not reflect an appropriate assessment to determine what care he needed."[53] The letter did not say what happened to this patient.

The experts found many cases in which care was unreasonably and unnecessarily delayed. Even when care was provided, it was often inadequate. The inspectors reviewed the records of 10 inmates for primary care by a nurse practitioner during a one-month period. Six received substandard care. Two had abnormal skin tests for TB but neither received treatment. One inmate said she had lumps in her breasts and armpits as well as chest pain and swollen legs. The nurse ordered a mammogram, but seven months later it had not been done. By this time, the swelling in her legs was so severe that when pressed, her flesh stayed depressed like "silly putty." This condition is known as pitting edema and requires urgent care. When the outside experts expressed alarm about the way this woman was treated, a doctor did an incomplete examination of her swollen legs but did not document whether he had checked her breasts or armpit lumps.

In another case in Santa Fe, an inmate was bleeding from the ear following trauma, a condition that typically indicates either a perforated eardrum or a skull fracture. The nurse practitioner prescribed a painkiller and never referred the patient for an ear examination or neurological checkup. Yet another patient with high blood pressure and diabetes reported a sudden loss of vision on February 20, 2002. He should have immediately been sent to the emergency room but was referred to an optometrist. Optometrists measure eyes for eyeglasses but do not specialize in eye disease. It took until April 1 before the inmate was seen by an ophthalmologist, who immediately referred him to a retina surgeon. Two more crucial weeks passed before jail officials took him to see the surgeon. The surgeon wanted to operate immediately but needed permission from the jail. Another 10 days went by before the jail gave its permission and surgery took place. "Although this inmate's blindness could have been prevented had he received appropriate care, the delay in treatment caused him to lose his vision permanently," the letter said.[54]

The report described many other cases of inexcusable medical failures and delays—too many to list them all here. But the point is clear. Prison and jail inmates are highly vulnerable to poor treatment and mistreatment. They represent a uniquely vulnerable sector of society. They may be too sick or too ignorant to stand up for themselves. They are completely at the mercy of medical staff and other prison employees. The fact that a tiny minority of inmates or their surviving family members collect sizeable legal settlements after death or serious harm has occurred is little or no comfort. If an inmate dies and leaves no survivors, there is no lawsuit and no recompense. The body is quietly disposed of and the inmate is quickly forgotten.

The handling of medications is a major health issue for prisons and jails. It is important that inmates on courses of medicine take their doses regularly and finish the prescribed course. Failure to do so is often worse than not taking the medicine at all. The inconsistent use of antibiotics contributes to the emergence of drug resistant diseases that place both the individual and the community at risk. Surveys have shown that inmates often miss their doses because they are not in their cells or they do not hear medication calls. In Texas prisons, many patients must wait in long lines at "pill windows" to receive medication. Sick patients complain that they must stand for prolonged periods and often receive the wrong medication and in some cases no medication at all.[55] In Santa Fe, the nurse practitioner was the only person qualified to prescribe medication. She often changed doses that patients had been receiving in the outside world. Sometimes she switched them to cheaper, less effective drugs, apparently to cut costs.

At the Limestone Correctional Facility in Capshaw, Alabama, HIV patients have to get up at 3 a.m. and wait outdoors, summer and winter, for as long as 45 minutes to receive their medications. A paralegal from the Southern Center for Human Rights, armed with a court order, videotaped the scene in February 2003. Not surprisingly, the state's death rate for AIDS was more than double the national average. Limestone was housing HIV patients in an old warehouse with high, leaky ceilings. They were sleeping on bunk beds squashed close together so that infections were easily passed back and forth.[56]

In some jails, where there is a shortage of trained staff, correctional officers get landed with the job of seeing to it that inmates take their medicine. In a small jail with about 45 inmates in Jefferson County, Washington, a nurse visited once a week. During the rest of the time, untrained jail staff made medical decisions for the inmates, a task they were plainly unqualified for. Many medications have serious side effects and must be carefully monitored. Some drugs require regular blood tests. It is simply unfair to ask unqualified jail staff to do this, even leaving aside the fact that some guards may not have the best interests of inmates at heart. In 2002, the ACLU filed a class action suit against Jefferson County, alleging that staff often threatened to deny inmates their medications or did deny them as a punishment for misbehavior. In 2003, the county reached an agreement to settle the lawsuit. It agreed to improve conditions by meeting standards set by the NCCHC and appointed an outside monitor to check on its performance.[57]

In Texas, health officials came up with a new wrinkle in prisoner care—they used inmates as subjects in medical trials. A July 2000 inspection of the University of Texas Medical Branch (UTMB) found that medical experiments involving Texas prisoners were not up to standard. Prisoners were not told about potential risks, while benefits of participating were vastly overstated. Over half of UTMB research projects did not meet the standards set by the Office of Human Research Protection. In September 2001, UTMB was ordered to halt prisoner participation in 195 federally funded projects.[58]

Prison health is a lot broader than just the delivery of medical services. A jail can become a serious health hazard if the plumbing does not function properly or the toilets do not work. Insects and rodents must be kept out. Laundry must be done regularly and efficiently. The facility must have a functioning climate-control system. Inmates need adequate supplies of hygiene products. In Jefferson County, inmates said they were not provided with supplies of basic items such as toilet paper and feminine hygiene products and were forced to use pages from telephone books, towels or paper bags. Under its agreement with the ACLU, the jail agreed to address these shortcomings by ensuring that in future there would always be adequate supplies of these items on hand and agreeing to supply them to inmates on request as long as they were not misused.

In June 2004, a New York Times reporter toured the Los Angeles County Jail, where five inmates had been murdered in seven months. He found the jail housing up to six prisoners in a single cell, which meant two had to sleep on floors that were wet with toilet seepage. A staph infection was raging through the facility, and inmates crowded at the bars to show the visitor their lesions.[59]

Health professionals are increasingly alarmed about the spread of drug-resistant strains of staph—so-called super-bacteria—that are spreading from prison to the community. They are extremely difficult and expensive to treat, and if not treated can quickly become fatal.

Yet some jail authorities are making it harder, not easier, for inmates to maintain personal hygiene and fight illness. Since 1996, Polk County in Florida has been charging inmates $1.90 for a package of personal hygiene items when they are booked into jail. The package includes one bar of soap, one toothbrush, one .85-ounce tube of toothpaste, one safety razor, one comb, one washcloth, one 1.5-ounce container of roll-on deodorant and one 4-ounce container of shampoo. "Because inmates pay for these items, it has created a sense of ownership. Inmates are aware they need to get their money's worth—they have become less wasteful of the items overall," Sheriff Lawrence W. Crow, Jr., said.[60]

Increasingly, states are trying to pass health costs on to prisoners by charging them a co-pay, as if they were members of an HMO in the outside world. By 2003, at least 36 states were charging inmates between $3 and $9 per visit to the clinic, despite the fact that most inmates earned less than $1 an hour for prison work. Courts have upheld this practice. In some states there is a graduated system in which inmates pay less to see a nurse and more to see a doctor. Such fees are politically popular. "There is no way to justify handing convicted criminals free health care while law-abiding taxpayers are required to make co-payments for health services," said New York State Senator Michael F. Nozzolio, sponsoring a 2002 measure to introduce a $7 co-pay for prisoners. "By revoking this policy, we will bring justice to both the criminals who thumb their noses at the law and to the law-abiding citizens struggling to pay for their own health care."[61]

Clearly some inmates do abuse the health system, and this was one way to reduce the frivolous use of scarce medical resources. But what if such measures also discourage prisoners with chronic conditions or infectious diseases from seeking help? Delays of treatment probably end up costing the taxpayer a lot more than the amount prison systems can collect through co-pays. Preventive care is always a lot cheaper than treatment in a hospital emergency room. It also costs money to administer such co-pay programs. In California, the State Auditor reported in 2001 that it cost the state $3.2 million a year to collect $5 co-payments for every visit to a prison doctor, while the program only generated

$654,000 in income.[62] That kind of math simply does not make sense. The State Legislature passed a bill that year to revoke the co-payments, but then-Governor Gray Davis vetoed it.

Food preparation plays a big part in health. In Florida, the Department of Corrections signed a five-year contract in 2001 with Philadelphia-based Aramark Corporation to feed inmates in 126 of the state's 133 prisons. The contract aimed to reduce the state's food costs by over $80 million a year[63] by cutting spending on meals for prisoners from $3.07 to $2.36 a day.[64] How were these savings achieved? According to the *St. Petersburg Times,* daily logs kept by corrections officers described filthy kitchens, frequent meal delays, attempts to serve spoiled, watered down or undercooked food and a failure to obey rules requiring that each inmate receive the same meal—a security measure designed to prevent fights.

"Since the company took over prison kitchens last year, it has continually violated regulations designed to promote sanitation and safety," the newspaper said, adding that the state was taking big risks with the safety of inmates and staff alike.[65] In Marion County, an Aramark supervisor ordered prisoner workers to soak spoiled chicken in vinegar to get rid of the nasty smell before cooking. Guards, who also ate the same food, ordered 500 pieces of foul-smelling chicken thrown out. Inspectors in Brevard County found maggots on serving trays and on kitchen floors. In Hernando County, guards saw kitchen workers reusing chili con carne left over from the previous week. The state fined Aramark $110,000 for its practices but refused to end the contract.[66] This may not be a recipe for health, but it is surely a recipe for trouble. Hungry inmates are angry inmates. Sick inmates are costly inmates.

It does not have to be this way. Despite all the challenges, some jail systems have managed to build efficient and compassionate health systems that serve both inmates and the community. One is Hampden County in Massachusetts, which includes the city of Springfield. All prisoners receive a detailed health orientation upon admission, including a review of their medical history and screening for tuberculosis, sexually transmitted diseases and hepatitis A, B and C. Women receive pap smears and pelvic exams. The jail has found it is cheaper to contract with community-based providers to fill its health care needs than to hire its own staff. Each inmate is assigned a primary care physician, a nurse practitioner and a case manager from a health center from his own neighborhood. When they are released, inmates as well as their families can continue to receive care from these same professionals. Inside the jail, every cell block has a regular triage nurse who visits daily and takes care of minor complaints on the spot, referring more serious ones to the medical departments. "We are the community. Our inmates are members of the community from which they came—and to which they will return. We see ourselves as a point of entry into the health care system," said Thomas Conklin, director of health services at the jail.[67]

Many jail administrators would argue that it would be far too expensive to set up such an elaborate system. But Hampden County's costs, at $7.23 per inmate per day, were actually less than the $7.99 average paid by the 30 largest jails in the United States, according to a 2001 study. Administrators believe that inmates respond to the care they receive. They become involved in their own health care and learn positive behaviors that help them after they are released. A three-year study of inmates released from the jail from 1998 to 2001 found a reincarceration rate of 36.5 percent, compared to a national rate of 51.8 percent.

With the U.S. prison population aging rapidly, the costs of health care are likely soon to prove overwhelming for many states. This more than any other factor could undermine the philosophy of mass incarceration that has dominated the political debate for so long. It has started to happen already. In 2003, California was spending $730 a day—excluding medical procedures, drugs and the salaries paid to guards—to care for Steven Martinez, a quadriplegic who was paralyzed after fellow inmates stabbed him in the neck in 1998. Nurses bathed him, turned his body every two hours and spoon-fed him three times a day. If he lives another 30 years, just meeting his basic needs could cost California $8 million or more. And the state had another 120 prisoners who needed help with bathing, eating or other functions of daily life. State authorities have opposed releasing Martinez. He raped a woman; he should serve his time, they said.[68]

In January 2002, another unidentified 31-year-old California inmate underwent a heart transplant, the first time a state prisoner had received an organ transplant. The prison system bore the cost but did not publicly disclose it. The state was also spending millions of dollars transporting hundreds of convicts each month to city hospitals for kidney dialysis, at a cost of $233 per trip just for the vans, the gasoline and the guards.[69]

The fact is that removing parole and good time and forcing inmates to stay in prison until they die is going to cost society billions. Thirty-seven inmates whose medical expenses were classified as "catastrophic" cost Georgia $4.1 million in 2002. The bill for one inmate with lupus, diabetes and kidney failure came to $340,000. She died in prison.[70] Georgia, like other states, was extremely reluctant to give even dying inmates compassionate medical reprieves. In the summer of 2003, only five of the state's 41,000 inmates had been granted such reprieves. Farris Davis, 58, in prison on a life sentence since 1990 for murder and aggravated assault, was one who was denied. Davis, who suffered from poor circulation, high blood pressure and other health problems, had his leg amputated below the knee and had limited use of his right arm. His family lobbied for his release but Mike Light, a member of the state Parole Board, said he still needed to be punished for killing a man during a drug deal. "He's only served 13 years. The crime is still relatively fresh and there's some time still to be served here," he said.

In Angola prison in Louisiana, located on an isolated bend of the Mississippi River 50 miles north of Baton Rouge, warden Burl Cain told me that 90 percent of the 5,000 inmates in his charge would die in prison. They included prisoners with dementia and blindness, some who had been incapacitated with strokes and others with end-stage AIDS or cancer. As its population aged, the prison's annual medical budget ballooned to $12 million. It cost up to $400 a day to keep an inmate in the prison's medical wing. To meet the growing need, Cain established a hospice behind bars where inmates could die with dignity.

Ralph Dawson, serving life for second degree murder, was one of 37 inmates selected to work as medical aides, helping their fellow prisoners approach death. "I read to them, write letters for them, run errands, cook in the microwave, bathe them, shave them, pray with them, sing for them—whatever they need," he told me. "I logged 120 hours in the hospice last month. I'm trying to find something to focus on, something to live for. I'm trying to see a goal down the road. Is this really it for me? Is this my whole life, in here behind bars? If so, how will I deal with it? I'm looking to grab a hold of something to carry me through. I'm 35 and it crossed my mind recently that I might end up in here, in this hospice, with someone taking care of me. It gets hard sometimes just to put one foot in front of the other."

Ted Durbin, known to fellow inmates as "Animal," was working his way through a sentence of 140 years for multiple offenses. "Basically, I was a criminal. I have a parole hearing in 2021, but with my record, with 100 arrests, what are my chances?" he said. Durbin had a prison buddy who was admitted to the hospice as a patient. He began coming to visit, then started helping out and stayed on as a volunteer after his friend died. "I used to be an ugly person on the inside and the outside. Now I'm only ugly on the outside. I've been volunteering here three years. I've sat with quite a few men that died as I held their hands. We have to wipe their butts for some of the guys in here. You learn how to do it in a way that doesn't embarrass them. It's a privilege to be allowed to do that for someone at that stage of life. I'm in here three hours a day, five days a week. I have Hep C. I'd say 85 percent of the inmates have it. Right now, it's not active but in the future—who knows?"

Michael Shulark, serving life for second degree murder, vowed never to allow another inmate to die alone after one of his buddies died without a friend at his side. "When he died, all he had was correctional officers and nursing staff around him. I've been with 19 men since then. I'm on my twentieth one right now. His name is Tom. He's in and out of consciousness. It won't be long now. I'd like to go home someday, but I feel that I'm doing what I was meant to be doing. I'll probably die here too," he said.

Angola has its own cemetery called Point Lookout. Inmates' bodies are placed into coffins built in the prison carpentry and loaded on to a replica of an antique horse-drawn hearse, also made by inmates. Warden Cain said he would prefer to release terminally ill patients to their families, but the state did not allow it. "Do we really want old men in jail who can't hurt us any more?" he asked.

7

WOMEN BEHIND BARS

---

*"A woman is like a tea bag—
only in hot water do you realize how strong she is."*
Nancy Reagan[1] ∎

J ulia Strudwick Tutwiler (1841–1916) was an early pioneer of women's rights and prison reform in Alabama. Known as the Angel of the Prisons, she was instrumental in securing separate prisons for men and women in her state as well as the establishment of Alabama's first juvenile school. She campaigned successfully for a law to establish regular prison inspections and for night schools and vocational education for inmates. In 1941, 25 years after her death, Alabama opened the Julia Tutwiler Prison for Women in Wetumpka and named it in her honor. Unfortunately, as a class action lawsuit revealed, it is one of the worst prisons in the nation.

Originally built to house 364 inmates, by late 2002 the prison held 1,017. That year, it was the most violent institution in the state, with more assaults on staff and inmates than even the toughest male prison. Prisoners were held in large dormitories, hundreds squashed together in unventilated rooms with nothing to do all day. The summer heat was stifling, but there were not enough fans to cover all the dorms. Inmates had to take turns to have fans for four hours at a time. In any case, the fans did little other than move the hot air around.

"Bunk beds are laid in rows and arranged head to toe, within inches of each other. In some dorms, inmates can lie on their beds, reach out their arms, and touch other inmates. In dorm ten, some inmates have difficulty climbing to their top bunks because the proximity of other beds limits access to the ladders at the heads of their beds; inmates who sleep in top bunks often wedge their way between the bunks and then work their way to the top bunk," wrote U.S. District Court Judge Myron Thompson in a December 2002 judgment that ordered the state to improve conditions.[2]

"The health care unit is so short on space that three beds have been placed in the hall to house inmates who are waiting for or returning from an operation; these inmates share the hallway with everyone entering or leaving the health care unit. While Tutwiler's infrastructure has been modified in the past to handle more inmates, it is now so overcrowded that each inmate's living space is severely limited, and adding even one more bed would create an unacceptable burden," he wrote.

"During the summer, all inmates want relief from the unrelenting heat, putting fans and ice at a premium. Although fans are to be rotated every four hours according to a schedule, this does not always happen; aggressive inmates sometimes refuse to turn over the fan according to schedule, leading to fights and violence.... Similarly, the desire for ice also leads to fights. 'Ice call' is twice a day and some inmates push their way to the front of the line. Most inmates choose to leave these aggressive inmates alone, letting them move to the head of the line; those who do not acquiesce, however, face physical retaliation and violence for their refusal," wrote Judge Thompson.

In 1979, Tutwiler housed 196 inmates and had a security staff of 87. By 2002, the state had hired only five new officers to manage 884 additional inmates. When the prison was not fully staffed, one officer had to watch over 300 inmates in four different dorms at once. Dorm nine, which housed some of the more violent inmates, was known as the zoo. One officer was on duty alone most of the time. In dorm ten, an officer guarding 106 inmates on her own was attacked by a mentally ill inmate and was only saved when prisoners rushed to sound the alarm. Fights were common. Inmates easily made weapons from mop and broom handles and safety razors. One woman was cut from ear to chin during her sleep.

Reading Judge Thompson's opinion, one can only wonder what Julia Tutwiler would have thought of the prison that bears her name.

The growth of the inmate population in Tutwiler reflects the national trend. In the past decade, women have been the fastest growing segment of the U.S. prison population. The number of women incarcerated in prisons or jails more than doubled, from 44,065 in 1990 to 103,310 by midyear 2004.[3] Since 1995, the number of women in state or federal prisons has grown by an average of 5 percent a year—much higher than the 3.3 percent yearly increase in the male population.[4]

"Obviously judges are sentencing females at a higher rate than in the past. In the 1960s and 1970s, a woman typically had to commit several crimes before she was sent to prison. That's not the case any more. If you commit the crime, it doesn't matter if you are a man or a woman. You're going to do the time," said Ron Angelone, former boss of the Virginia Department of Corrections.

Whereas most men in prison have committed a violent offense, 70 percent of women in state prisons were convicted of nonviolent crimes, mainly drugs, property or petty financial offenses. Women have been special targets of the war on drugs. Even when judges want to be lenient, their hands are often tied by mandatory sentencing guidelines. The effect on families, especially black families, has been catastrophic.

"Studies show that the absence of a woman from the family is far more devastating than the absence of a man. When mothers are not in the family, the family is likely to deteriorate," said Evette Simmons of the National Bar Associate, a black lawyers group. "The harsh sentencing that came out of the war on drugs has become the war on the family."[5]

Women in prison face some of the same problems as men. Like men, many have mental health and substance abuse issues. Most are poor and uneducated, and many are in poor health. Despite the situation at Tutwiler, prison violence is less common than at male prisons, but it does exist. However, women in prison also face a slew of serious problems—personal, medical and sexual—that are specific to them. Over two-thirds of women in prison are mothers, and being separated from their children imposes extraordinary psychological stress. Added to this is that many female inmates are victims of abuse. A Bureau of Justice Statistics survey in 1999 found more than 57 percent of women inmates of state prisons had been physically and/or sexually abused at some point in their lives.[6] A third said they had been raped, and over half had suffered abuse by spouses or boyfriends. A third were the victims of parents or guardians. Appalling as these figures are, some scholars, like Harvard University social psychologist Angela Browne, believe they are too low because of methodological flaws in the survey, especially the way the questions were asked.

Browne spent several years studying inmates at Bedford Hills Correctional Facility, a maximum security women's prison in Westchester County, New York. She conducted detailed interviews with 150 newly incarcerated inmates. Their average age was 32; about half were African-American and a quarter were Hispanic. Most had never been married but 80 percent were mothers. In Browne's survey, an astounding 82 percent said they experienced some sort of assault during childhood.[7] Fifty-nine percent had experienced sexual abuse during childhood or adolescence, and 70 percent had suffered severe physical violence from a parent or caretaker. The pattern continued into adulthood, when 75 percent were abused by their partners.

Browne gives a chilling breakdown of the kinds of abuse these women suffered: 60 percent were kicked, bitten or punched; 57 percent were beaten up; 50 percent were hit with an object; 40 percent were choked, strangled or smothered; 36 percent were threatened with a gun or knife; 25 percent were actually cut or shot. Thirty-five percent had been raped by their partner.[8]

For these women, sexual abuse started early. Two-thirds had already been molested by age 11. Moreover, early abuse was a good predictor of later abuse—80 percent of those physically abused as children were later abused as adults. Typically, around the age of 12 to 14, these young girls began dropping out of regular education. Some ran away from home. They associated with young men several years their senior who introduced them to drugs and crime. Often, they became pregnant. "You see an onset of substance abuse, early depression and posttraumatic stress responses," said Browne.

One study of admissions to a big Midwestern jail suggested that twice as many women as men had serious mental illnesses and over one-fifth were diagnosed with Post Traumatic Stress Disorder.[9] Clearly women represent an extraordinarily vulnerable segment of the prison population. In many ways, their needs are greater than those of men. Unfortunately, they are often not met. Women prisoners have specific medical requirements, physical as well as mental. Some need mammograms because of a family history of breast cancer or other risk factors but do not always receive them. A 1998 study in a Southern prison found 70 percent of women who should have had mammograms under the standard medical protocol had not been tested.[10]

It took Sherrie Chapman two years to convince authorities at the California Institution for Women in Frontera that she needed an urgent mammogram and examination after she felt a lump in her right breast in 1991, her lawyer said. By 1995, she required an immediate radical mastectomy and the removal of four lymph nodes. Correctional officers were not very sympathetic to her needs during chemotherapy, and she often missed appointments. In 1997, Chapman lost her left breast as well. Then she discovered lumps in her neck. Her attorney, Cassie Pierson, recalled, "Sometimes they would send her out for tests—but usually she would call and tell me that the prison doctors didn't seem concerned. 'You've just got swollen glands; don't worry, they're not cancerous.'" They were cancerous. Denied parole in June 2002, Chapman died six months later in a community hospital with a prison guard outside the door. She was 45.[11]

While some women prisoners die, others give birth. Every year, hundreds of babies are born to women in prison. A study by the Bureau of Justice Statistics found that in 1997 more than 2,200 pregnant women were imprisoned and more than 1,300 babies were born behind bars.[12] Being pregnant in prison is terrifying. Most state prisons give pregnant women the same food as other inmates, which is not a healthy prenatal diet.[13] But the scariest part comes when it is time for the woman to give birth. In 1999, Amnesty International highlighted several cases of women in labor transported to the hospital in shackles and then actually forced to go through labor and give birth while chained down to a bed. "Maria Jones,"[14] a nonviolent drugs offender held in Cook County Jail in Chicago, described her labor: "I told the nurse that my water broke and the officer took off the handcuffs so that I could put on the hospital gown. I was placed on a monitoring machine with the leg shackles still on. I was taken into the labor room and my leg was shackled to the hospital bed. The officer was stationed just outside the door. I was in labor for almost 12 hours. I asked the officer to disconnect the leg iron from the bed when I needed to use the bathroom, but the officer made me use the bedpan instead. I was not permitted to move around to help the labor along." As the moment of birth neared, the doctor had to work the chain around so that Maria could find a comfortable position. She couldn't place her feet in stirrups or get her legs apart because her ankles were still chained together. "The doctor called for the officer but the officer had gone down the hall. No one else could unlock the shackles and my baby was coming, but I couldn't open my legs. Finally the officer came and unlocked the shackles from my ankles. My baby was born then. I stayed in the delivery room with my baby for a little while, but then the officer put the leg shackles and handcuffs back on me and I was taken out of the delivery room. I was in the hospital for about three days, with one hand and one foot shackled to the bed."[15]

A woman about to give birth presents no security threat and no escape risk. Women in labor need to be able to shift positions to stay comfortable. Chaining them to their beds puts the health of both the mother and child at risk if complications arise. Sometimes, a woman must be moved to an operating room immediately for an emergency Caesarian. There isn't time to waste unlocking shackles. But beyond that, women need to be able to give birth with dignity. This is hard to do while chained to a bed with a prison guard hovering in the room. Yet most states still allow this to happen, and a few even require it.

As of 2001, only 15 states banned the restraint of pregnant women during labor and delivery. Thirty-three states usually required women about to give birth to be chained while they were driven to the hospital. Eighteen allowed women to be restrained during labor and/or delivery. Four states—Connecticut, Louisiana, Minnesota and Oklahoma—followed written policies requiring that inmates be restrained at all times during all medical procedures and made no exceptions for childbirth.[16]

Following the Amnesty report, Illinois did pass legislation saying women in labor should not be transported to the hospital in shackles. But, according to Gail Smith of the group Chicago Legal Advocacy for Incarcerated Mothers, women were still giving birth wearing handcuffs, and one woman in the summer of 2003 actually gave birth in the jail because officials ignored her cries that she was going into labor until it was too late to get her to the hospital.

What if a woman prisoner decides that rather than go through all this she would rather terminate her pregnancy? Under the law of the land, a woman has a constitutional right to do so and that right does not end just because she is serving a prison term. In practice, prison authorities in some states place obstacles in her way. In 1999, a woman identified as Victoria W. entered the Terrebone Parish Criminal Justice Complex in Louisiana. When she received her health screening, she found out that she was pregnant and immediately told prison personnel she wanted an abortion. They told her she could not have one unless she hired a lawyer and obtained a court order. She tried to do so, but the process dragged on for three months. By the time she was released after serving her sentence, she was already 25 weeks pregnant and no longer able to have an abortion in Louisiana.[17] She had the child and gave it up for adoption. In April 2002, the Center for Reproductive Rights went to federal court seeking damages on her behalf. Five months later, U.S. District Court Judge Jay Zainey dismissed the case without hearing arguments. Zainey, a former chair of Louisiana Lawyers for Life, had been voted to the federal bench by the U.S. Senate in February 2002.

In 1998, Yuriko Kawaguchi was brought up before Judge Patricia Cleary in the Common Pleas Court in Cuyahoga County, Ohio, on charges of credit card fraud. She had already spent four months behind bars awaiting trial and was 21 weeks pregnant. Kawaguchi was eligible for release on probation based on the time she had already served and asked the judge to set her free without delay so that she could have an abortion. Cleary told the woman she would only release her if she agreed to carry the pregnancy to term. When Kawaguchi refused, the judge sent her back to prison for another two months. "I'm saying she's not having a second-term abortion," Cleary stated from the bench.[18] By the time Kawaguchi was released it was too late to have the abortion.

In September 2000, the Ohio Supreme Court suspended Cleary, who by then had been voted out of office, from practicing law for six months after finding that she had acted in a "manner prejudicial to the administration of justice." Justice Deborah Cook wrote that Cleary's statements in this case "displayed partiality toward certain conduct that Cleary thought morally appropriate. Such displays of partiality toward certain conduct injected a bias and prejudice...that should not be tolerated."[19]

As anxious as some authorities are to force women to carry their pregnancies to term, they are equally anxious to separate newly born babies from their mothers as soon as possible. In at least 40 states, babies are removed from their imprisoned mothers soon after delivery or when the mother is released from the hospital.[20] Moreover, under the 1997 Adoption and Safe Families Act, women inmates risk losing custody of their children, whether born in prison or not, forever. The law requires states to begin proceedings to sever a parent's right to a child if he or she has spent 15 months of the preceding 22 months in foster care. The act was an attempt to establish more stable lives for foster children and improve their chances of being adopted. But many children, especially older children past the "cute" age, have little chance of being adopted. Removing their one familial tie condemns them to a future as legal orphans drifting from one foster home to another. Once parental rights are terminated, the decision is usually final. No further contact is allowed between the birth mother and the child.[21]

Bedford Hills is one of a small number of prisons where authorities have tried to keep inmates in contact with their families. If a woman is pregnant when she enters the prison, she may be able to keep her baby with her for a year in a special nursery unit. Usually, only women serving short sentences who can expect to leave prison with their babies are admitted to the program. Anyone convicted of a violent offense is excluded. The mothers and their babies sleep in a special wing of the prison apart from the rest of the population. The well-equipped day-care center looks much like a nursery on the outside with books and toys and posters on the walls. It is a bright and cheerful place, full of the sounds of young infants. The mothers do regular prison jobs or take educational courses but get frequent breaks to feed, wash and cuddle their babies. They also receive guidance on parenting. When I visited in 2001, there were 16 babies in the crèche, including one set of four-month-old twins—Caleb and Paige Durham. Their mother, Lisa Durham, serving her second prison sentence for drugs possession, had lost custody of two other children, aged six and four. This time, she said she intended to do better.

"I've learned a lot about myself. I learned I am very self-destructive. I set myself up for failure. But I've learned to make better choices. The nursing managers and volunteers here have been wonderful. I used to be ungrateful. I was always moaning. I've changed. I've learned it's okay to ask for help. My family will be there for me when I go home. But not the twins' father. He's a drug addict. He doesn't even know they exist," she said.

Prison staffer Judith MacCalla said that was fairly typical. Fathers and husbands usually disappeared when a woman was sent to prison. "During visiting hours, this room is filled with women and children. You can count the men on the fingers of one hand. The boyfriends and husbands—they aren't here," she said.

Inmates with older children can spend long weekends with them in mobile homes within the prison grounds. They can cook their own food, eat on picnic tables and experience a form of normal family life for two or three days. The children spend the nights with host families in the community. The prison also sponsors a summer camp for inmates' children so that kids can visit their mothers frequently during school vacations.

Worrying about the breakup of their families and the loss of their children is perhaps the largest single stress factor facing women behind bars. Family times like Christmas and Thanksgiving are especially tough. Prison authorities used to make allowances, but many no longer do. Bonnie Foreshaw, serving a 45-year murder sentence in York Correctional Institution in Connecticut, recalls when the authorities tried to make Christmas special for inmates to ease the pain of separation. Staff gave prizes for the best-decorated housing units, and inmates enjoyed a special Christmas meal with table decorations and small gifts. Now the rules are stricter and these little niceties have disappeared. The focus has switched from rehabilitation to punishment.[22]

Because there are fewer women's than men's prisons, women are more likely to be locked up further away from home, making it more difficult for children to visit. A 1993 study found that more than half of the children of women prisoners never visited their mothers. Most lived more than 100 miles away from their mother's prison. If they do visit, the experience can be frightening and confusing for children. They must confront officers wearing uniforms, some carrying weapons. They must pass through electronic gates to mingle in a noisy, crowded visiting room with a mother they may hardly know who has looked forward for weeks to these few precious hours. Still, visiting is better than not visiting. Enforced separation between a mother and her children hurts both. Studies have shown that women in prison are twice as likely as those outside to have grown up in a single parent household. According to the Bureau of Justice Statistics, almost half of women in prison had at least one immediate family member who had been incarcerated.[23] The danger is that this terrible pattern will extend to yet another generation.

Diana Delgado, a mother of four, survivor of domestic violence and former addict, served two prison sentences and gave birth to her daughter behind bars. "My incarceration was a painful and traumatic experience for my children. I was a four-hour drive from my home, which made it nearly impossible for my family to bring my children to see me. It will take them years to heal from this separation. They feel abandoned and hurt, and their reaction was to rebel in school and at home. They have low self-esteem and feel like nothing matters," Delgado said.[24]

"My daughter is the one who has been affected the most, for we were never able to bond like a mother and a daughter should. She was born while I was in jail, and we were separated soon after her birth. Because of that separation in her earliest months of life, we do not have a solid mother-daughter relationship. She lacked the affection and attention she needed to develop a strong sense of self. We can never reclaim that lost time."

In 2003, authorities in Alabama began transferring 300 women from Tutwiler to a private prison in Louisiana to comply with Judge Thompson's order to reduce overcrowding. The decision meant many of these women would no longer be able to see their children, who would have to travel much further to visit. So in fulfilling an order intended to help inmates, the state found a new way to hurt them. "It doesn't mean we don't care about whether or not they see their families," said Brian Corbett, a spokesman for the Alabama Department of Corrections. "We had to have immediate relief to comply with the court order. It's not what we wanted to do, but something we had to do."[25]

A year later, Brent Coreil, District Attorney of Evangeline Parish, where the private jail was located, said he was investigating charges against an unspecified number of guards accused of improper sexual contact with female inmates from Alabama. "There is definite misconduct that did occur, and we will follow through with it," Coreil said. One guard admitted assaulting an inmate and was terminated.[26] And so, there was no end to the suffering of the unfortunate inmates of Tutwiler.

Apart from family issues, the daily demands of prison life impose enormous strains on women in a different way than it does for men. In prison, there is no privacy. Incoming and outgoing mail may be read and censored. Officers may periodically search cells for drugs and contraband, dumping inmates' personal belongings on the floor. Routine procedures such as being restrained or searched are incredibly traumatic for women who have already experienced so much abuse. Women in maximum-security prisons have to submit to intrusive searches of their bodies at any time of day or night. Even in lower security prisons, inmates are routinely searched whenever they enter or exit the facility.

Doreen O'Shea, an inmate of the Bristol House of Corrections in Massachusetts, wrote of her feelings of intense humiliation and degradation each time she is strip-searched. "No matter how many times the feelings are repeated, I cannot get past them. Being strip-searched. 'Take it all off, open your mouth, shake your hair, lift your breasts, turn around, lift your feet, now squat over a mirror....' I do not do this for my husband, let alone a total stranger, and even though I am strip-searched each time I leave and re-enter the building, the two feelings will not subside."[27]

Being searched by a man intensifies the trauma many times over. A 1997 survey of prisons in 40 states found that on average 41 percent of the correctional officers working with female inmates were men. In some states, the proportion was much higher. Two-thirds of the correctional staff guarding women in California were men; in Kansas, the figure was 72 percent.[28] The presence of male officers in a female cell block, where they may see prisoners in states of undress on the toilet or in the shower, can cause deep shame.

There is nothing particularly new about men guarding women. However, in the past the role of male guards in women's prisons was restricted to functions that limited actual physical contact. Civil rights and antidiscrimination laws passed since the 1960s swept many of these restrictions away. Ironically, this was partly a result of lawsuits launched by female corrections officers to win the right to work in men's prisons. States responded by writing "gender-neutral" employment policies. Still, most states do not allow male officers to conduct strip searches or intimate body searches of women except in emergency circumstances. Courts have differed on the crucial point of what constitutes an emergency.

Take the experience of Sandy Skurstenis, whose case came up to the Eleventh Circuit Court of Appeals in 2000. Skurstenis was arrested in Alabama for driving under the influence of alcohol, and the arresting officer found a gun in her car for which she had an expired permit. She was taken to the stationhouse, where a female officer asked her to strip, squat and cough. She was held in a cell overnight. Next morning, she was brought to the infirmary, where a male nurse carefully examined her hair, including her pubic hair, for lice. An hour after this second search, she was released. The court ruled that the search was both constitutional and reasonable in its scope and manner because it was conducted by a health official.[29]

For several years throughout the 1990s, officials at the Suffolk County Jail in Boston routinely strip-searched every single woman booked into the facility—over 5,400 women in total. This policy was for women only. Male prearraignment detainees were held in a Boston police lockup and were not automatically strip-searched.[30] Among the victims was Denise Gasparini, who was arrested in December 1998 for failing to return an overdue video game her children had rented. Then there was Joanne Maiscalco, arrested for selling sausages outside the Fleet Center basketball arena without a permit and taken to jail because a bail bondsman could not be found. Both had to strip naked and bend over while a female guard searched them. Only five of the 5,400 searches came up with anything illegal. A class action lawsuit on behalf of the women who had been strip-searched led to a $10 million settlement in 2002.[31]

The Supreme Court ruled as far back as 1986 in *Weber* v. *Dell* that strip-searching a person arrested for a minor offense who has not been arraigned violates the Fourth Amendment, which protects citizens against unreasonable searches and seizures. But that message apparently still has not filtered through to many jurisdictions. In 2001, New York City settled a class action brought on behalf of 60,000 people, male and female, arrested and strip-searched in 1996 and 1997. The cost to city taxpayers—a cool $50 million. There was nothing subtle about the procedure. Some of those arrested had to undress in groups; some were threatened if they did not disrobe quickly enough; others had their clothes thrown across the room by abusive guards.[32]

One might think that jurisdictions would learn a lesson from these two examples and stop strip-searching women arrestees. But no! In April 2005, Miami-Dade County agreed to pay more than $6 million to settle a lawsuit filed by three women who were strip-searched after their arrests during 2003 protests over a free-trade gathering. [33]

One of the women, Judith Haney, a 50-year-old project manager at a California biotech company, described her experiences to the Commission on Safety and Abuse in America's Prisons. [34]

> "After I removed all my clothes, the guard told me to turn around, bend all the way over, and spread my cheeks. I'm not sure that I can really convey the emotional and physical complexity of the situation. Bending over and "spreading my cheeks" exposed my genitalia and anus to a complete stranger, who had physical authority over me, so that she could visually inspect my body cavities. The only way I could cope with this was to stay very focused in my head and just separate from my body. The feeling was sort of like floating while also feeling like a big lump."

> "The guard's next set of instructions were to squat —and then— to hop like a bunny. Remember, I'm still "spreading my cheeks," so I can't use my arms to balance or assist me in the hopping process. Hopping-like-a-bunny was physically very difficult for me to do since I've had bad knees for over thirty years. I didn't do it to the guard's liking, so I had to do it over several times—even though I explained to her that I physically couldn't do it. When that process was complete, the guard then told me to turn around and to remove my navel piercing. I explained that it was unlikely that I would be able to remove it since it wasn't made to be removed. Using a threatening tone of voice she told me to remove it or she would "cut it out." I tried to remove it, but I just couldn't unscrew the jewel. The guard then left and returned with large clippers and cut the navel ring off me. She then told me to put my clothes back on. I stood, bent over, and hopped naked under orders and in view of at least two guards in a small room with a door open to a hallway that passersby could see in for about 10 to 15 minutes. My genitalia and anus were exposed and viewable to anyone passing through the hallway for over 5 minutes."

Again, as in Boston, men who were arrested at the event were not strip-searched. When Haney's lawyers investigated, they found women had been routinely strip-searched in Miami-Dade for seven years in violation of state and federal law, and as many as 20,000 had suffered this indignity.

Prisons in different states, guided by the courts, are still searching for an answer to the question, What, if any, limits should be placed on male officers supervising female inmates? Take the issue of prison "pat-downs" in which male guards frisk female inmates through their clothes. One 1993 case, decided by the U.S. Court of Appeals for the Ninth Circuit, arose after a prison in Washington State tried to institute cross-gender pat-downs to placate female prison guards who were fed up with having to interrupt their meal breaks to frisk women prisoners. The majority decision, written by Judge Diarmuid O'Scannlain, described how such a search was conducted:[35]

> During the cross-gender clothed body search, the male guard stands next to the female inmate and thoroughly runs his hands over her clothed body starting with her neck and working down to her feet. According to the prison training material, the guard is to "use a flat hand and pushing motion across the (inmate's) crotch area." The guard must "push inward and upward when searching the crotch and upper thighs of the inmate." All seams in the leg and the crotch area are to be "squeezed and kneaded." Using the back of the hand, the guard also is to search the breast area in a sweeping motion, so that the breasts will be "flattened." Superintendent Vail estimated that a typical search lasts forty-five seconds to one minute. A training film, viewed by the court, gave the impression that a thorough search would last several minutes.

The policy was enforced for only one day. An inmate with a long history of sexual abuse by men became so distressed by a male guard pawing her that her hands had to be pried loose from bars she had grabbed during the search and she vomited after returning to her cell block. The same day, she filed a civil rights action. The court decided that such searches amounted to cruel and unusual punishment. Judge John J. Noonan, concurring with the decision, wrote an interesting addendum:[36]

A bland American civil servant can be as much of a beast as a ferocious concentration camp guard if he does not think about what his actions are doing.... Half the cruelties of human history have been inflicted by conscientious servants of the state. The mildest of bureaucrats can be a brute if he does not raise his eyes from his task and consider the human beings on whom he has an impact.

There should not be male guards at a women's prison. There should not be a male superintendent of a woman's prison. Our statutes should not be construed to require such mechanical suppression of the recognition that in our culture *such a relation between men in power and women in prison leads to difficulties, temptations, abuse, and finally to cruel and unusual punishment.*[37] That is the broader context of this case.

However, that decision was just one of several on this issue, which has never come to the Supreme Court. Consequently, states are free to follow different policies. In another case in Nevada in 1995, the court decided that it was permissible for men to search clothed female inmates, including touching their breasts and genitals, unless there was evidence that the women would suffer severe distress. Even if this was shown, the court held the searches would still be legal if there were not enough female correctional officers to conduct all pat-downs.[38]

These rulings both addressed the situation of searches conducted by the book. But can there possibly be any doubt that many officers disregard procedures and take the opportunity to grope or fondle the women they are searching? One group of prisoners in New York described how officers stroked their breasts, grabbed their crotches and made sexual or obscene comments while they were conducting searches.[39] It may be a minority of officers, but when the temptation is so manifestly there, when the person doing the searching has all the power and the person being searched has none, some guards will abuse their authority.

States have different rules governing when male guards may see female inmates naked. Frequently, women on suicide watch are made to undress. In theory, they should be given paper gowns to wear. If they do not take them, they must remain naked. In Florida in 1999, the

Department of Corrections declared it would no longer allow guards to keep unclothed women in their cells after an inmate committed suicide. Before hanging herself, Florence Krell had written to her mother and to the judge who sentenced her complaining of her despair after having been left naked in her cell where male officers could see her.[40]

Then there was the case of "Jane Doe," arrested in Story County, Iowa, for public intoxication. She was taken to jail, where she yelled and cursed at officers. She pounded and kicked the door of a holding cell until staff decided to place her in a padded cell. Under jail procedures, she was stripped. It is not clear whether this woman was offered a paper gown, but she did not receive one. A male officer watched as she was undressed and marched naked into the cell. Some time later, there was a shift change at the jail. As the new officers came on, the woman was still shouting sporadically. So officers decided to strap her, spread-eagle and face down, on a wooden board, where she was left naked for three hours. They later testified that they did this because they were afraid she might hurt herself in the padded cell. While she was on the restraint board, a camera transmitted nude images of her to monitors in the front office, where most of the deputies on duty were men. Eventually, someone covered her buttocks with a towel. When this case reached the Eighth Circuit Court of Appeals in 2002, the court ruled that requiring the woman to undress in front of a male officer did not violate her rights because she was loud and violent at the time. Nor was her march naked from the padded cell to the restraint board a violation because she remained unruly. However, the court said leaving her naked and exposed on the board crossed the constitutional line and intruded into her privacy.[41]

In 1995, the Department of Justice began an investigation of four prisons in Arizona. Two years later, the Department filed suit against the state, saying women inmates had been subject to sexual misconduct and unlawful invasion of their privacy, including "prurient viewing during showering, toileting and dressing."[42] In 1999, the parties settled the lawsuit and Arizona agreed to revise employee training and strengthen investigations of sexual misconduct complaints. Male officers were ordered to announce their presence when entering areas in which female inmates might be undressed. The agreement also created two 15-minute periods each day when only female staff would be present so that inmates could dress and shower with no men around.[43]

Did that solve the problem? Hardly. In 2002, two Arizona prison officers were indicted on numerous charges of sexual misconduct. One allegedly had sex with a prisoner in exchange for perfume, music tapes, and marijuana, which he smuggled into the prison. In 2001, when the inmate became pregnant, he forced her to take a "morning after" pill. The second officer was charged with harassing at least four women, fondling their breasts, demanding oral sex and making suggestive comments.[44]

One of the longest running legal sagas involving the role of male guards began in Michigan in 1996 when a group of female inmates sued the Department of Corrections for sexual misconduct and harassment. The case eventually settled for over $3.7 million.[45] The Department of Justice also investigated women's prisons in the state, uncovering widespread abuses, and eventually reached a settlement that called for reforms similar to those enacted in Arizona. But that was not the end of the matter. In 1999, Bill Martin, a political appointee with no prior prison experience, became head of the Michigan Department of Corrections. A few months later, Martin announced his intention to remove all male officers from women's prisons. Several correctional officers, both male and female, immediately launched a lawsuit. In July 2002, U.S. District Court Judge Avern Cohn ruled in their favor and against Martin. He rejected the notion that only female officers should guard women prisoners.[46] However, Judge Cohn gave a list of specific tasks male officers should not do.

"Females being viewed by males is qualitatively different than males being viewed by females," he wrote. "Strip-searches, observation of female inmates while undressed and staffing of medical visits are all discrete tasks that should be limited to female corrections officers, as is transport under some circumstances. Pat-down searches are of the same order."[47]

In his decision, Judge Cohn seemed to be implicitly admitting that the risk of sexual abuse always exists in women's prisons. But how much abuse really goes on? Nobody knows. A report in 1999 by the United States General Accounting Office into the federal prison system and prisons in California, Texas and the District of Columbia found that none of these jurisdictions had comprehensive data on the number, nature or outcomes of alleged sexual misconduct complaints. Officials had to go back and examine their files one by one to come up with any kind of numbers. In California, Texas and in federal prisons, the report said 506 allegations of staff sexual misconduct had prompted investigations in the previous three years, of which 92 were sustained. Most ended with the employee resigning or being fired. Only 14 federal prison employees, and none in the state systems, faced criminal prosecution. All 14 were convicted, receiving sentences ranging from three months of home confinement to 232 months in prison.[48]

The report acknowledged that these 506 incidents were probably only the tip of the iceberg. As stated, prison systems did not have organized data on complaints about sexual misconduct. The figures covered only those deemed credible enough to merit investigation. Many grievances filed by women are simply ignored or dismissed. A class action suit in New York, filed by 15 women in 2003, described case after case in which women's complaints were disregarded or rejected. In some cases, several women complained about the same officer, but officials still did nothing. In one case at Albion Correctional Facility, a sergeant brought Lucy Amador into a room in the basement of the administration building and forced her to participate in oral sex. He then made her clean herself and drink water to destroy any physical evidence. But he was not thorough. Back in her cell, Amador discovered a semen stain on her shirt. There had been other complaints about this officer, but only now was he fired and later successfully prosecuted. Lucy Amador hardly benefited. She was placed in segregation without her belongings and later transferred to another prison and held in protective custody, otherwise known as solitary confinement. Feeling desperate and even suicidal, she begged to see a psychiatrist. Over the next two months, she had two five-minute sessions with a psychologist.[49]

Is it any surprise that in most cases of sexual misconduct, prisoners are afraid to complain? If there is no medical or physical evidence and no witnesses, allegations come down to "he said, she said" situations. An inmate's word is never as good as an officer's, and both sides know this. Guards tell their victims, "Who are they going to believe? I have a badge and a uniform, and you are a convicted criminal."

Beyond that, women prisoners have good reason to worry about retaliation if they come forward. Officers can make life easier or harder for inmates in a thousand ways, small and large. They can limit family visits so a woman never sees her children. They may deny commissary rights so she cannot buy food treats or personal hygiene items. They may confiscate mail as contraband or subject prisoners to extra body searches that are especially intrusive and unpleasant. If several officers are abusing women, they may band together to protect each other.

In Michigan, many of the women who were plaintiffs in a 1996 class action lawsuit suffered retaliation. Women were harassed, threatened, subjected to abusive pat-downs and written up for rules violations they did not commit. In a 1998 report, Amnesty International said the most vicious retaliation was aimed at those women seen as the most articulate and charismatic. Stacy Barker, serving a life sentence for a 1986 murder, was placed in punitive segregation for 200 days after officers alleged finding drugs in her cell. She denied the charge and had never tested positive in random drugs tests before then. Officials canceled her visitation rights for the duration of her sentence, which was the rest of her life. That meant she would never again see her daughter.[50]

But Barker was a fighter who repeatedly beat the authorities in court. In 1995, she won a six-figure settlement after alleging she had been raped repeatedly by the same guard over a period of months. In 2000, she was among the 29 women who split a $3.7 million settlement. When she was denied visits, she fought that too. A federal judge eventually voided the order.[51] In 1999, her first-degree murder charge was overturned, and she won a new trial. Finally, in December 2001, she agreed to a plea bargain deal under which she could be free by 2008.[52]

Although they settled her cases, the Michigan Department of Corrections continued to deny that Barker had ever been abused. A department spokesman, Matt Davis, said any sex between Barker and guards was consensual. That comment revealed a profound lack of understanding. No sex between prison guards and female inmates should be treated as consensual. There cannot be truly consensual relations where the balance of power is so lopsided. This is one of the biggest problems in attempting to estimate the extent of the problem. Many sexual relationships in prisons have the outward appearance of consensual sex.

Typically, a male officer grants favors to a female inmate in exchange for sex. Nobody ever complains and no reports are written. Both parties, it could be argued, get something out of the relationship. In fact, this kind of relationship is no different from the sex between a slave owner and a bondwoman. It is coercive because one party does not have the ability to choose freely. Thirty-nine states agree and define any sex between a guard and a prisoner as felony rape.

Events at Suffolk County House of Correction in Boston, where eight officers were fired or suspended from 1999 to 2001 for sexual misconduct, give a good picture of how these things work.[53] Inmates described how they ate home-fried chicken and Chinese food provided by guards, received early morning coffee, access to cellphones and extra cigarettes and watched TV with officers outside their cells once they agreed to have sex. Guards kept watch for one another, blowing into their radios when a supervisor was coming.[54] This went on for some years until one of the inmates became pregnant. It turned out this inmate had been having sex with three officers, one of whom was the father of the child she eventually gave birth to. What if a woman did not agree to have sex? Then, like inmate Karen Passanisi, she might wake up in her cell to find an officer pulling down her pants with his fingers stuck inside of her body.

Every so often, pockets of sexual abuse come to light in the U.S. prison system. Authorities always say they are isolated incidents and there is no pattern of abuse. Since 1997, seven employees of the Carswell Federal Prison in Texas have been fired, indicted or convicted for sexual misconduct. They include a chaplain, a kitchen supervisor, a gynecologist at the prison hospital and a staff counselor as well as guards.[55] In June 2003, a Fort Worth jury took half an hour to award $4 million to Marilyn Shirley, a 47-year-old mother of two children and five stepchildren, who was smart enough to guard her sweat pants with the guard's semen stains until her last day in custody. Shirley testified that as he was raping her in a supply room at Carswell, the guard told her, "Do you think you're the first? This happens all the time." Shirley probably won't see a cent of the $4 million. The guard, who was also facing federal charges, had no way of paying her. Meanwhile, Marilyn Shirley must live the rest of her life with the effects of the rape. "I have panic attacks. I'm in a terrible state of depression all the time. I have terrible nightmares. I am in fear of losing my husband. I want to be a mother to my kids," she said.[56]

Previously, I described the good work being done at Bedford Hills to keep mothers and babies together. So it was doubly disappointing to learn of serious allegations of abuse at that prison in a lawsuit filed by 15 New York inmates in 2003. It would be too depressing to go through all 15 allegations listed in the complaint. Here is just one:

Shenyell Smith was a model prisoner at Bedford Hills, to the point that she earned a spot in the Honor Block, an area reserved for inmates with outstanding disciplinary records. Within weeks of her arrival, Officer T. allegedly began pestering her with intrusive personal questions. When she rejected his advances, he told her, "No prisoner tells me 'No.'" A month later, he raped and sodomized her in the kitchen. When she sought medical help, he had her locked in her cell and threatened to remove her from the honor floor. He said it was a waste of time to complain, since no one would believe her.[57]

Whether or not the officer was correct, the allegations showed that even in a place like Bedford Hills, filled with good-hearted, well-intentioned staff and volunteers who really care about the inmates, the awfulness and ugliness of prison life cannot be banished.

Nineteen months after the women had filed their suit, the case had not moved foward. "We've heard nothing from the judge," said lawyer Lisa Stark. In the meantime, most of the women had served their sentences and been released. But their hopes of finding redress from the court had faded.

8

SUPERMAX

---

*"Conditions must not involve the wanton and
unnecessary infliction of pain, nor may they be
grossly disproportionate to the severity of the crime."*
Supreme Court Justice Lewis Powell[1] ■

The town of Boscobel in southwestern Wisconsin (population 2,706) has a small but honored niche in history. On September 14, 1898, two traveling salesmen, John Nicholson and Samuel Hill, were sharing a room in the crowded Central House Hotel on Wisconsin Avenue. They got talking and discovered a common devotion to Christianity. We do not know who came up with the idea of starting a Christian traveling man's association, but the seed was planted and from it grew The Gideons International, which annually places 59 million Bibles in hotels, motels, hospitals, ships, doctors' offices and jails.[2] The Central House is now called the Boscobel Hotel and room 19 carries a plaque memorializing the event.

For the next century, Boscobel continued on its quiet way, content to be known as "Wisconsin's Wild Turkey Hunting Capital." Then, in 1996, Republican Governor Tommy Thompson decided to build a super-maximum security prison there. "Prisons work," Thompson declared in his annual address to the state. "They keep violent people from harming good people. It's that simple. So tonight I am committing to build a supermax prison. If we don't get federal funding, we must build it ourselves. And once this plain, stark and austere facility is built, that's where Wisconsin's most vicious criminals will go. The supermax will be a criminal's worst nightmare."[3]

In the 1990s, constructing supermax prisons became the hottest trend in corrections. They were sold to voters as places that would punish the most dangerous, incorrigible, violent, unremorseful, worthless and evil criminals in America by holding them in places that were both appropriately harsh and perfectly secure. Having a supermax became a point of pride—a symbol for how "tough on crime" a jurisdiction had become. By 1997, 30 states and the federal government were operating at least one such unit, keeping inmates in continuous segregation with little or no interaction with other people.[4] They included California's Pelican Bay and Corcoran state prisons; Virginia's Red Onion and

Wallens Ridge; Tamms in Illinois and the federal supermax in Colorado. Several other states were building more such prisons.

Over the years, prison administrators have tried two ways to manage difficult and dangerous inmates: either dispersing them widely in many different prisons or concentrating them all in one institution. The notorious Alcatraz penitentiary, on a rocky island in San Francisco Bay, symbolized the concentration method. Established in 1934 as a special prison for kidnappers, racketeers and predators, "The Rock" housed many of the federal government's most infamous criminals for almost 30 years. But by the time it closed in 1963, the prevailing correctional doctrine had swung to the dispersal theory. It was not a success. Assaults and violence in federal prisons grew through the 1970s. In 1983, there was a serious riot at the federal penitentiary in Marion, Illinois, in which two guards were stabbed to death. In response, authorities put Marion on indefinite lockdown and placed inmates in permanent solitary confinement. The number of violent incidents fell sharply; prison administrators all over the country paid attention. The modern supermax had been born.[5] In 1995, Marion was superseded in the federal system by the Administrative Maximum Security (ADX) prison in Florence, Colorado.

By this time, technology had moved a long way from the days of Alcatraz. For the first time, it was possible to build a prison that totally separated inmates from the world around them and from interaction with either staff or fellow prisoners. That was the kind of place Governor Thompson wanted to build in Boscobel. A proud, tough-on-crime Republican, Thompson presided over a growth in Wisconsin's prison population from 5,736 when he took office in 1987 to 20,682 in August 2000.[6] Still, prison wardens in Wisconsin weren't sure they needed a whole new facility. They first suggested adding 25 segregation cells at each of four existing prisons. Thompson nixed that idea. The wardens' second choice was a 200-bed supermax. Thompson vetoed that too. Eventually, the state legislature went along with his plan and built a 500-bed prison at a cost of $44 million. The new facility won a prize from an engineering magazine and was portrayed as a source of state pride. When it was opened to great fanfare in 1999, authorities organized a six-day open house.[7] Tens of thousands of people toured the empty prison while vendors sold hot dogs, sodas and commemorative T-shirts.

What was life like inside the Wisconsin supermax? District Judge Barbara Crabb described conditions in a 23-page ruling in 2001: "Inmates on Level One at the State of Wisconsin's Supermax Correctional Institution in Boscobel, Wisconsin, spend all but four hours a week confined to a cell. The 'boxcar' style door on the cell is solid except for a shutter and a trap door that opens into the dead space of a vestibule through which a guard may transfer items to the inmate without interacting with him. The cells are illuminated 24 hours a day. Inmates receive no outdoor exercise. Their personal belongings are severely restricted; one religious text, one box of legal materials and 25 personal letters. They are permitted no clocks, radios, watches, cassette players or televisions. The temperature fluctuates wildly, reaching extremely high and low temperatures depending on the season. Visits other than with lawyers are conducted through video screens."[8]

The judge went on: "Because of the heavy walls and boxcar doors at Supermax, there is a constant muffled sound broken intermittently by loud yells and slamming gates. A five-inch strip of opaque glass runs along the top edge of one wall of each cell. By standing on the bed and craning his neck, an inmate can glimpse the sky through a small sealed skylight.... At night, inmates are required to sleep in such a way as to allow guards to see skin when they perform hourly checks of the inmates. Guards will wake inmates if they have covered their faces in such a way that the guards cannot see any of the inmate's skin.

"There is no air conditioning and the solid cell doors and lack of windows prevent air from circulating. On August 9, 2001, Daniel Feldt, an industrial hygienist, monitored the temperature and humidity at Supermax when the outdoor temperature was 91 degrees. According to his report, the average cell temperature at bed height was 91.75 degrees and the average relative humidity was 59.4 percent. These figures produce a heat index in excess of 100 degrees. Although the cells contain showers that could provide some relief from the heat, inmates are permitted to use the showers only three times a week.

"Inmates in Level One Unit are allowed four hours of exercise a week in an exercise cell, which is nothing more than a slightly larger version of a regular cell. It has no windows. There is no exercise equipment of any kind, although it would be possible to install equipment that would not pose a security threat to staff or inmates. The room is too small for jogging. All it will accommodate is pacing or exercises such as sit-ups or jumping jacks that inmates could do in their own cells."

"Inmates are not allowed face-to-face visits, other than with their lawyers. The institution provides only video visitation. Inmates remain in their cell block and visitors at the front of the institution. Inmates and visitors see each other on small video screens that are located across the room from the inmate. The audio quality is poor.... During the video visits, inmates remain handcuffed, shackled and belly chained. Prison log books show that only 10 percent of inmates receive visits, an unusually low number.... Level One inmates at Supermax are allowed only one six-minute telephone call a month. They are not allowed to have any electronic equipment in their cells or to participate in any programs. Their canteen privileges are limited. Inmates in Level One are not allowed to have library books in their cells.... At Supermax, inmates must stand in the middle of their cells with the lights on and their trousers on in order to receive food or medication. If they do not comply, they are deemed to have refused the food or medication."

Governor Thompson was pleased with his creation. Touring the facility in October 2000, he said, "It's accomplishing its purpose. The toughest of the tough, the worst elements of our prison society are in this institution. They're in here because of their behavior and they can get out because of their behavior. They don't like being here but they are not being abused in any way. None of their civil rights are being adversely affected. They would like to be outside and I can agree with them. So would I."[9]

Warden Gerald Berge was also pleased. He told a reporter the idea that prisoners were isolated was nonsense. He said there were at least six interactions between inmates and staff every day—when meal trays were dropped off and picked up. He did not mention that these "interactions" took place through closed doors.[10] Inmates who survived the place said the only thing that kept them from going completely insane was their ability to communicate with their immediate neighbors through ventilation ducts. This, according to Berge, was the one design fault in the building. Prison engineers tried to correct the problem, but without success.

Whenever a politician or a prison chief exalts the virtues of a supermax, they always use the same phrase. They always say that it is only for "the toughest of the tough" or "the worst of the worst." This argument was used to justify both the conditions in such institutions and the massive costs of building them. A study by the Florida Corrections Commission in 2000 found that constructing a supermax would cost $47,500 per inmate bed, compared to an average of $28,700 per bed in other state maximum security prisons.[11] A supermax is also much more expensive to operate than a regular institution. "Providing meals and other services at individual cell fronts, multiple officer escorts, and maintenance of elaborate electronic systems are examples of things that add up quickly," wrote chief Chase Riveland, a former head of corrections in Washington state. "The number of correctional officers required to assure both internal and external security, movement of inmates, security searches of cells and the delivery of food and other supplies and services to individual cells generally drives staffing ratios, and therefore operating costs, much higher than those of the general population prisons."[12] This wasn't an issue in the 1990s when states were flush with cash. It became more of a factor a few years later when these same states were forced to cut health and education spending to deal with massive budget deficits.

The problem with the "worst of the worst" argument is that experience has shown that it just isn't true. A better slogan would have been, "Build it and they will come." Once a state built a supermax, it was under enormous political pressure to fill it. After spending tens of millions of dollars to erect these costly penal palaces, governors were not anxious to have them standing half-empty. In state after state, it became abundantly clear that a high proportion of supermax inmates were severely mentally ill. They were not so much the "worst of the worst" as the "sickest of the sick." Wardens of other prisons were all too happy to get rid of them because they were disruptive and difficult to control. Supermax wardens took them to fill as many beds as possible.

Like other states, Wisconsin did not have enough "worst of the worst" to fill a 500-bed supermax. The new prison soon became a dumping ground for anyone who might be rebellious or troublesome. Any prisoner who got into a fight with a fellow inmate went straight to the supermax. When this still didn't fill even half of the available beds, wardens started using the facility to relieve congestion at other prisons. Some inmates convicted of nonviolent offenses and even a number of juveniles wound up at the supermax.

In his study for the U.S. Justice Department, Chase Riveland warned against this very danger. "Prison staff have always had to deal with uncooperative inmates. They continuously test the limits, frequently break minor rules and consume an inordinate amount of staff time. As comforting as it may be to an institution staff to be rid of such persons, the use of costly high-custody beds for this population is probably not only inefficient, but arguably overkill. *These facilities are inappropriate for the nuisance inmate*," he wrote.[13]

Other states faced the same problem as Wisconsin. Virginia found itself with excess capacity after building two supermaxes in the 1990s—Wallens Ridge and Red Onion, both in Wise County in Appalachia. Virginia found an innovative solution to fill its empty beds. It began renting out supermax space to other states where prisons were overcrowded. Connecticut sent several hundred inmates to Wallens Ridge. It turned out that 23 percent were serving sentences of five years or less and 41 percent 10 years or less. They included many prisoners convicted of nonviolent crimes such as burglary or drugs offenses—hardly the worst of the worst.[14]

At the 1998 opening of the Red Onion State Prison, Virginia Corrections chief Ron Angelone had mocked the idea of rehabilitating supermax inmates. "What are they going to be rehabilitated for? To die gracefully in prison. Let's face it, they're here to die in prison," he said.[15] Angelone's words came tragically true in the case of David Tracy, a mentally ill 20-year-old. With less than a year of his sentence to serve, Tracy could not handle the extreme conditions at Wallens Ridge and committed suicide by hanging himself with a sheet. Connecticut paid his family $750,000 in compensation.

Even slight infractions by Virginia prisoners could earn them a trip to a supermax. Johnnie Wood, an inmate at a less restrictive Virginia prison, had the nerve to complain to Angelone personally about the climate control system during a tour by the state Board of Corrections. Angelone ordered Wood, a small-time drugs offender with a low security rating, sent to Red Onion the same night.[16]

In Wisconsin, a May 2001 report by the state's Legislative Audit Bureau found that more than 15 percent of supermax prisoners were mentally ill.[17] That year, prison officials also admitted that eight teenagers were locked up at Boscobel. Two were only 16 when they arrived. Canyon Aaron Thixton had been diagnosed with various mental disorders from the age of nine. By the time he was 17, he had experienced the full majesty of the American criminal justice system. He had been pepper sprayed, beaten, stripped of his clothes and bedding and left naked in a "clinical observation" cell after a failed suicide attempt.[18] Thixton told a therapist he felt his life was totally hopeless and worthless. Was it for people like this that Governor Thompson built the supermax? Was there no other place he could be sent?

As word spread about conditions in Boscobel, inmates' families began to complain. One mother[19] said she had to travel three hours for one-hour video "visits" with her son, during which she could not hear his voice over the audio system. "He presents for the one-hour visit in shackles, in a tiny cubicle. He reported that at our last visit the prison staff 'forgot' him in the hot, tiny cubicle for one hour after the visit. We have also learned from our son that many inmates are given anti-anxiety and antidepressant drugs, handed to them through the opening in their cell doors, and to the best of our knowledge, without one-to-one personal medical attention. It was for the worst of the worst but they filled it up with people who should never have been there," this mother said. Her son was eventually released and began trying to recover from the year he spent at Boscobel.

Judge Crabb went through the medical histories of seven prisoners at the supermax. Prisoner 2, for example, was admitted to the prison twice, with an intermediate stay at a mental health institute. Judge Crabb wrote, "He has been diagnosed at various times as schizoaffective, bipolar, obsessive-compulsive disorder, borderline character disorder, antisocial personality disorder and histrionic personality disorder. He is currently prescribed Librium (a tranquilizer), Paxil (an antidepressant) and Depacote (a mood regulating drug). A February 5, 1998, psychiatric examination indicated that Prisoner 2 was diagnosed with schizophrenia and that the antipsychotic medication Haldol and the mood regulator Valproic Acid were prescribed for him. Prisoner 2 has attempted suicide two times since February 2000."[20] The other six cases made for similar reading. What were they doing there?

The judge summed up: "Without exception, Prisoners 1 through 7 have suffered intensified symptoms, whether increased depression, severe hopelessness, attempts at suicide, command hallucinations or bizarre behavior. Although in most cases the prescribed medications have lessened these symptoms, plaintiffs point out that the severe conditions are likely to have triggered or exacerbated the symptoms in the first place. Moreover, it is not surprising that the medications reduce symptoms; this is what these medications are designed to do. What is surprising is that some inmates, such as Prisoners 1 and 2, are still experiencing symptoms despite the strong medications they are being prescribed."

Faced with Judge Crabb's opinion, Wisconsin decided to settle the lawsuit and to remove all seriously mentally ill inmates from the supermax. Prisoners who remained would be allowed to spend more time out of their cells and have more reading and religious materials. The state also agreed to build an outdoor recreation area so prisoners could see the sky from time to time and to maintain cell temperatures at 68 to 72 degrees in winter and 80 to 84 degrees in summer.[21] By this time, Governor Thompson had moved on to serve as Secretary of Health and Human Services in President George W. Bush's first administration, leaving Wisconsin lawmakers to deal with the expensive white elephant he had left behind. In 2001, the state legislature's joint finance committee voted 15–1 to ask the Department of Corrections to study ways to convert the supermax back into a conventional prison. Thompson's successor, Governor Jim Doyle, said he was ready to consider this but it might not be possible. "My understanding is it is going to be a very difficult prison to retrofit to make it more of a standard prison, and that's a problem," he said.[22]

As the Wisconsin case was going on, supermax opponents won another temporary victory in Ohio. Judge James Gwin of the U.S. District

Court for the Northern District of Ohio ruled that the state had violated prisoners' right to due process when it placed them in the Ohio State Penitentiary (OSP), a supermax in Youngstown.[23] He ordered the state to rewrite its rules and not to send mentally ill inmates there any more.

Judge Gwin described conditions at Youngstown as even worse than on Ohio's death row, where prisoners at least were able to see the sky and breathe fresh air from time to time. "Death row inmates have access to true outdoor recreation and have direct access to attorneys. Most significantly, death row prisoners can interact with other inmates during recreation or by conversations in their cells. In contrast, inmates at the OSP have extremely limited contact with other individuals," the judge wrote.

On the meat of the case, Judge Gwin ruled that Ohio's procedures in selecting inmates for the supermax were arbitrary and inconsistent. Any prisoner dispatched to Youngstown automatically lost the right to parole, yet inmates were sent there without any kind of due process. Ohio prisoners were not told why they were being transferred to the supermax. They had no opportunity to appeal or even to hear the reasons for the transfer. The first most knew about it was when they were already on the bus. "Inmates were awoken in the early morning hours and shipped off to the OSP. This denial of notice was intentional, apparently because Department officials believed the transfers would be easier to make. In addition, most of the class were never told of the grounds used to support their incarceration at the OSP," Judge Gwin wrote.[24] He ordered Ohio to clean up its selection procedures, and the state did in fact make some changes.

Judge Gwin's decision was upheld by the 6th U.S. Circuit Court of Appeals. The case eventually reached the U.S. Supreme Court in March 2005. Ohio Attorney General Jim Petro, who intended to run for governor in 2006, asked the justices to reverse the lower court and uphold the state's new procedures for transferring prisoners to the supermax, arguing that, "the government needs to have the capacity and ability to make the best possible decision in light of all possible factors."[25] The Supreme Court ruled in June 2005, upholding the state's procedures as well as its right to place some inmates in the supermax. However, the justices did recognize the extreme conditions of confinement in supermax prisons and made it clear that prisoners must have the right to challenge decisions to place them in such draconian facilities.

The Ohio and Wisconsin cases only tinkered at the edge of the problem. No court has yet held that prolonged segregation, in and of itself, constitutes cruel and unusual punishment. In fact, in *Wilson* v. *Seiter* in 1991, the Supreme Court held that "nothing so amorphous as 'overall conditions' can rise to the level of cruel and unusual punishment when no specific deprivation of a single human need exists."[26]

Despite the Wisconsin and Ohio rulings, there can be no doubt that a large number of mentally ill individuals continue to be held in supermaxes around the country. James Washington, an inmate of Red Onion in Virginia, wrote to me that there were at least seven mentally ill prisoners in his control unit. "There were three who yelled, screamed and batted the door day and night. One of them was moved to another unit. He was putting urine and feces in the ventilation system. He was one of the screamers and door kickers. The second door kicker was sent to a mental institution—he smeared feces and urine on the door/sink/toilet combination and on the shelf, desk, walls, floor—everywhere. He would sing Christmas carols at two or three o'clock in the morning, loudly banging on the door. The third door kicker, the mentally ill prisoner below me, the prison guards aggravate him as though he is a dog on a chain, rattling the door, which makes him kick the door. This prisoner appears to be between 50 and 60."[27]

At the Tamms Correction Center in Illinois, a $73 million facility opened in 1998, Chris Marcum, serving time for two burglary convictions, was one of several prisoners who reacted to the harsh conditions by mutilating themselves. In letters to attorney Jean Snyder of the University of Chicago, Marcum described his experiences. "I was in the shower and got upset. I broke a razor and sliced myself 18 times. I was taken to the hospital and placed in a suicide cell for five days," he wrote in February 2000. "The same day I was sent back to the pod. I was upset because the doctor told me that if I wanted to cut myself, I would have to deal with the scars because he wasn't going to stitch me up. So I decided to start again."

May 5, 2000: "I took a bunch of pills and sliced my arm up and had to be rushed to the hospital to have my stomach pumped."

August 31: "At about 12:15 a.m. I cut myself up. I was put in a cell on suicide watched naked. I didn't receive a blanket until hours later. The cell I was put in was filthy. It had shit, blood and food everywhere."

Another Tamms inmate, Ashoor Rasho, became so desperate and disturbed that on August 20, 1998, with his arms already infected from self-inflicted wounds, he cut himself and began eating small pieces of his own flesh in front of a correctional officer. He was eventually stitched up and returned to his cell, where he cut himself again, pulled his stitches out and lost more than half a pint of blood. Staff at Tamms said Rasho was trying to manipulate them to gain concessions.[28]

Psychologist Craig Haney said self-mutilation was pretty common among supermax inmates. "Prisoners start to believe that cutting themselves is the only way to get a response from the world around them. It's the only way they convince themselves that they still exist," he said.

Another Tamms prisoner[29] complained of hallucinations and hearing voices. "I don't know what kind of mind control devices they have or are using against myself, but it's endless and I'm dying, as well as dead. They are able to talk to me through the mind by throwing their voice in my head somehow.... Then I started going through changes. I'd forget things. I'd wake up not knowing. Then the window. I started seeing birds, bees, flies, bugs doing strange things, things that weren't normal. Then my food. When I chewed it turned into water. Dead souls were in my cell, the living came. I was made to believe I had some kind of power that will change the world and so on. I'll be insane. I have no head. A soul is complete, mine is cut off at the shoulder while the head is completely gone."

Don Cabana, who served for five years as warden of the maximum security death row prison in Parchman, Mississippi, testified about the atmosphere inside supermax facilities to the Commission on Safety and Abuse in America's Prisons in April 2005. He said:

> "The environment inside supermax units actually increases the levels of hostility and anger among inmates and staff alike. The sense of hopelessness and despair on the part of inmates in these units becomes problematic for prison staff who are ill equipped to deal with the increased signs of mental illness, psychosis, suicidal behavior, and a plethora of other aberrant behaviors that manifest themselves... While there can be no doubt that a substantial

number of prisoners require closed monitoring and supervision, supermax frequently takes management problem inmates and makes them worse. Officers and staff who are selected to work in supermax are often ill equipped and poorly trained. Abuse of authority and power by officers is exacerbated in the volatile supermax environment."[30]

Psychologists and prison administrators have long known that prolonged isolation not only worsens existing mental conditions but causes breakdowns in previously sane prisoners.[31] When Alexis de Tocqueville visited the Eastern State Penitentiary in Philadelphia in 1831, a well-educated inmate told him he often had "strange visions. During several nights in succession, I saw, among other things, an eagle perching at the foot of my bed." Another inmate told the visitor his soul was sick; two others were too disturbed to speak coherently.[32]

In a paper presented to a conference funded by Tommy Thompson's U.S. Department of Health in January 2002, Craig Haney noted, "This kind of confinement creates its own set of psychological pressures that, in some instances, uniquely disables prisoners for free world reintegration. Indeed, there are few if any forms of imprisonment that produce so many indices of psychological trauma and symptoms of psychopathology in those persons subjected to it. My own review of the literature suggested these documented negative psychological consequences of long-term solitary-like confinement include: an impaired sense of identity; hypersensitivity to stimuli; cognitive dysfunction (confusion, memory loss, ruminations); irritability, anger, aggression, and/or rage; other directed violence, such as stabbings, attacks on staff, property destruction, and collective violence; lethargy, helplessness and hopelessness; chronic depression; self-mutilation and/or suicidal ideation, impulses, and behavior; anxiety and panic attacks; emotional breakdowns and/or loss of control; hallucinations; psychosis and/or paranoia; overall deterioration of mental and physical health."[33]

This collection of symptoms even has a name—the SHU (Special Housing Unit) syndrome, coined by Harvard Medical School psychiatrist Stuart Grassian in 1979. Grassian studied inmates confined to their cells for 23 hours a day at Attica Prison in New York and found they exhibited depression, increased paranoia, agitation, manic activity, delusions, florid psychotic illness and suicidal tendencies.[34]

Psychiatrist Terry Kupers has also studied SHU syndrome. He said even those inmates who did not become completely psychotic manifested a number of psychosis-like symptoms, including massive anxiety, hyper-responsiveness to external stimuli, perception distortions and hallucinations, acute confusion, difficulties with concentration and memory and others.[35] Kupers made the point that most supermax prisoners would eventually be released to the community on completing their sentences. They would emerge from years of total isolation mentally destroyed and full of rage.

Not all supermaxes are exactly alike. At Red Onion and Wallens Ridge in Virginia, some inmates live two to a cell, which is arguably even worse than total segregation if one's cellmate is mentally ill and has unpleasant personal habits. Red Onion houses some inmates in "general population" and some in segregation. Those in general population are locked up with their cellmates most of the time. They are allowed out for meals and for an hour a day of recreation in a bare yard with a basketball hoop. Correctional officers carrying firearms loaded with rubber bullets watch their every move. New arrivals are read a warning:

"Everywhere you go throughout this prison, there are officers with weapons who will be observing you. Any attempt on your part to assault staff or other inmates will be met with the use of firepower. Any failure on your part to follow verbal instructions from the staff—for example, refusal to leave the mess hall, refusal to clear the yard, refusal to lock up—will be met with the immediate use of firepower. If you threaten the safe, orderly operation of this prison, we will use the force necessary to ensure that you comply."[36]

Ron Angelone, who instituted these rules, insisted they were for the safety of all, including inmates. "When we first started, prisoners tested the limits to see if we meant business, because that's what prisoners always do. When they found out we did mean business, incidents fell off. Guns are rarely fired now," he said.

Angelone said prisoners in supermax prisons deserved to be there, either because of the crime they committed or because of their behavior in prison. "When someone is sentenced to a very long term, say 60 to 80 years, we start him in that prison. Their behavior determines how long they will be there. If they follow rules, they can work their way to a less restrictive prison. It gives them something to live for. Or they could just be self-destructive individuals who do not want to follow anybody's rules but their own."

Even a prison like Red Onion depends on prisoners following rules to run smoothly. Its architects did not match the degree of isolation achieved by the prizewinning designers of the Wisconsin supermax, where there was a shower in every cell. In Red Onion, prisoners leave their cells to shower. Before a prisoner exits his cell, he has to push his hands through a small opening in the door to be cuffed. Then, officers place shackles on his legs and attach a chain to his waist. Two officers then lead him to the shower, one holding the lead and the other pressing an electronic stun gun against his body. This procedure applies even to prisoners with no record of violence.[37]

But what if a prisoner refuses to obey the rules? Many mentally sick prisoners find it very difficult to understand and follow instructions. What if a prisoner refuses to shove his hands through the slot to be cuffed, or refuses to leave his cell when ordered? Then, the prisoner becomes subject to one of the most potentially dangerous and violent prison procedures—the forcible cell extraction. Captain James H. Topham, a senior prison chief in Maryland and an experienced instructor, has written a guide on how this should be done using five officers.[38]

First, Captain Topham lists the basic equipment needed for the operation: extraction shield, protective vest, helmet with face shield, gas masks, protective gloves, groin protector, elbow and knee pads along with shin protectors, handcuffs, leg irons and/or flex cuffs, OC spray and baton. That's the minimum. Where possible, he also recommends a flash bang device, "Pepper Ball" System (a high-pressure air launcher of pepper ball projectiles), 37-mm "less lethal" impact munitions, 12-gauge "less lethal" impact munitions, electronic stun gun, capture nets and, in life or death situations, firearms.

Having dressed and armed themselves, the extraction team moves into position. "The officers line up in a pre-planned configuration, march to the cell and line up in front of the cell door. The Team Commander will in some, but not all cases, allow the offender one more chance to comply with the order. In some circumstances the fact that the team has been observed marching into the dayroom or onto the tier and is now poised outside the cell is enough to make the offender comply with the orders.

"The team commander can have (if allowed by the institution) the option to use OC (pepper spray) or chemical munitions on the offender before the team enters the cell … If the offender still does not comply and the order is given to go into the cell, the shield officer (1) is the first through the door and the other officers follow right along in the order of their position, i.e., 1, 2, 3, 4, 5. The officers push each other forward onto the shield officer so the collective weight of all of them pushes the offender back and pins him or her with the shield. When the offender is pinned the officers immediately break off to their respective quadrants.

"The two upper officers (2 & 3) go for the hands and arms while the lower two officers (4 & 5) go for the offender's legs and lift up and then pull them out so the offender can be placed in a prone position on the cell floor if the offender is not already on the floor. The shield officer continues to pin the offender and follow the offender to the floor, keeping the offender confined under the shield.

"Because of the speed and explosiveness at which this takes place and, in some cases, the lack of room to move, all officers must be familiar with each other's responsibilities … Once the offender is restrained, the shield officer can pass the shield out to the team commander or one of the support staff outside. This frees up the shield officer to restrain the offender's head."

That's how it's supposed to go down. In 1995, Thelton E. Henderson, Chief Judge, United States District Court for the Northern District of California, described how some cell extractions happened at Pelican Bay.[39]

"On January 31, 1991, Arturo Castillo refused to return his food tray in protest against a correctional officer who had called him and other inmates derogatory names. After leaving the tray near the front of the cell, Castillo retreated to the back and covered himself with his mattress for protection, in anticipation of a cell extraction. It is undisputed that Castillo, who is small in stature, made no verbal threats or aggressive gestures. Nor did he possess, or pretend to possess, any kind of weapon.

"Shortly thereafter, Sergeant Avila warned Castillo that if he did not give up his food tray, it was going to be very painful. Castillo refused to hand Avila the tray, stating that if they wanted the tray, they would have to come and get it. The supervising lieutenant then authorized his sergeants to forcibly remove Castillo from the cell. To accomplish this removal, two rounds from a 38 millimeter gas gun were fired to the cell. A taser gun was also fired, striking Castillo in the chest and stomach. Then, without attempting to retrieve the tray (which remained near the front of the cell), some number of officers entered the cell, walked past the tray, and advanced toward Castillo. Castillo testified that one of the officers then hit him on the top of his head with the butt of the gas gun, knocking him unconscious. When he regained consciousness, he was on the floor with his face down. An officer was stepping on his hands and hitting him on his calves with a baton, at which point Castillo passed out a second time. When he regained consciousness again, he was dragged out of the cell face down; his head was bleeding, and a piece of his scalp had been detached or peeled back. At that point, it became clear that Castillo had been seriously injured, and he was taken to the infirmary and then to the hospital by ambulance. According to the medical report, the wound on Castillo's head was a seven centimeter by eight centimeter avulsion with a 'deep groove under flap (of scalp) that appeared one half centimeter-plus deep, running from the frontal to the parietal area of the skull.'"

Judge Henderson said he had no doubt that many correctional officers at Pelican Bay did their jobs honorably and well. Others were upset at the kinds of excesses they saw but felt they could do nothing to stop them. Still, he concluded, "The use of unnecessary and excessive force at Pelican Bay appears to be open, acknowledged, tolerated, and sometimes expressly approved." Prison records showed that in the early 1990s, officers at Pelican Bay were conducting around 95 cell extractions per year—around one every four days. Officers were obviously using cell extractions as a form of punishment for real or perceived infractions. These extractions were extremely violent. In one, after an inmate refused to give up a cup, spoon and extra clothing, staff hit him with three electric taser stun darts, fired three gas rounds into his cell and also sprayed him with mace. The court heard testimony that being struck by a single taser was like "being hit on the back with a four-by-four by Arnold Schwarzenegger."

One evening, inmate Luis Fierro was miffed because he was not able to get his hair cut and he refused to return his dinner tray. Instead of letting him calm down, officers decided on a cell extraction. First they fired a rubber pellet through the food port, which struck him in the groin. They followed this with two bursts of mace and several tasers, hitting Fierro in four places. Then the officers burst into the cell, took him down and beat him. The officers reported that Fierro suffered "minor abrasions and bruises." Judge Henderson listed them: "(1) multiple areas of bright red bruising on back, especially upper back; (2) scratches on left neck, left cheek and right cheek; (3) abrasion and bruising of left shoulder; (4) bruising and swelling about both eyes at edges of eyebrow; (5) small scratch on right calf; (6) large abrasion on right chin; (7) large areas of bruising around both ankles; (8) bruising on left upper outer thigh; (9) abrasion on left shin, and (10) abrasion on right calf."

Judge Henderson concluded, "Based on these unexplained injuries, I believe that Mr. Fierro was subjected to an extensive beating to the head and back after the extraction team entered the cell.... In conclusion, from defendants' own reports it appears almost certain that Mr. Fierro was subjected to blatant and brutal punishment for disobeying an order—in this case, the order to turn over the dinner tray."

The judge also described the case of inmate Kenneth Ward, who insulted a female officer. Next day, a male officer ordered him to put his arm through the slot to be handcuffed. Judge Henderson wrote, "At this point, (Officer) Kelly repeatedly threw his body weight against Ward's left arm. It is undisputed that as a result, Ward's upper left arm snapped and broke. Ward immediately became light-headed and he felt a lot of pain. He recalls that he felt as if he were in shock and was unable to move. As a result of this injury, Ward has suffered recurring problems with nerves in his arms, including numbness and spasms." The judge noted that the amount of force the officers needed to break Ward's thickly muscled arm had to have been "enormous."

At Pelican Bay, prisoners were often hog-tied as a punishment for disobeying orders. This involved handcuffing an inmate's hands in front of his body, placing him in leg irons, and then drawing a chain between the handcuffs and legs until only a few inches separated the bound wrists and ankles. Prisoners were sometimes held like this for up to nine hours. Others were kept naked in cages exposed to the elements or to public view.

Judge Henderson: "Violet Baker, a former educational program supervisor at Pelican Bay, gave a frank and credible account of one such incident. She testified that one day in late January or early February, she was walking from her office toward another facility. It was very cold (she was wearing gloves and a heavy jacket), and it was pouring rain. She observed two African-American inmates being held naked in two cages. When she passed by again one hour later, one inmate was still there, and she observed that he was covered with goose bumps. He said he was freezing, and asked her to request a pair of shorts and a T-shirt. She then saw an officer coming in her direction. When she looked at him, he looked back and just shrugged his shoulders, saying it was 'Lieutenant's order.' When she determined that it was Lieutenant Slayton on duty, she let the matter drop. Although the incident upset her, Slayton had a reputation for causing problems if crossed, and she did not want her educational program or teachers to suffer by her interference in this matter."

When correctional officers, armed with the latest high-tech weapons, are told the prisoners they are guarding are not only highly dangerous but morally worthless, there is a grave danger they will be treated as less than human. Prisoners complain that guards are very fast to activate their electronic weapons and often discharge them "accidentally." In August 2003, accused Washington sniper John Allen Mohammed was zapped when he refused to have an X-ray that had not been ordered by a court. Attorney Jonathan Turley wrote, "The guard holds a simple remote control that sends an eight-second 50,000 to 70,000 volt charge through a prisoner, causing immediate loss of muscular control and incapacitation. When shocked, many individuals will defecate or urinate on themselves. Some can experience fatal cardiac arrhythmia. Muscular weakness and temporary paralysis continue for 30 to 45 minutes. Last spring, Wisconsin sheriffs held a public display to show the media how harmless tasers and stun belts are by shocking one of their own deputies, appropriately named Krist Boldt. Boldt was hit with a five-second jolt and was sent to the hospital with a head wound after he hit the floor."[40]

In Virginia, Tom Deardorff, a former employee of Wallens Ridge, testified that he saw guards kick and beat prisoners, shoot them with rubber pellets and spit in their food. Officers forced prisoners wearing leg irons to run, and if they fell, the guards dragged them along the ground. These allegations helped spark a Department of Justice investigation.[41]

At Wallens Ridge, the officially sanctioned punishment of choice was strapping a prisoner to a table for 48 hours at a time. This policy was liberally applied, despite medical advice that such restraints should never be used for more than 12 hours, and the prisoner should be released for 10 minutes every two hours to stretch his limbs and restore blood circulation. In Virginia, prisoners were briefly released every eight hours to use the toilet. The ACLU acquired scores of incident reports describing such punishments. Here is one:

A prisoner identified as Inmate Hatton grabbed an officer's hand while he was removing handcuffs, pinching him between his index finger and thumb. At the time, the inmate was in the cell, with his hands extended through the slot in the cell door, while the officer was outside. The officer gave Hatton a five-second jolt with an Ultron stun gun and jerked his hand away, after which the inmate offered no further resistance. As punishment, Hatton was put into restraints. Both his arms and legs were secured and another strap went around his torso so that he could not move at all and he was then left alone in a room. This happened on April 5, 2001, at 8:35 p.m. According to the report, he was released at 8:25 p.m. on April 7, exactly 47 hours and 50 minutes later.[42]

In 2002, three guards from Wallens Ridge were charged with beating a shackled prisoner in his cell and falsifying their report of the incident. All three had been fired from their jobs, but when the case came to trial in rural Wise County, Virginia, the court found it difficult to select a jury. Many potential jurors knew the defendants; some were related to them. When a jury was eventually empaneled, it heard testimony from three other officers who described how they had seen the accused guards kick and beat the inmate. It took the jury less than an hour to acquit the guards. Judge Robert Stump immediately ordered the Virginia Department of Corrections to reinstate them with full benefits and back pay.[43]

A similar tale unfolded when eight guards from Corcoran Prison in California's Central Valley—an area that provides some 10,000 prison jobs—were brought to trial in 2000. The guards were accused of setting up "gladiator fights" between rival gang members in the prison. The trial judge allowed several people to sit on the jury who had reason to favor the guards. One was a corrections officer at a local county jail and another had submitted an application to become a state prison guard and was awaiting a response. The judge also barred testimony about a "code of silence" among corrections officers. After the not-guilty verdicts, jurors posed for pictures with the acquitted guards.[44]

In 2002, a jury in rural Bradford County in north Florida also acquitted three guards of murdering death row inmate Frank Valdes, who died after a cell extraction. Valdes was sentenced to death for murdering a correctional officer. The day before he was stomped to death, he had threatened to kill another officer. The guards decided to remove him from his cell so that they could search it for hidden weapons. Prosecutors claimed the extraction turned into a brutal beating. Valdes was treated at the prison clinic. When he was returned to his cell, the officers beat him again. An autopsy found Valdes suffered 30 rib fractures as well as a broken nose, jaw, clavicle and sternum. His chest was crushed so severely that he suffocated.

It was incredibly difficult to seat a jury to hear the case. Attorneys called nearly 3,000 potential jurors and questioned nearly 1,000. Scores of people were dismissed after they expressed sympathy for the guards. After three months, a panel of six jurors and five alternates emerged. The prosecution produced 51 witnesses and stacks of documents, but their key witness, a former guard who had turned state's evidence in return for immunity, changed his testimony on the witness stand. Several inmates testified, but the jury chose to believe the defense, which argued that some of Valdes' injuries might have happened after he climbed the bars of his cell and threw himself on to the concrete floor.[45] The defense also appealed to their emotions. "Corrections officers form a thin line of law enforcement to protect us from society's worst and most violent people," said defense lawyer Ted Curtis during closing arguments. Pointing to the defendants, he declared, "These are the good guys." Following the verdict, the state prosecutor decided to drop charges against five other officers he believed had taken part in the lynching, saying it would be a waste of time and money bringing them to trial in Bradford County.

Valdes was undoubtedly a deeply reprehensible character, yet it is worth asking in what way he was different from those who so brutally killed him. He was sentenced to die, but not like that.

A discussion of the death penalty does not fall within the ambit of this book. However, since death row prisoners in most states are held in segregated SHUs under supermax conditions, it is worth discussing their lives. An individual does not lose all of his or her rights after being sentenced to death. The state retains the responsibility of looking after the inmate's physical and mental well-being until all judicial procedures are exhausted and the moment of execution arrives. With the large number of death row inmates exonerated in recent years, this responsibility looms even larger.

Until 2000, Texas's death row was housed at the Ellis Unit near Huntsville, where inmates could look out of their cells through bars and interact with one another. They were even allowed to work four hours a day in a garment factory and participate in group recreation. However, after seven inmates escaped in November 1998, authorities shifted death row to the Polunsky Unit, 43 miles east of Huntsville. Six of the escapees were quickly recaptured, and the seventh drowned.

In Polunsky, prisoners are held in the familiar supermax pattern, alone in their cells for 23 hours a day with one hour for solitary recreation in an empty room. Lawyer Meredith Martin Roundtree said guards often used pepper spray at any hint of prisoner defiance. "Because of the ventilation system, the gas is spread throughout the pod each time they use it," she said. Prisoners complain of frequent lockdowns, when they are deprived of hot meals and recreation and do not receive clean clothes or towels for weeks at a time. Their cells frequently flood with toilet runoff.[46]

The trend in recent years has been to make death row conditions more and more unpleasant. In Florida, authorities added a heavy mesh to the outside of cells so death row prisoners could no longer see out. They also removed art supplies and pencils on security grounds. Prisoners were given a memo: "Effective Monday, November 29, 1999, standard ink pens and pencils are now considered contraband. A new security ink pen will be issued to each inmate. These will be replaced on an as-needed exchange basis only. This will mean that drawing pencils or calligraphy pens are no longer authorized."[47]

In Oklahoma, where death row is underground so there is no natural light, a death sentence means never seeing the sun again, which perhaps explains why one in three inmates give up their appeals and ask to be put to death quickly. This phenomenon, known as volunteerism, is growing throughout the country. From 1995 through 2001, at least 61 of the 409 people put to death in the United States were "volunteers."[48] Some were clearly mentally incompetent; others were deeply depressed. "With inadequate medical and psychiatric attention, I have seen rapid deterioration and personality changes in these men, which is what is leading to volunteerism," said Texas defense lawyer Yolanda Torres.

Mississippi's death row is at Parchman State Penitentiary, a prison with a particularly grim history. Parchman was one of the notorious prison farms that grew up in the South during the Jim Crow era. It was basically a plantation that used convicts as slave labor. Parchman inmates worked from before dawn until after dusk in chain gangs and died by the hundreds. Abuses at Parchman continued until 1972, when Federal Judge William C. Keady ordered an end to the forced labor system. Keady visited Parchman and found prisoners living in conditions of unbelievable squalor. Raw sewage collected in vast stinking pools next to their living quarters. The water supply was polluted and the kitchens overrun by insects and rats. Inmates told him shootings and beatings were common, murders went unreported and the segregation unit was a torture chamber.

In 2003, Parchman was the subject of another federal trial, this time concerning conditions on Unit 32C, where Mississippi's 66 death row inmates were held. A group of experts visited the prison on August 8, 2002. A day before the tour, prison officials tried to clean the place up. They sprayed it with insecticide and washed and bathed some of the prisoners who had had excrement smeared all over their bodies. They also gave the prisoners fans and repainted part of the cell block.[49]

The experts were not impressed. Questioned by the plaintiff's attorney, Susi Vassallo, who studies how heat affects the body at New York University Medical School, said nothing had prepared her for the experience of entering Unit 32C. "I'm not particularly claustrophobic, but as you stood there, you absolutely could not breathe, and it really made you wonder how somebody could tolerate being in there and keep control of themselves," she testified.

Q: Do you believe that the heat during the Delta summer at Parchman prison on death row poses a serious medical risk to the inmates there?

A: There's no question in my mind that that is the case.

Q: And what is the serious medical risk posed?

A: At its worst, death from heat stroke, which can occur relatively rapidly with no warnings. At the least, just heat exhaustion, heat illness.

Q: In those medical records did you see evidence of anyone on death row who was at a heightened risk for heat stroke or other heat-related illness?

A: There are a number of people, first of all, who seem to be well-recognized as being psychotic, so that those individuals are not going to be able to recognize their heat stress, to respond to it, to take certain behavioral precautions that others might do who are not psychotic. It's very well-known by physicians that people who are psychotic are at great risk for heat-related illness.

Q: Based on everything you've seen and reviewed and learned, do you think it's likely that, under current conditions, a death row inmate will die of heat stroke or some other heat related incident?

A: I think it's very likely.

James Balsamo, director of environmental health and safety at Tulane University, said he had measured heat indexes of 136 degrees in the unventilated cells. Prisoners could not open the windows without being attacked by swarms of mosquitoes. There was no effective netting to keep them out.

Q: When you were in the cells did you, in fact, observe insects, bugs, mosquitoes?

A: Yes, sir, I certainly did. Spiders, mosquitoes, live ones. And also, I went along the window ledge of the cells, I actually took my finger and scraped it along there and layers of dead bugs would just be moved about. I could move it with my hand.

Q: I want to move now to the sewage disposal system. I want you to tell the Court what is a ping-pong toilet?

A: It's a descriptive term. Like you're watching a ping-pong match where the ball goes back and forth. The adjoining cells have toilets and if you flush one with fecal material, whatever's in it, it then just goes directly over into the next cell and comes up. The toilet bubbles up in the toilet of the person in the adjacent cell.

Q: All right, sir. Did you observe the existence of these ping-pong toilets in the cells at unit 32C?

A: Yes, sir, I did. And pretty much uniformly. I had the inmates demonstrate by putting toilet paper in one and then watch it come bubbling up on the other side. Yes, I did observe it numerous times.... The material also overflows when the toilets overflow and they have the fecal material...that gets in the cell where the inmate is, and all his living utensils, his toothbrush, his towels, everything else is in there.

Dr. Balsamo described the general state of the cell block.

"The conditions there, except for the ones freshly painted white, were extremely filthy. The paint was peeling and chipping. There was evidence of water leakage coming down on the walls. There was brown-colored material with a 3D rim, meaning you could see it—it wasn't just a flat thing. I've been told that inmates sling fecal material at the walls and especially some of the ones with mental problems and that that's what that material was."

Q: How do inmates clean their cells?

A: The inmates are provided a bucket of water and a mop to mop their cells and I was told on a frequency of once a week. Inmates have told me that when they beg or plead for them to give it to them, they can get a brush to clean the toilet or a short handle one, a very large brush that does not fit into the neck of the toilet at the bottom, but that is what they get to clean their cells.

Q: Do inmates get regular cleaning supplies and materials that are adequate to clean their cells?

A: No, sir.

Q: All right. Describe for the Court how that operates.

A: Okay. There's one bucket, one mop for the whole 20 cells. I was told that it does not contain soap or bleach or anything, no sanitizing agent or anything in it. And that many of them told me they would not even use it because it just spreads the dirt from somebody else's cell into their cell, rather than help clean it. They indicated to me that they use their own bar of soap that they're given that they use for showers, and some use their own towels to clean the areas.

Q: And the water, as the bucket is passed from cell one to two to three to 20, is it changed?

A: No, sir. All indications were, from the numerous inmates I spoke to, that no, it was not changed.

Vincent Nathan, who has worked for nearly 20 years as a court-appointed monitor and expert in prison cases, testified that he could barely stand the heat and the insects during his tour. "The insect problem was so serious to make it almost impossible for me to complete my tour of the place," he told the court.

Q: The heat?

A: It was unbearable. I mean I wasn't in a coat and tie. I think I had a short sleeve shirt on and was very unhappy that I hadn't brought a long sleeve shirt because of the mosquitoes. And it was unbearable. One couldn't draw a breath. I became almost panicked when I walked into that cell.

Psychiatrist Terry Kupers testified he found six inmates who were among the most psychotic he had ever seen, as well as several others with diagnosable mental conditions.

Q: Where are the severely mentally ill prisoners housed? On the tiers with the other prisoners?

A: Not only housed right in the middle of the tiers with the other prisoners, but they are moved around so that various prisoners reported being put in a cell that had been occupied by one of the prisoners and having to deal with the mess in the cell.

Q: Have you formed an opinion as to the mental health care provided to prisoners on death row?

A: Yes. It is grossly inadequate. It essentially boils down to warehousing people with severe mental illness in a cell with no activity. They are idle all day long. Some are medicated, but there is essentially no other mental health service.

Q: Given the fact that all of these men are death sentenced, does it really matter from a mental health point of view if they suffer mental deterioration or breakdown?

A: Well, I think it matters in two ways. First of all, all of these men are not going to be executed; 183 death sentences have been granted since 1976. Of those, only five in Mississippi have been executed. Four convictions have been reversed. The Mississippi Supreme Court has reversed the death penalty in 41 percent of the 166 direct appeals it has ruled upon.... But besides that, I think we in the United States have a certain level of human decency. We don't treat anybody in the terrible way that I heard people are treated on death row at Parchman. There's a certain level of human decency and human rights....

The court also heard from William Joseph Holly, a 28-year-old prisoner who had spent 10 years on death row.

Q: So how has this routine over the past 10 years affected you?

A: I'm not sure how to explain. How do you explain what it's like to do the same thing continuously over and over basically without little variation over and over and over again for 10 years? And the variation you do get is usually not in a good form. Your fires, your floods, you know, things along those natures, you know. It's pretty bad.

Q: Pretty bad how? Can you expand on what pretty bad means to you?

A: Well, first, you would have to basically imagine yourself locked in a concrete box about the size of your average person's bathroom for 10 years, and then in those 10 years, basically you read, you sleep, you eat, you get up. You know, just the same routine continuously over and over. Don't have anything to do. So your choices are pretty limited. You know, after a while the idleness just eats at you. Just slowly steals your sanity bit by bit.

Christopher Epps, Commissioner of the Mississippi Department of Corrections, said that in his opinion Unit 32C met national standards. "I opened 32. It's in better shape now, in my professional opinion, [or] almost as good a shape as it was from the day we opened it. We just painted it. It's in good shape," he said.

Q: The state of Mississippi is not too poor to provide fans to these inmates. Isn't that a correct statement?

A: Depending on who you talk to, sir. We're $400 million below revenues today. I'm $32 million. I go to bed every night owing vendors $32 million, and I'm told I'm going to be $40 million come July 1.

Q: But fans on death row on July 1 wouldn't present an insurmountable financial problem?

A: I just told you I was $32 million in debt. In my budget, it would. I'm $32 million in debt today to vendors.

Judge Jerry Davis ruled in May 2003. He found Mississippi death row inmates suffered from excessive heat, insects, human excrement, the rantings of psychotic inmates and poor mental health. This, he said, amounted to cruel and unusual punishment. "No one in a civilized society should be forced to live under conditions that force exposure to another person's bodily wastes. No matter how heinous the crime committed, there is no excuse for such living conditions. It is the duty of the state of Mississippi to meet these minimal standards of decency, health and well-being," he said.[50]

Judge Davis, a former federal prosecutor, ordered the state to provide inmates with fans, a shower and ice water when the temperature rose above 90 degrees. He ordered better insect screens to be installed and told the state to fix the plumbing and get rid of the ping-pong toilets. He ordered that mentally sick inmates be housed separate from the rest.

Corrections Commissioner Christopher Epps said, "The Mississippi Department of Corrections respectfully disagrees with Judge Davis's findings."

The state appealed, but in June 2004, the U.S. Court of Appeals for the 5th Circuit upheld Judge Davis and rejected most of the state's arguments. It ordered Mississippi to fix the ping-pong toilets, provide fans and ice to prisoners on exceedingly hot days, stop mosquito infestations, and properly treat prisoners suffering from mental illness. [51]

9

SHORT-TERM PROBLEMS

> *"Jail life must be very satisfactory, for those who have been compelled to spend a few days there come out of it completely satisfied. They don't want to go back, nor stay any longer than they can help, under the polite attentions of the man who carries the key."*
> **Mark Twain**[1] ■

On January 28, 2001, Malik Jarno, a 16-year-old orphan from Guinea in West Africa, arrived at Dulles International Airport outside Washington, D.C., seeking sanctuary from a conflict in which most of his family had been killed. Malik's mother died when he was 12. His father, who was an Imam, a prominent community leader and a government opponent, was jailed in 1998 in a massive army sweep against his neighborhood and died in prison. Malik's brother took him to a family friend; then he too disappeared and was presumed dead. The friend got Malik out of the country to the Ivory Coast. Eventually, with the help of well-wishers, he made it to the United States.[2]

Malik, who is mentally retarded, was interviewed by an immigration officer at the airport. The officer asked him why he was not carrying valid papers, shouted at him, called him a liar and sent him to an adult jail in Arlington, Virginia. Later, he was moved to another jail in Virginia Beach and then to Piedmont Regional Jail, located in the small country town of Farmville, Virginia, about halfway between Richmond and Roanoke. The jail serves several counties in southern Virginia and has been increasingly used to house immigration detainees.

In recent years, incarcerating foreign detainees has become a highly profitable business for a growing number of U.S. jails. Tough immigration laws passed by Congress in 1996 required that all asylum seekers and foreign residents facing deportation be detained while their cases were decided instead of being released to the custody of relatives or friends. The law led to a mini–population explosion in the number of foreigners behind bars. On any given day, there are approximately 20,000 such individuals in detention; in the course of a year the total exceeds 200,000.[3] A few smart sheriffs quickly realized that locking up foreign detainees could mean fat profits. The Immigration and Naturalization Service (INS) pays $50 a day to house immigrants in jail. The actual cost for most jurisdictions, especially rural counties, is less than half that. In Farmville, profits from housing immigrants made the Piedmont jail self-supporting. In York, Pennsylvania, a new jail wing built exclusively for immigration detainees financed a property tax cut.[4] In Montgomery County, Maryland, a new $90 million jail was deliberately built larger than needed so the county could compete to house immigration detainees. County leaders said it was the only way to close a $2.5 million budget gap.[5]

As usual, along with profits went abuse. A 1998 Human Rights Watch report found poor conditions and mistreatment of foreigners in jails all around the country.[6] At Tensas Parish Detention Center in Louisiana, INS detainees and local inmates were severely beaten by sheriff's deputies, and three deputies pleaded guilty to civil rights violations. In Jackson County Correctional Facility in Florida, detainees were shackled to concrete slabs and shocked with electrified batons. In Krome Detention Center near Miami, women detainees were molested, harassed and raped by at least 15 male guards.[7] In 2000, the Justice Department launched a probe of the Wicomico County Detention Center in eastern Maryland, where immigrants were mixed with the general population. It found inadequate medical care, inappropriate use of force by guards, chronic overcrowding and unsanitary conditions that posed a health risk to inmates. Prisoners were forced to wear soiled underwear and jumpsuits and slept on mattresses that were old, soiled and flaking off, making them impossible to sanitize. The showers often ran hot water that reached 152 degrees Fahrenheit, 32 degrees above scalding temperature.[8] Warden John F. Welch told the *Washington Post* he liked housing foreigners, not only because they were highly profitable but also because they were easy to intimidate. "Throw a troublemaker in a jail cell with 30 American thugs. That adjusts his attitude," he told the newspaper.[9]

With this record, it should have come as no surprise when the Department of Justice Inspector General released a scathing report in June 2003 on the treatment of 762 aliens held in the aftermath of the 9/11 attacks on the World Trade Center and the Pentagon. It found that some detainees who were held at the Metropolitan Detention Center in Brooklyn were subjected to highly restrictive 23-hour lockdowns. The lights in their cells were kept on around the clock. They were allowed only one brief telephone call a week. Whenever they left their cells, they were placed in leg irons and heavy chains. The report also found a "pattern of physical and verbal abuse by some guards."[10] Guards slammed detainees against walls and walked on their leg shackles. Detainees said guards told them, "You will feel pain" and, "Someone thinks you had something to do with the World Trade Center, so don't expect to be treated well."[11] None of the detainees were connected to the attacks.

Long before 9/11, Piedmont Jail in Virginia had acquired a fearsome reputation among immigrant advocates and human rights activists as a dangerous and violent place for Americans and foreigners alike. Malik Jarno was particularly poorly equipped to handle its rigors. A psychologist who examined him in February 2001 concluded he suffered from "very delayed intellectual functioning." His IQ was approximately 47, placing him in the bottom 0.1 percent of those tested.[12] As if that were not enough, Malik spoke only Puhlar, a West African language, and some very basic French. He did not understand what was happening to him or why and there was no one to explain it to him. Unlike U.S. citizens, foreign residents, refugees and asylum seekers do not have the automatic right to legal representation, and many can languish for many months or even years in jail while their cases are decided. It took nine months before Malik was brought before an immigration judge for a preliminary hearing.

His plight was grim. The authorities had decided to treat him as an adult, despite the fact that he carried a birth certificate, which had not been altered or tampered with, clearly stating that he was a minor. A small, slight figure who looked even younger than his age, Malik was unable to defend himself against abuse from other inmates. Finally, after several months, he managed to get the attention of one of the volunteer lawyers who occasionally visited the jail. The lawyer took the case and tried initially to get Malik transferred to a juvenile facility where he could be given appropriate services. But when the lawyer produced Malik's birth certificate, the authorities simply locked him in solitary confinement with a card on the door reading "Juvenile." While in solitary, he had to provide guards with written requests for permission to telephone his lawyers or even to take a shower, despite the fact that he could barely write in Puhlar and not at all in English or French. After a week, his lawyer managed to get him transferred back to the cell block.

On October 31, 2001, there was an altercation in the block when another inmate, Ousman Nabe, complained he was unjustly being deprived of food. Corrections officers decided to forcibly remove Nabe to solitary confinement and told other inmates to get out of the way. One detainee, Kopandru Singo, described what happened next in a legal affidavit.[13]

"I was sitting on my bunk with Mr. Jarno while trying to eat our food that just got served. Officer M[14] was the first person to put his hands on Mr. Ousman and he received assistance from other officers, including Officer C as Mr. Ousman was struggling with them. At that time, people were trying to back off to give them more room. Meanwhile Officer W ordered people to back off, so they did. Mr. Malik and I tried to do the same thing by getting up from the bunk and walking away. But Officer W took her pepper spray and directly sprayed it in Mr. Malik's face. I was closer and I turned my face away to protect my eyes. I tried to go, but remembered that Mr. Malik was more hurt than I was. I turned my face back and I saw Mr. Malik, eyes closed, pepper spray liquid on his face all over. I forced myself and kept my eyes open and I led Mr. Malik to the bathroom where I washed his face with cold water. It wasn't enough; he couldn't open his eyes. I couldn't take it anymore, my eyes were burning. They opened the door, people went out in the corridor. I led Mr. Malik out there and came back to wash my face and take some toilet paper.

"They took Mr. Malik to the medical department and took us on the recreation yard. A few minutes later, Mr. Malik joined us. 'What happened in the medical department?' I asked. 'They washed my face with hot water and when I screamed cause it was burning more and more, so they used cold water and a few minutes later they asked me to join you out here.' That's what he told me in French, of course. 'Nothing else?' 'No,' he answered, as I asked him.

"A few hours later, we were asked to go back to our pod and I was six persons away from Mr. Malik as he asked Officer W who was in the corridor why she used the pepper spray on his face and why he didn't get medical attention. His questions were all in French as he couldn't speak English. 'Blah, blah, blah, the same to you,' replied Officer W.

"Automatically, another officer who was far away came running. They jumped on that little boy. At least six persons as I could see pushed him, twisted his arms, held his legs, put him on the wall pressed, and then on the floor. It was so horrible that I turned my eyes away. None of them tried to know what was really going on. They just used force against him without any reason. When I turned my eyes back, I saw Mr. Malik carried, handcuffed so tightly that he almost cried. I could read fear, intense fear and confusion in his eyes. He disappeared from my sight and I saw a fellow inmate crying, wiping tears from his own eyes."

As a result of articles I wrote about Jarno in 2002, members of Congress started asking questions and he was transferred to a juvenile facility. He turned 18 and was sent back to adult jail, this time in York, Pennsylvania. Finally, in late December 2003, after almost three years in jail, Jarno was released, although immigration authorities were still fighting in court to have him sent back to Guinea, where he feared he would be killed. A month before his release, Jarno sued three officers from Piedmont in federal court. But the jury in Alexandria, Virginia, never heard testimony that Jarno was mentally retarded, and they accepted the officers' explanation that they were acting to enforce discipline within jail guidelines.

In April 2002, I visited Piedmont Jail with a group of human rights lawyers. I was able to move around the cell blocks and talk to inmates. Many independently told me identical stories, which could not have been rehearsed. They said guards had beaten them, slammed them against walls and floors and shot at them with pepper spray pellets from close range. Inmates had been deprived of medical care and medication, denied regular outdoor recreation and often placed in isolation for no good reason. Women inmates told me that an entire female cell block had been ordered to stay in bed for over a week and allowed to get up only to use the toilet and shower. They said they had been forced to strip naked directly under a video camera. The images were transmitted to a screen outside the cell block, which male guards could see. "They made us line up right under the video camera and strip completely naked. Why I don't know," said Sayedeh Jahanmir, an Iranian woman. There had also been allegations of rape at Piedmont and one guard had been fired. A woman from Cameroon said she had developed sores and abscesses all over her body, but it took three weeks until she was allowed to see a doctor. The doctor said she might be allergic to the laundry detergent being used by the jail, but the authorities did nothing to help her. Detainees received one set of clean clothes only once a week. They were issued with one toilet roll a week and had to hand in the empty roll to get a new one. They were not provided with soap. The cell block was stiflingly hot, but the fans did not work. The water in the showers was a dribble.

Allen Beaton, a British citizen, who was jailed pending deportation for trying to enter the United States with invalid papers, described how some inmates threatened a hunger strike to protest the temporary removal of a television set from the cell block. "At four in the morning, I get yanked out of my bunk while I was still asleep. There's a knee at the back of my neck and my hands are cuffed behind my back. The guards took me downstairs and threw me against the wall. They said if I told anyone, they would split my head wide open," he said. Several detainees described how one elderly Somali detainee was using the toilet at the time. Guards threw him against the wall without provocation. The INS declined to respond to these allegations, but said it would investigate. After my story appeared, the jail authorities closed the facility to lawyers visiting foreign detainees, ensuring that asylum seekers would get no legal representation whatsoever.

If this kind of treatment was only meted out in U.S. jails to foreign citizens who lack lawyers, that would be worrying and shocking enough. However, the sad fact is that American citizens in jails across the nation routinely face the danger of similar treatment or worse. In recent years, major brutality scandals have shaken several of the nation's largest jails in cities like New York, Chicago and Boston as well as in many smaller jurisdictions. Does this constitute a pattern of abuse? Obviously, with over 665,000 people held in more than 3,000 jails around the country at any one time and 10 million passing through the jail system each year, it is hard to generalize.[15] No doubt, many jails and corrections officers make valiant efforts to do a good job with the available resources, though a large number have to grapple with chronic overcrowding and budget shortfalls. But sufficient abuse occurs in enough different places with enough regularity to raise serious questions.

Jails have a much more complex and varied mission than prisons. The key point is that for a great number of people, jails are not supposed to be places of punishment. They are holding facilities. According to the Department of Justice, jails have ten distinct tasks:

- to receive individuals pending arraignment and hold them awaiting trial, conviction or sentencing.
- to readmit probation, parole and bail bond violators and absconders.
- to temporarily detain minors pending transfer to juvenile authorities.
- to hold mentally ill people until they can be transferred to appropriate health facilities.
- to hold individuals for the military, for protective custody, for contempt and for the courts as witnesses.
- to release convicted inmates to the community upon completion of sentence.
- to transfer inmates to federal, state or other authorities.
- to house inmates for state or other authorities when prisons are overcrowded.
- to sometimes operate community-based programs as alternatives to incarceration.
- to hold inmates sentenced to short terms, generally of one year or less.[16]

These overlapping tasks can make jails busy and bewildering places, with people constantly entering and exiting the system. In fiscal year 2002, New York's Rikers Island operated 322,142 inmate transports. It admitted 108,464 inmates during the year, and its daily population was usually a tad below 14,000. Detainees stayed an average of 45.2 days and annually cost the city a staggering $62,595 apiece.[17]

Like the prison population, the nation's jail population has been growing fast in recent years. From 1990 to 2002, it expanded by 40 percent, from 163 per 10,000 members of the general population to 231.[18] In 2002, 17 of the 50 largest jail jurisdictions in the country operated at over 100 percent of capacity. Clark County, Nevada, which encompasses Las Vegas, was at 166 percent capacity; Maricopa County, Arizona, was at 152 percent. In Philadelphia, the jails were operating at 132 percent of capacity.[19]

Overcrowding coupled with budget and staff shortages may excuse or at least explain many things. They may explain why a Los Angeles

County Grand Jury report in 2003 found the city jail in Long Beach, California, which is undergoing a two-year renovation, to be "filthy" with "roaches and rodents scampering across the floors." In response, Tim Jackman, deputy chief of the Long Beach Police Department, admitted, "Our jail is not clean. It's dirty. But it's not filthy." [20]

In Charleston County Detention Center in South Carolina, a state Department of Corrections report in October 2002 found numerous violations, most due to severe overcrowding. The jail, opened in 1994 with a capacity of 661 inmates, was holding an average of 1,388 a day in the summer of 2002. Violent and nonviolent inmates were housed together; sentenced criminals were mixed with those awaiting trial. Inmates were not receiving health screenings, and inspectors found a serious rodent problem, with about 22 rats being killed each month. "I've caught three in my office," said Chief Deputy Keith Novak.[21]

In Marion County, Indiana, U.S. District Judge Sarah Evans Barker said conditions in the overcrowded county jail "violate all our senses of human dignity." The judge held Sheriff Frank Anderson in contempt but did not order him detained. She set a 1,135-inmate cap on the jail to be phased in over nine months and said she would fine the county $40 a day for each inmate over the limit. The jail population had been running 100 to 300 over the limit.[22]

Overcrowding and confusion may also explain incidents like the death of Dr. Eduardo Miranda in 1997 in the El Paso County Jail in Texas. Miranda, a Mexican doctor who was taking medication to avoid seizures, was detained in the border town on a traffic violation. A jury in 2003 found that he asked jail staff to let him have his medication but was refused. He suffered a seizure and suffocated when staff tried to restrain him. The jury awarded his widow $2.5 million.[23]

One could also argue that many cases of brutality are the fault of individual bad apples among the great mass of honest, straight jail correctional officers and not endemic to the system. This appeared to be the case in Multnomah County Detention Center in Portland, Oregon, where four guards in 2000 were fired after viciously beating a taxi driver in the jail. At least two bore identical tattoos that read, "Brotherhood of the Strong," a neo-Nazi slogan. The fatal incident closely followed the violent deaths of two other inmates under suspicious circumstances.

One officer was later convicted of harassment and official misconduct.[24] In the Tulsa County Jail in Oklahoma, black inmates were forced into a cell known as the "Aryan Tank," where they were made to confront inmates believed to belong to a white supremacist group. Undersheriff Bill Thompson said it was a "legitimate attempt to integrate a cell." A brawl ensued. One black and one white inmate later each won a $25,000 settlement for their injuries.[25]

Jail abuse cases are often costly. In May 2002, a federal jury in South Bend, Indiana, awarded $56.5 million to the family of Christopher Moreland, the largest verdict in the state's history.[26] In the early morning of October 5, 1997, the thirty-year-old Moreland was arrested on suspicion of drunk driving and taken to the St. Joseph County Jail in South Bend. A surveillance video captured the gruesome details. Moreland got into a confrontation with another inmate. Deputy Paul Moffa entered the cell and sprayed Moreland with an extremely potent pepper spray called OC 10. The deputy then choked him and slammed his head against a concrete bench. Two other deputies took Moreland upstairs to wash off the pepper spray. Instead of putting him under cold water, the guards threw him into a hot shower, amplifying the effect of the powerful chemical. They then placed him in a restraint chair, sprayed him again and threw him back into the shower, where he banged his head on the floor. Finally, they tossed him, naked and comatose, back into his cell, where he was found dead the next morning. The damages awarded by the jury exceeded the $39.6 million the county paid to build the brand new jail, though whether the family would ever see the money remained doubtful.

Reading through a litany of cases from around the nation, an awful sameness emerges. In November 2002, the city of Shreveport, Louisiana, paid $4.9 million—its highest settlement ever—to Carl Janski, an inmate who was severely beaten in his cell while being held on drunk charges. Janski died a month after the settlement was reached.[27] In Santa Fe, New Mexico, the county jail had a rash of incidents that attracted the attention of Department of Justice investigators. They included the arrest of a guard in 2001 on charges of raping a mentally retarded man, four women inmates who alleged rape or sexual abuse and a guard sentenced to a year in jail for helping three inmates to escape.[28] In Grant County, Kentucky, in 2003, five inmates filed civil rights lawsuits for injuries suffered in the county jail. One, Billy Jo Killion, said he was badly beaten by fellow inmates. A nurse at the jail recommended speedy surgery, and a date was fixed. But Killion never kept the appointment. Instead, officers allegedly locked him in isolation in an attempt to cover up the assault. Killion said that after the beating his eyeball was partially hanging out of its socket. He suffered three skull fractures, possible fractured ribs and a broken mandible as well as extensive damage to his right eye, making it doubtful he would ever see out of it again.[29]

We expect a lot from our jail system. In the absence of other social safety nets to care for the physically and mentally sick and those addicted to drugs and alcohol, a modern jail is supposed to operate almost like a hospital emergency room triage. As well as taking custody of dangerous criminals, it is supposed to screen all entrants and direct those who need help to appropriate services. Clearly, many guards and wardens are not psychologically prepared or properly trained for these tasks. Understandably, they remain focused on protecting themselves and each other against violent felons and preserving order rather than dispensing services to needy clients.

The most prestigious units in many jail systems are the special squads that many sheriffs deploy, called CERT or SERT teams (Corrections or Sheriff's Emergency Response Teams). Dressed in paramilitary black uniforms or camouflage fatigues and armed to the teeth with the latest supposedly nonlethal weapons, members of these teams are a carefully selected elite. They undergo elaborate weapons and physical training and stand ready around the clock in many facilities to quell not only riots, but any form of inmate unrest or disobedience. Each year, the best get to strut their stuff and compete against one another at industry fairs, such as the Mock Prison Riot sponsored by the federal National Institute of Justice's Office of Law Enforcement Technology Commercialization, which is held in a disused prison in Wheeling, West Virginia.

The year I attended, teams participated from 17 states, acting out 36 "real-life" scenarios, each one demonstrating a different aspect of prisoner unrest, resistance or violence. Volunteer students and corrections officers played the parts of rioting prisoners. One CERT squad from

Alabama, dressed from head to foot in black body armor and carrying stun guns, crushed a protest by inmates who barricaded themselves in the recreation yard. The team fired fake tear gas and pepper balls and rushed the yard swinging their sticks. The protesters were quickly immobilized, brought to the ground and handcuffed. Another team quelled a food fight in the cafeteria with a "flash-bang" stun grenade followed by a charge of officers wearing padded gloves, plastic shin guards, Kevlar helmets and flak vests. A third scenario dealt with a hostage situation in a cell block. The liberal use of fake blood made the proceedings seem more realistic. Scores of commercial companies from around the world were also on hand, trying to sell the latest innovations in "corrections technology."

In CERT training, enormous emphasis is placed on the correct technique of applying appropriate and not excessive force. The general rule, according to Lieutenant Vince Wasilewski, a CERT commander in New York's Onondaga County, is to apply a level of force that is slightly higher than the resistance the subject is using.[30] Plainly, officers in prisons and jails should not be reaching for the OC spray at the first sign of perceived noncompliance. Equally plainly, they often do.

In Cook County Jail in Chicago, the elite squad is called the SORT team (Special Operations Response Team). It has been implicated in scores of incidents of violence and brutality in recent years. One of the most dramatic took place on February 4, 1999, when SORT members accompanied by four guard dogs without muzzles ordered 400 prisoners to leave their cells in response to a gang-related stabbing three days earlier.[31] According to a 50-page report by the Sheriff's Internal Affairs Division, the guards ransacked cells, then herded inmates into common areas where they were forced to strip and face the wall with hands behind their heads. Unit commander Richard Remus stood on a table shouting, "SORT runs the jail," as guards went from prisoner to prisoner examining them for gang tattoos. Anyone who looked away from the wall was struck with a wooden baton. Some prisoners were forced to lie on the floor, where they were stomped and kicked. One inmate, who did not leave a cell fast enough, said he was beaten with fists and batons until he urinated on himself and went into convulsions. At least 49 inmates told investigators they had been beaten. One, Leroy Orange, told the *Chicago Tribune*, "Everybody who had a tattoo got their ass whipped. It was scary.

The dogs were barking and the guards were just beating the [expletive] out of everybody. I've never seen anything like it." After the beatings, guards prevented inmates from receiving immediate medical care.

As a result of the report, Remus was demoted and kicked off the squad in March 2003, four years after the incident. He resigned a few days later, protesting his innocence and saying he did not want to work for an organization that would "kowtow to the media." But this incident was far from the only case to bubble to the surface. Two guards came forward to describe another vicious beating that took place in July 2000. On January 17, 2003, corrections officer Roger Fairley testified in a deposition about what he saw that day.[32]

"I saw inmate Scott, inmate Fields, inmate Sanchez and inmate Mitchell on the floor, handcuffed and shackled with the exception of inmate Mitchell because he had a cast I believe on his left leg, so he didn't have any shackles on. I saw Officers F., B., P. and G.[33] violently beating the inmates on the floor."

Q: What do you mean, violently beating?

A: I saw them jumping up in the air, coming down on their heads with their knees. I saw them kicking them in every part of their bodies with all their might. At one point I saw Officer F. kicking Mitchell and Mitchell's body completely lifted off the floor and he flew into the wall. I saw them hitting them with elbows, stomping on their faces and heads, kicking them in the face. So I yelled at them to stop because what I saw was too violent. But they didn't. Nurse Lorense arrived on the scene. She put her hand over her mouth because she couldn't believe what she was seeing, so she started yelling.... I heard Lieutenant B.'s voice behind me—and I know Lieutenant B.'s voice because I worked with him for a long time— override our voice, gesture and say, 'They want to hurt my officers? Fuck'em. Kill'em, they deserve to die.'"

In 2003, the U.S. Department of Justice launched a criminal investigation of these and other incidents. Ernesto Velasco, who was director of the jail when some of the worst violence occurred, had been nominated by Governor Rod Blagojevich to become head of the Illinois Department of Corrections and was about to begin confirmation hearings.

He was forced to resign.[34] Attorneys representing the county recommended settling 35 lawsuits brought by inmates.

Fairley was asked at his deposition why he had not come forward earlier. He responded that there was a wall of silence in the department. Guards simply did not "snitch" on each other.

"I was angry for a long time after that incident. I thought about reporting it. But I couldn't, because it's a very complicated situation when you work in a jail. If you report other officers doing wrong, you can end up getting hurt by those officers. I've seen it. You can be harassed, they vandalize your cars. You can no longer depend on anybody for back up," he said. "All I can say at this point (is that) on many and many occasions I witnessed excessive force, abuse of power, intimidation. And all the things that I've witnessed, the way the County operates, it's all designed so that it can be covered up. This incident was one of them."[35]

On July 27, 2003, there was yet another brutal incident at Cook County Jail. Seven inmates described how some 50 officers hit them and kicked them without provocation even after they were handcuffed. University of Chicago lawyer Jean Snyder, in a letter to Illinois State's Attorney Richard Devine, wrote, "One guard used a pool stick to beat the inmates; others put on leather gloves or rolled handcuffs around their wrists. One inmate's arm was bruised from being struck with the pool cue while he was trying to protect his head; another inmate had a bloodied and torn lip that required several stitches to close; a third had splinters lodged in his back from being struck repeatedly with a pool stick."[36]

While this was going on in Chicago, the sheriff's department in Suffolk County, Massachusetts, which includes Boston, was also in the throes of upheaval. The incidents took place in two relatively new jails that had opened in the early 1990s to replace two ancient facilities that were notorious for riots, escapes, overcrowding and brutality.[37]

Accounts of the events in Boston and Chicago were remarkably similar. As in Chicago, the elite squad in Boston, known as the SERT, was at the center of the storm. A former jail officer, Bruce Baron, said he witnessed more than 20 beatings of inmates during three years as a guard from 1995 to 1998. He said that 95 percent of the time, it was because a guard didn't like an inmate, not because the inmate had done anything wrong.

"They would try to provoke the inmates and then call in the SERT or try to take care of it themselves. It was a macho thing," Baron said.[38]

When Baron came forward to report abuses, he had to endure a year of harassment from colleagues, who threatened him, shoved him and called him a "rat coward." His wife, who suffered from multiple sclerosis, received a threatening phone call. A voice said, "We're going to make your husband a cripple like you." Baron eventually won a federal jury award of $500,000.[39]

In one 1998 incident, detainee Reginald Roscoe refused to have his bag searched. He was handcuffed, thrown against a wall, splitting the skin on his forehead, and taken into a cell for more punishment. Lieutenant Eric Donnelly, an officer with the unit, left off the beating for a moment and shouted, "This is my jail!"[40] Roscoe later needed five stitches to close his head wound.

In Chicago, it was Remus shouting, "SORT runs the jail." In Boston, it was Donnelly shouting, "This is my jail!" The mentality was the same.

On March 31, 2003, Michael J. Sullivan, U.S. Attorney for the District of Massachusetts, announced that a federal jury had convicted Suffolk County Jail Officer Brian Bailey of criminal civil rights violations in connection with the beating of a pretrial detainee. The jury also found him guilty of conspiracy to obstruct justice, obstruction of justice and perjury. Four other defendants—Lieutenants Eric Donnelly and Randall Sutherland and Deputy Sheriffs Anthony Nuzzo and Melvin Mansucco—decided to plead guilty on the eve of their trial.[41]

The Justice Department had verified four separate acts of brutality, all in 1999. On April 15, two pretrial detainees started fighting with a third inmate. The CERT team commanded by Donnelly responded and was told to take the two detainees to another unit. On the way, Donnelly ordered CERT team members to give the two "a tickle"—he meant give them a beating. The two were taken into separate cells and viciously beaten.

Eight days later, another inmate got into a fight with an officer. The CERT team, under Donnelly, handcuffed him and beat and kicked him so hard that he had to be taken to the hospital. Immediately after the incident, members of the team discussed how to cover up the beating. Then, they wrote and submitted false and misleading reports.[42]

On September 24, a pretrial detainee locked in a cell on suicide watch was stripped naked without a blanket. After several hours of the detainee yelling for a blanket, Bailey and another officer decided to enter the locked cell and "slap him around" to get him to shut up. They subsequently falsified their report of the incident and Bailey later lied about it to a federal grand jury.

On October 16, Leonard Gibson, an 18-year-old detainee awaiting trial on car theft charges, was assigned to a cell in the medical unit because he suffered from Tourette's syndrome, a neurological disorder that causes involuntary movements or tics and uncontrollable vocal outbursts. His outbursts annoyed Donnelly and one of his CERT colleagues so much that they decided to shut him up the only way they knew how. Another inmate, Rene Rosario, described what he saw to the *Boston Globe*.[43] "Donnelly came in and Lenny starts having his problem and the officer yells, 'Shut up.' And Lenny said, 'I'm sorry. I can't help it. This is a disease.' Then they promised to slap the Tourette's out of him. He was screaming. He was pleading, 'Please don't hit me! Stop! I can't help it!' But all you could hear was the pounding. The pounding. He was really hurt."

In a press release announcing the officers' guilty pleas, Assistant Attorney General for Civil Rights Ralph F. Boyd Jr. asserted that only the "smallest fraction of law enforcement officers abuse their power." But was this really true? In Boston and Chicago, the beatings went on for years before they were exposed. Many officers knew what was happening but kept quiet, even if they disapproved and did not take part in the abuse themselves. It was a rerun of the Stanford Prison Experiment. Did the chain of command really know nothing, or did senior officers choose to turn a blind eye?

Some faults were relatively easy to fix. The American Correctional Association found in 2001 there was not even the most rudimentary system to log, track and record grievances in Boston's Nashua Street Jail. There were no cameras in key areas, despite the fact that it was a new state-of-the-art facility. After the report appeared, cameras were installed.

But human faults cannot be fixed merely by installing cameras or other technology. The violence in Boston did not take place in a vacuum. Brutality went hand in hand with financial corruption, not to mention the sexual abuse scandal described in Chapter Seven that eventually left the department staggering under the weight of a $10 million class action settlement. In 2002, a Special Commission headed by former U.S. Attorney Daniel K. Stern concluded that a lack of leadership in the Sheriff's Department, exacerbated by a corrupt hiring system, lay at the root of the problems. He found a jail system riddled with cronyism.

"Many of the staff at all levels owe their jobs to well-connected politicians. Because the Sheriff made promotions without clearly defined criteria (or even an employee evaluation process), many staff members concluded that their own advancement depended on politics rather than merit," the report said. Brutality and sexual misconduct "occurred in a deeply troubled institution where conditions were ripe for officers so inclined to abuse their authority."[44]

While some jail guards were abusing inmates, many were also milking the system financially. In fiscal year 2000, Suffolk County guards piled up $5.8 million for overtime compared to $6.3 million for the 4,300 officers who worked for the Massachusetts Department of Corrections across the entire state.[45] In September 2002, Suffolk County Sheriff Richard J. Rouse announced he would accept a buyout of his contract and step down. He left on November 29, the same day the department failed to pay $5 million that it had promised to settle the sex abuse scandal and incurred a further penalty of $150,000.[46]

One could argue that the Boston and Chicago examples show that even though many defenseless inmates suffered grievous physical and mental harm, the system did work. Bad behavior was eventually rooted out and punished while those at the top of the system paid a political price. The problem is that even after a system is cleaned up and brutality and corruption appear to have been stamped out, never to return, they remain lurking close below the surface, ready to sputter back to life at any time. Events at Rikers Island provide a sobering lesson.

Rikers actually consists of 10 separate jails on an island of 415 acres between Queens and the Bronx, close to La Guardia Airport. Several hundred detainees are also held on former Staten Island ferries converted into floating detention centers. In the late 1980s, Rikers seemed almost out of control. Hundreds of inmates and guards were injured in riots, and a vicious turf war between black and Latino gangs raged virtually unchecked. In the early 1990s, authorities were reporting an average of 150 inmate slashings and stabbings a month. Even after that was cleaned up, problems reemerged with disturbing regularity. In the first half of the 1990s, 26 Rikers officers were charged with drug smuggling. In 1995, nearly a dozen corrections officers were charged with assaulting inmates over a 10-year period and falsifying reports, and three were sent to prison.[47] More than 50 inmates suffered broken bones, and about three dozen had perforated eardrums.[48] Inmates won a $1.6 million settlement.

But by 2000, all these problems seemed to be in the past. Bernard Kerik, Commissioner of New York City's Department of Corrections, later to be the city's police commissioner and later still to be put in charge of building a new Iraqi police force after the U.S. invasion of 2003, had taken command. He introduced a corporate management style, cleaned up the jail, improved its appearance, reduced inmate violence to close to zero and made the institution a model for the rest of the country to emulate.

But in 2002 and 2003, after Kerik had departed, the shadows returned. Among the headlines of those two years:

- Seven jail workers were charged with accepting bribes to smuggle drugs to inmates.[49]
- A gang leader was investigated for allegedly ordering his girlfriend to have sex with a jail guard so the officer would allow her to smuggle drugs into the facility.[50]
- A New York TV station aired video of corrections officers renting cars on primary day in September 2002 to help the Republican Party and alleged that officers were pressured to conduct unpaid campaign activities while in uniform.
- Corrections Department Commissioner William Fraser denied allegations of wrongdoing but resigned, saying he could no longer carry out his duties because of the media furor.[51]
- Anthony Serra, the former three-star general who was head of all 10 jails on Rikers, was indicted on 89 corruption charges. He was accused of using prison guards to do landscaping and house improvements on his home and run personal errands while on city time.[52]

Wearing handcuffs, Serra was led into a Bronx courtroom on February 13, 2003, and listened as prosecutors accused him of violating the public trust by systematically looting the jail of materials and supplies.

Most surreal of all, four veteran Rikers workers were charged with stealing a Salvador Dali sketch worth possibly $600,000 from a locked display case in the jail lobby. The composition, depicting the Crucifixion, was taken from a double-locked display case during an unscheduled fire drill on March 1, 2003, and replaced with a crude copy. The painter had donated the work to the prisoners of Rikers in 1965.

10

MONEY, MONEY, MONEY

"He who opens a school door, closes a prison."
Victor Hugo ■

The Canon City Public Library in Fremont County, Colorado, is eager to make local history come alive for young people. On its Internet site, it provides a historical timeline of the area.[1] Children learn that dinosaurs roamed this part of America 130 million years ago and left fossilized remains behind. Humans first arrived around 2,200 years ago, but whites did not begin settling until 1838. In 1871, the first territorial prison opened its gates on the western edge of town. In 1929, the deadliest prison riot in Colorado history killed 12 people. During World War II, German prisoners of war were housed in the area. The timeline reaches a fitting climax in 1990, when ground was broken for a federal supermax prison. "Fremont County becomes known as the Corrections Capital of America with a total of thirteen facilities," the text proudly proclaims.

The library also offers a lesson plan for teachers, with all the materials needed to make local history exciting and relevant. At the middle school level, one project asks students to imagine they are prisoners in the state penitentiary. They are required to write letters to their families describing life behind bars and to keep a journal. In lesson two, the students have to imagine they are running the prison. They must create a map with a simple key to label the buildings within the compound and answer questions like, "How many prisoners would you put in one cell?" and "What problems do you see with the way you have placed inmates together?" Finally, they must write a statement to the state legislature convincing lawmakers to fund a new prison building.

Students may well find these lessons interesting, since some will probably end up working in a prison if they stay in Canon City. In Fremont County, the number one employer is the Colorado Department of Corrections with nine prisons, and the number two is the Federal Bureau of Prisons with four. Prisons have become the backbone of the local economy. And Canon City is just one of hundreds of "prison towns" that have multiplied across America in the past 20 years. In many communities, prisons have been hailed as economic saviors. Towns that once might have hesitated to bring a prison to town now rush to put together incentive packages, as if they were competing for a major sports franchise. Abilene, Texas, offered the state incentives worth more than $4 million to get a prison. The package included a 316-acre site and 1,100 acres of farmland adjacent to the facility capable of generating $500,000 in cotton per year. The city also pledged to upgrade its roads, improve its communications and public works infrastructure and provide state officials with the use of a private plane and hangar.[2]

"There are a lot of economic pluses to prisons. You're talking about stable jobs, which is something you don't get from some other businesses. Prison jobs seem to be pretty recession-proof. You're also bringing in employees who will buy houses and spend money in your community. It adds up quickly," said Michael Bourn, executive director of Amarillo Economic Corporation in the Texas Panhandle. Amarillo bid successfully for three prisons to be built on the northeastern edge of town in the late 1980s and 1990s. The prisons employ 1,300 people and may have helped generate another 2,000 jobs indirectly, which helped keep the unemployment rate at around half the national average as the economy slowed after 2000. "We haven't experienced any negatives at all," Bourn said. "If we got the chance, we'd try to get more prisons out here. People are decently paid, although the work is not for everyone."

There are also all kinds of indirect benefits. For example, low security prisoners are allowed to work outside, cleaning up trash, maintaining grounds and buildings and beautifying the city. In Amarillo's maximum security prison, inmates grow produce, most of which goes straight to the community food bank."

Buckeye, located 35 miles west of Phoenix, used to be a sleepy little outpost in the Arizona desert with a population of around 5,000 until it competed successfully for a major state prison to be built 15 miles west of town. Just getting the place built was a huge undertaking. The complex covers 284 acres. It contains 23 miles of road and 20 miles of fencing. Twenty-seven contracting companies and many hundreds of workers were involved in its construction. It has its own electrical plant, generators and a vast computer data center as well as a wastewater treatment plant designed to process 750,000 gallons of raw sewage per day. The six kitchens produce 12,450 inmate meals every day; the laundry washes 53,000 pounds of clothes and linens each week, and the maintenance crew keeps almost 6,000 locks and 11,000 light fixtures working.[3]

The prison helped transform Buckeye. The state upgraded the road leading to the town, and the population began to explode. A new movie theater and a $2.5 million swimming complex opened. There was one hitch. The prison was built on land outside official municipal limits, which meant Buckeye was not getting any tax revenue from the facility. No problem. The city changed its bylaws and annexed the land. Developers paid attention. Because Buckeye was sitting on ample supplies of water, it suddenly became prime real estate. "We'll probably be a town of 35,000 within five years," said Mayor Dusty Hull. After that, the sky is the limit. According to the Maricopa Association of Governments, the town could eventually support a million people.[4]

Life has already changed forever. "We have a lot of jobs here now. Almost all the guards live in Buckeye, but they are not all that well paid so we have had to provide affordable housing. Also, quite a few inmates' families have moved here so they can visit more easily and often. Sure, we get more money from the state and more revenues from our local taxes, but we also have more crime and more demand for social services and welfare than we had before the prison came," said Mayor Hull.

One reason the city was so anxious to expand its limits was that the U.S. Census Bureau counts inmates as if they were citizens of the towns and counties where they are incarcerated rather than of where they actually come from. More residents means more federal aid and grants. Buckeye stood to gain subsidies of $600 per inmate per year from the 2000 census. When this effect was multiplied across America, the result was to drain a significant amount of money away from inner cities, where most prisoners originate, to white, rural areas where most prisons are sited.

"The near-doubling of the prison population since the last census and a rural prison boom during the 1990s portends a substantial transfer of economic and political power from urban to rural America," wrote criminologist Tracy Huling. "The prisoner 'share' of the nearly $2 trillion in federal funds tied to population counts distributed nationwide over the next decade will go to the mostly rural hometowns of their keepers."[5]

Moreover, since prisoners earn little or no money, they also artificially drive down average income rates, making towns and counties eligible for federal housing funds. Census figures are also used to redraw political boundaries. Even though most prisoners cannot vote, their presence helps boost the political clout of rural districts, most of which are staunchly conservative.

Before 1980, only a third of prisons were located in non-metropolitan areas. By 1999, the number had risen to 57 percent.[6] According to the Department of Agriculture's Economic Research Service, 245 prisons sprouted in 212 rural counties during the 1990s.[7] In West Texas, where oil and farming both collapsed, 11 rural counties acquired prisons during that decade. The Mississippi Delta, one of the poorest regions in the country, got seven new prisons. Appalachian counties of Virginia, West Virginia and Kentucky built nine, partially replacing the collapsing coal mining industry.[8]

"The unemployment situation was so bad, we were almost desperate," said Scott Davis, county administrator for Wise County in southwest Virginia. Salvation arrived in the shape of the Wallens Ridge and Red Onion supermaxes. By the late 1990s, each prison was pumping around $13 million into the economy in direct wages. Local civic leaders as well as state authorities were pleased. "They're happy, we're happy, the people inside are the only ones who are unhappy," said Chuck Miller, executive director of the Big Stone Gap Redevelopment Authority.[9]

In counties acquiring prisons, the population rose by 12 percent during the 1990s, compared to a growth rate of 1.5 percent the previous decade. Sussex County, Virginia, which got two maximum security prisons, became the fastest-growing county in the United States. In Corcoran, California, 11,000 of the town's population of 21,000 were prisoners.[10] Del Norte County in northern California was an economic disaster until Pelican Bay opened in 1989. Only four of the area's 17 sawmills were still operating, and commercial salmon fishing had all but dried up. During the mid-1980s, 164 businesses went belly-up. Pelican Bay brought hundreds of new jobs and new commercial development—an Ace Hardware, a Safeway, a K-Mart.[11] The county population grew by 17 percent in the 1990s to 27,500.

Studies have found that prisons create around 35 jobs for every 100 inmates housed.[12] But there is some controversy about their overall economic impact. One study that compared seven New York counties that had prisons to seven that did not found little discernible difference in unemployment rates or per capita income over the past 25 years.[13] Most of the best jobs within prisons tended to be filled by people who lived outside the host community, and most of the contracting work was also done by outsiders. Inmates themselves, working for less than a dollar an hour, replaced some local low-paid workers.

This result seems to contradict anecdotal evidence from around the country that suggests that prisons do indeed spur economic development. Further research is needed. Still, it is indisputable that the emergence of so many prison towns has created a dependency. If the number of people incarcerated in America was ever to begin seriously falling, prison communities would become part of a powerful political lobby campaigning to keep their beds filled.

Whether or not local communities reap the full benefit, there is no doubt that there is big money to be made in prisons. As recently as 1980, there were no private companies operating U.S. prisons and jails for profit. The change began in 1984 when Hamilton County, Tennessee, awarded a contract to Corrections Corporation of America (CCA) to run a jail. That year, the federal Immigration and Naturalization Service also turned to CCA to run a lockup in Houston. In 1985, Kentucky became the first state to hire a company to run a prison. Privatization picked up steam in 1987 when Texas awarded two 500-bed facilities to CCA and another two to Wackenhut Corrections Corporation, the other leader in the field.

By the end of 2002, 31 states and the federal system reported 93,771 prisoners in privately operated prisons. They accounted for 5.8 percent of all state prisoners and 12.4 percent of federal inmates. Five states held at least a quarter of their prisoners in privately run facilities—New Mexico (43 percent), Alaska (31 percent), Wyoming (30 percent), Montana (29 percent) and Oklahoma (28 percent).[14] Wackenhut was also managing prisons in Australia, New Zealand, South Africa and Canada.

Few areas of "corrections" have aroused as much debate as privatization. There is no doubt that the primary motivation pushing states to opt for private prisons was the desire to get new facilities built as quickly and cheaply as possible. As University of Oklahoma economist Alexander Holmes explained, allocating $40 or $50 million from a state budget to build a prison is a significant commitment even when the economy is doing well. "As a result, financing new prisons most often requires the issuance of bond debt. In most states, this requires a vote of the people and the dedication of a tax source to repay the debt. Legislators are often reluctant to invoke this mechanism. Private prison contracts, which allow the repayment of the debt embedded within the per diem fee, become particularly attractive alternatives to major prison construction programs," he wrote.[15] In the 1990s, private companies were so confident in their ability to fill prisons that they began to build some "on spec" in the certain knowledge that they would not be left standing empty for very long.

Private prison companies also claim to be able to operate more cheaply than state facilities. Professor Holmes examined this claim carefully with respect to the six private prisons operating in Oklahoma. He found that private prisons were able to bring costs down as they built up experience, but there were certainly no dramatic savings. In 1996, private prisons spent $50.41 per inmate per day, compared to state medium security prisons, which were spending $35.35. By 2001, state costs had risen to $46.12 while private costs had fallen to $45.75. But this really begs the question: If private prisons are indeed cheaper, how are their savings achieved? Is it by paying their staff less than in the public sector? Prisons are extremely labor-intensive, with 65 to 70 percent of operating costs going to staff salaries, benefits and overtime. Private firms usually employ non-unionized labor and offer less attractive benefits packages. Or do private prisons achieve savings by cutting corners on security and by providing fewer services to inmates?

One comprehensive study conducted for the Department of Justice concluded that promises by private prison companies to achieve 20 percent savings in operational costs "have simply not materialized." In fact, the average savings from privatization was only about 1 percent, and most of that was achieved through lower labor costs. Still, the mere presence of private alternatives might have forced down costs in the public sector. "Certainly in those markets where correctional officer salaries and fringe benefits have been excessive, privatization has fostered a reexamination of those costs, which has led to cost savings," the report said.[16] On the other hand, studies suggest that staff turnover rates in the private sector are much higher and officer morale is lower, which in turn can lead to abuse.[17] There can and should be other ways of measuring performance by private prisons. One would be to compare recidivism rates in the private and public sectors. Unfortunately, the data is scarce and unreliable. In any case, private prisons reflect the incarceration philosophy of the clients that hire them. In Oklahoma, Professor Holmes noted that there was a heavy emphasis on punishment and almost no attention paid to rehabilitation. "Currently the state is contracting for incarceration services almost exclusively and provides little in the way of incentives for rehabilitation services," he said.[18]

Private prisons in other states offer more vocational, educational and behavioral programs. In Lawrenceville Prison in Virginia, operated by CCA, inmates can take courses from a local community college at their own expense. The prison also offers vocational training in computing, interior renovation, industrial cleaning, plumbing, carpentry and horticulture. It also has programs for alcohol and substance abuse and anger management. "Every inmate here has to be either in a program or in a job," said Warden Steve Dotson.

Lawrenceville represents the bright side of privatization. There is also a dark side. Take the case of the Northeast Ohio Correctional Center, in Youngstown, that was built on spec by CCA in 1996. Soon after it opened, the District of Columbia contracted to send prisoners to Ohio because the prison in Lorton, Virginia, that housed inmates from Washington was closing. Under the terms of the contract, only minimum or medium security prisoners were supposed to be sent to Youngstown. In fact, as a report to the Attorney General later made clear, many maximum security inmates were transferred with the knowledge and approval both of the District and CCA.[19] The results were predictably awful. Within the first 15 months of operations, six inmates escaped, two were murdered, 17 others were stabbed and numerous other serious assaults against staff and inmates occurred. For long periods, the prison was locked down to prevent further violence. In March 1999, a U.S. District Court in Washington approved a $1.6

million settlement to inmates who complained they were abused, denied adequate medical care and not properly separated from other prisoners.

After two inmates broke out of a CCA prison in Bartlett, Texas, in August 2000, a state investigation found numerous security infractions. Three months later, five prisoners at this same facility were injured in a disturbance. In April 2001, guards at Cibola County Correctional Facility in New Mexico, operated by CCA, teargassed 700 inmates who had staged a nonviolent protest against conditions. In Arizona, there were repeated disturbances at the Florence Correctional Center, operated by CCA, where prisoners shipped from Hawaii were being held together with INS detainees. When officials from Hawaii showed up to inspect the prison, they were told most areas within the facility were too dangerous for them to enter. According to media reports, a gang had taken control and was practically running the place, intimidating or buying off guards, terrorizing fellow inmates and engaging in sex with female INS detainees.[20]

In Texas, Brazoria County leased 512 beds in its local detention center to Mississippi-based Capital Correctional Resources, Incorporated (CCRI). Missouri contracted to send 415 inmates to the facility to relieve overcrowding in its own prisons. On September 18, 1996, guards staged a drugs raid inside the jail, which was videotaped for training purposes. The tape showed several inmates, who had arrived from Missouri that same day, forced to strip and lie on the ground. A police dog attacked several prisoners; the tape clearly showed one being bitten on the leg. Guards prodded prisoners with stun guns and forced them to crawl along the ground. Then they dragged injured inmates face down back to their cells.[21]

That incident became notorious after the Abu Ghraib scandal broke. ABC Nightline tracked down an interview given by then Texas Governor George W. Bush to a local Austin TV station in which he said: "I think in retrospect, had I known the videotape existed, and I'm confident that had other state officials known the videotape existed, we would have pushed for harsher action, quicker action."[22] The Bush administration's response to Abu Ghraib was strikingly similar.

Again, the attitude seemed to be that it was not so much the abuse that was the problem as the pictures of the abuse.

In New Mexico, Wackenhut Corrections Corporation was given a contract to operate two prisons. In the first nine months of 1999 alone, four inmates were murdered at the two facilities and scores injured. The violence culminated in a riot at the Guadalupe County Correctional Facility in Santa Rosa in August 1999. As guards lost control of the situation, a group of prisoners rushed corrections officer Ralph Garcia and stabbed him to death. A former rancher, Garcia had been forced off his land by drought and had signed on with Wackenhut for $7.95 an hour. He had not even completed the short training course the company provided when he was left alone in a cell block with 60 prisoners. After the murder, as many as 290 inmates rampaged through the prison for several hours, setting fires, as authorities struggled to regain control. State officials later said Wackenhut tried to disguise the extent of the disturbance and even held up state police at the prison gates for half an hour before allowing them to enter.[23]

A board of inquiry subsequently found plenty of blame to share around. It criticized Republican Governor Gary Johnson for rushing to build prisons quickly without proper planning. Johnson had run campaign ads vowing to make prisoners serve "every stinking minute" of their sentences and promising to save large amounts of taxpayer money by completely privatizing the state prison system. He directed that new prisons should be built without electrical outlets in cells to prevent inmates from operating TVs or radios.[24]

The report found that the Wackenhut prison in Santa Rosa had serious design flaws allowing prisoners to hide weapons. Inexperienced guards and supervisors failed to note the signs of impending violence. The staff-to-inmate ratio was grossly inadequate, and the facility suffered from high turnover.[25] Panel member Jerry O'Brien noted that corrections officers were being paid less than Wal-Mart salespeople. Fellow member George Vose observed that guards generally had less than a year of experience and were unprepared to handle gang members. On the night Garcia was murdered, there were only 18 staff on hand to manage 418 inmates.[26]

Reducing staff to a minimum was and remains part of Wackenhut's corporate credo. On the company's Internet site, it declares, "By designing out staffing redundancies, a private company is able to save significant costs over the long term. We estimate that the operating costs of a prison over its lifecycle are at least 80 percent of its total costs and that labor costs represent approximately 70 percent of that total; any reduction of redundant staffing costs will obviously generate huge efficiencies and savings over time. A single post can cost an operator between $150,000 and $250,000 a year in wages and benefits."[27]

In its corporate statement, Wackenhut put forward a powerful statement of prisoners' rights. "WCC knows that the loss of freedom, and not the conditions of confinement, is the only punishment that an offender should face. Our offender regimes are strict and well organized, but they are not punitive or demeaning," it said. Unfortunately, actions sometimes spoke louder than these words. Wackenhut lost the right to operate a juvenile facility in Louisiana after a judge complained that inmates were treated no better than animals. "They wound up in a place that drives and treats juveniles as if they walked on all fours," said Judge Mark Doherty. Some were kept in solitary for months and deprived of shoes and blankets, all in the name of cutting costs. Untrained guards threw inmates against walls, twisted their arms and shoved them to the ground because they had never been taught other ways to enforce discipline.[28]

The Justice Department had to sue the state for emergency relief to protect inmates from "dangerous and life-threatening conditions" due to abuse and neglect. The department said juveniles were subjected to unreasonable isolation; they were often placed in four- and five-point restraints, and they suffered corporal punishment.[29] Wackenhut said the accusations were overblown, but Louisiana settled the lawsuit six months later, abandoning its experiment in privately run juvenile facilities.

By 2000, with all these problems, the financial position of both CCA and Wackenhut had worsened. Investors, who had bid up shares in both companies, suddenly soured on them. Prospects for future expansion no longer seemed so rosy. Some of the facilities they operated were targeted for closure and others stood empty. The companies intensified their lobbying of state and federal officials, winning some notable battles. In Mississippi in 2001, Governor Ronnie Musgrove vetoed the state's corrections budget so he could spend more money on schools. The legislature overrode the veto, after Wackenhut President Wayne Calabrese wined and dined two key state senators.[30] Prison lobbyists then persuaded legislators to write a bill allocating the same amount of money for private companies, whether or not their prison beds were filled. State corrections chief Robert Johnson complained he was being forced to pay $6 million for 600 "ghost inmates" in empty beds.[31]

In Georgia and Florida, bills to limit private prisons died in committee. Florida legislators rejected a request from the Department of Corrections for 4,100 new beds in public prisons and instead authorized 1,086 additional slots in private prisons.

Wackenhut and CCA seemed to model some of their tactics on the tobacco industry. While employing top-notch lobbyists, they also quietly financed a Private Corrections Project at the University of Florida, headed by Professor Charles Thomas. Thomas soon emerged as an influential "expert." He produced a series of research papers and was invited to lecture at academic conferences and testify to state legislative committees. Reporters quoted him often. Few were aware of his ties to the private prison industry until ethics complaints were filed against him in 1997. He was fined $20,000 and forced to resign.[32]

The outlook for private prisons improved again in 2002 as the U.S. prison population resumed its upward climb. A crackdown on illegal immigrants after the attacks on the World Trade Center and the Pentagon also boosted their prospects. CCA won a contract to house 1,500 foreign residents serving criminal sentences in a prison it had built on spec in McRae, Georgia, that had been standing empty for more than a year. The company said the contract would be worth over $100 million in its first three years. By mid-2003, CCA was reporting a dramatic turnaround in profits. In the second quarter, it earned $12.1 million, compared to a loss of $31.4 million the previous year. President and CEO John Ferguson commented, "Our second quarter results reflect considerably higher occupancy levels, revenues and operating margins than the previous year and provide additional evidence supporting our contention that industry fundamentals are particularly compelling. This belief is also confirmed by the recent report by the Bureau of Justice

Statistics showing that in 2002 the U.S. prison population grew at its highest rate since 1999, while 25 states and the federal prison system operated at or above highest capacity. Given state budget deficits and the lack of new bed construction, we believe these trends will continue. Ongoing prison overcrowding and the lack of new prison construction should provide numerous opportunities to fill our remaining empty beds and, in appropriate situations, to deliver new beds to meet our customers' needs."[33]

Wackenhut, where profits rose by 17 percent, also looked forward to a bright future of more and more prisons. "It is inconceivable that anyone could pick up a newspaper or watch a television today and believe that private prison operators need to work at increasing demand for their services. It is an unfortunate fact that the 'market' continued to develop and grow despite all best efforts to address the causes and symptoms of crime," it said.[34]

A third leg of the "prison-industrial complex" is made up of labor unions such as the 31,000-member California Correctional Peace Officers Association (CCPOA). Led from 1980 to 2002 by Don Novey, a former guard at Folsom State Prison, the union became a force no California politician could afford to ignore. It poured around a third of the $22 million it collected each year in dues from its members into political action committees.[35] According to California Common Cause, the union was the largest contributor to 25 lawmakers in the 2000 election, including Governor Gray Davis and state Senate Speaker John Burton.[36] In 2002, when he was running for reelection, Davis signed a pay deal with the officers granting them pay increases of 33.7 percent over five years. Two months later, the union sent his campaign a check for $251,000.[37] Davis's links to the prison guards and the generous pay deals he signed with them later became an issue in the 2003 recall election.

The CCPOA uses its money shrewdly. With many of its members concentrated in sparsely populated rural counties, its influence can be paramount in elections. The union puts many of its resources into electing supportive judges and district attorneys in these small jurisdictions. When a local lawmaker dares to go against the union, the results can be politically fatal, as former King County District Attorney Greg Kirkland discovered in 1998. Kirkland prosecuted officers from the Calipatria State Prison suspected of choking, punching and beating 36 shackled inmates in 1995. He also investigated allegations of abuses by guards at Corcoran Prison. The union put $30,000 into a campaign to defeat Kirkland—a huge amount in a county of only 136,000 voters. A few days before the election, the CCPOA sponsored a flyer that implied that Kirkland did a better job representing the interests of inmates than citizens. He lost the election.

In 1999, the union also killed a bill in the state legislature that would have removed prison brutality cases from the purview of local prosecutors and placed them in the hands of the state attorney general. The bill easily passed the senate but died in committee in the state assembly. "The CCPOA torpedoed this thing. One of the assemblymen who voted against it pulled me aside and said, 'Bill, sorry, but I'm whoring for the CCPOA.' At least he was honest," said Attorney General Bill Lockyer.[38]

The union has a longstanding alliance with crime victims' groups, two of which it helped to create. It was a brilliantly successful association for both sides. The small, disunited victims' groups received access to CCPOA's money and organizing expertise. The union got to use the faces and stories of victims, placing human faces on its drive for stiffer sentences and more prisons. Voters may not sympathize too much with prison guards but would hardly resist the stories of actual victims—ordinary people like themselves. Within a few years, the victims' rights movement became a national political force to reckon with. In 1994, the alliance of prison guards and victims rights groups played a major part in persuading California voters to adopt the "three strikes" initiative. The union spent $101,000 to get the proposition placed on the ballot. The result was the continued expansion of the California prison system.

While it is quite expensive to incarcerate prisoners, prison labor is extremely cheap—a factor behind the explosive growth of prison industries in recent years. In 2003, 21,000 inmates worked for Federal Prison Industries, also known by its trade name UNICOR, which was earning over $600 million annually for the federal government. Inmates were making Kevlar helmets, camouflage fatigues, lighting systems, sandbags, blankets and night vision eyewear for the military.[39]

Nationally, sales of products made by prison labor topped $1.8 billion that year. Critics noted that creating jobs behind bars was no different than sending them to Mexico or China. The net result was still fewer jobs for American workers. Inmates were normally paid around $1 a day, though in some states, rates could rise as high as $2.75 a day, and in others go as low as 50 cents.

One of the big hidden costs of the U.S. prison system is the millions of dollars paid out each year by states and local authorities to settle lawsuits. There are no figures, and many lawsuits are settled quietly without a dollar amount being made public. Still, a newspaper database search of lawsuits settled in California alone since 2001 suggests that the total figure is fairly massive. Some of the alleged offenses settled out of court include the following:

- Santa Ana paid $95,000 to a man attacked by a neo-Nazi in a county jail.
- Los Angeles paid $1 million to a jail inmate who was raped.
- Contra Costa County paid $365,000 to the family of an inmate who committed suicide in jail.
- Los Angeles paid $5 million to jail inmates who were hog-tied, one of whom died.
- Los Angeles also paid $27 million to inmates who were held beyond their release dates and improperly strip-searched.
- Sacramento paid $50,000 to a man beaten in jail and $1.3 million to inmates and staff injured during a prisoner transport.
- Sutter County paid $366,000 to a lawyer attacked by his own client in jail.
- Newport Beach paid $172,867 to a man beaten by fellow inmates.
- Los Angeles paid $2.8 million to women raped by a deputy sheriff.
- Santa Clara paid $3.5 million to a youth whose failed suicide left him paralyzed and unable to speak.
- The state of California paid $600,000 to the family of an inmate at the Pleasant Valley State Prison shot by a guard; it also paid $201,000 to the family of a woman denied appropriate treatment for hepatitis C.

Lawmakers in at least 12 states and the federal government have attempted to limit "frivolous lawsuits" through legislation. For example, Oklahoma passed a bill in 2002 imposing a one-year statute of limitation on inmates filing suit. Anyone who files a habeas corpus writ requiring that a prisoner appear in court now has to pay the prisoner's transportation costs. Prisoners who file what are deemed to be frivolous or malicious claims will lose their "good time" toward early release and may also lose the right to have a TV or radio in their cells. Additionally, they face fines of thousands of dollars and must pay court costs.[40]

While powerful interests back the continued expansion of the U.S. prison system, many states and counties by 2003 were beginning to feel the fiscal pain. Despite the tremendous prison building boom of the 1990s, prisons and jails in many jurisdictions continued to operate at or beyond full capacity. And the money was no longer there to just keep building and building. In California, prisons already accounted for 5.1 percent of a state budget drowning in red ink; another 3.8 percent went to the legal machinery that put people behind bars. Candidates in the recall election of Governor Gray Davis had to grapple with tough questions. Where could they cut? The 56 percent of the budget that went to K-12 education? The 14 percent the state was spending on health care? The 9.3 percent that went to social services? The 5.1 percent spent on infrastructure? Not surprisingly, most candidates, including actor Arnold Schwarzenegger, were not very specific.

In Colorado, which underwent a population boom in the 1990s, several counties had to start releasing jail inmates to relieve congestion. In Denver County, an aging county jail designed to hold 1,350 inmates was squeezing in almost 2,000. The county stopped automatically jailing convicts for parole violations and started releasing inmates convicted of nonviolent crimes after serving half their terms. In Pueblo County, a jail built in 1980 to hold 189 inmates had almost 500. Most cells were triple bunked—three men to a 10-foot by 10-foot cell. Sheriff Don Corsentino called the jail a "powder keg" and said he might have to close it to all but felony and domestic violence arrestees.[41]

Arizona reported it had 4,130 more prisoners than beds to put them in and sent 624 to a private prison in Texas. The Department of Corrections asked for an additional $31 million to alleviate overcrowding, but the legislature was slow to release any money.[42] Florida lawmakers were less reluctant. Although they refused new funding to meet anticipated growth in college enrollment, they approved $66 million in emergency funding for prison expansion. The crisis arose after the state reported admitting more prisoners in June 2003 than in any single month since 1992. Many were drugs offenders. The number of people sentenced to state prison for drugs crimes had risen 13.4 percent in a single year. In its haste to expand, lawmakers allowed the Department of Corrections to bypass normal bidding laws in choosing contractors. Governor Jeb Bush said, "What we are trying to avoid, and what we will avoid, is any early releases."[43]

Politicians who for years have run on "tough on crime" platforms find it exceedingly difficult to change their tune. But something has to give. State revenues plummeted after 2000. Although they recovered by 2005, states still face the same dilemma: Every extra dollar spent on corrections requires a dollar cut from some other state budget. If prison populations continue to rise, there will be a lot of pain to share around.

Most states and most lawmakers have failed to face the difficult facts and are tinkering around the edges of the problem. In 2003, Colorado cut inmates' pay from an average of 85 cents a day to 60 cents a day. Total savings to the Department of Corrections: around $1.7 million. Total budget for the Department of Corrections: $536 million.[44] The State Planning and Budgeting Office reported that Colorado's prison population grew by 7.9 percent a year in the 1990s and was expected to grow another 25 percent by 2008. Corrections accounted for 8.2 percent of the state budget. Spending on inmate health care alone had grown by over 35 percent since 1999.

Under the new inmate pay system, it will take prisoners nearly six days of work to buy a bottle of shampoo in the commissary and four days for a packet of potato chips. When some prisoners at the Sterling State Prison stopped working in protest, 16 strike leaders identified as ring leaders were immediately sent to a much tougher maximum security facility, the Colorado State Prison, located in Canon City, the "Corrections Capital of America."[45]

11

AFTER PRISON

"True compassion is more than flinging a coin to a beggar. It is not haphazard and superficial. It comes to see that an edifice which produces beggars needs restructuring."
Martin Luther King, Jr.[1] ■

obert, a Vietnam veteran with a drugs habit, was arrested in Washington, D.C., in a police sting in 1984 with marijuana and PCP in his pocket. At the time, he was working as a junior auditor for the Internal Revenue Service and supporting a son and daughter. He described himself as a recreational user. "I wasn't a junkie. I had it under control. I wasn't hurting no one," he said. The judge was not impressed. He sentenced Robert to four to 16 years in prison. If he had behaved himself behind bars and stayed clean after his release, Robert could have been done with his sentence relatively quickly and gone on with his life. That's not the way things worked out.

Behind bars, Robert did behave well. He was an education aide, helping fellow inmates to get their GED high school equivalency certificates and also worked as a control room clerk. After five years, he was released on parole. But Robert had not kicked his habit in prison and soon resumed using drugs. He found a job but failed to report regularly to his parole officer. In 1994, he was sent back to prison for violating the terms of his parole. Three years later, he was released again; this time he stayed out for seven months before failing a drugs test. Back he went. In November 1999, Robert emerged yet again but was free for less than two months before a dirty urine test sent him back once more. When I met him in March 2000, Robert was living at a halfway house in Washington, D.C., where he was closely supervised and regularly tested for drugs. He had a clerical job that paid $8.75 an hour and was due to move in with his sister six weeks later. He was full of good intentions. "I'm 46 years old. I'm getting too old for this. I want to stay out this time. Since 1984, I have spent 11 years in prison and five years outside, all for one drugs conviction. I have lost my family. I have not been a father to my children. I want to get my own place and take care of myself. I call it regaining responsibility over my life," he told me.

I intended to write a series of articles about Robert, hoping to follow his progress over the following months as he tried to rebuild his life. But the series never materialized. Two weeks after I met him, Robert failed a drugs test yet again and was sent back to prison. He broke off contact and refused to talk to me again. His story, which is all too typical, raised serious issues. Robert had committed one drugs possession offense, for which he had served 11 years in prison and counting. Yes, he was an addict with a harmful habit. But he had never committed a violent offense, he was never a big-time or even a small-time dealer, he was never connected to a gang. Who was he hurting other than himself? Did society get its money worth for the many thousands of dollars spent on his incarceration? Or might there have been a better way?

Robert's case illustrates the dilemma facing the 600,000 prisoners being released from U.S. prisons every year. Many emerge angry and bitter and even less well equipped to lead an honest life than they were before. As we have seen, drugs are widely available behind bars. According to the Office of National Drug Control Policy, 70 to 85 percent of state prison inmates need substance abuse assistance, but only 13 percent receive treatment in prison.[2] A California study found that half of those released from that state's prisons were functionally illiterate.[3] Joan Petersilia, a criminologist with the University of California, Irvine, has studied the lives of parolees. "They remain largely uneducated, unskilled, and usually without solid family support systems—and now they bear the added burdens of a prison record and the distrust and fear that inevitably results. Not surprisingly, most parolees do not succeed, and failure occurs rather quickly—re-arrests are most common in the first six months after release," she wrote.[4]

The Bureau of Justice Statistics has found that two-thirds of those released from prison on parole were re-arrested within three years. In 1980, parole violators were 18 percent of state prison admissions. By 1997, the proportion had almost doubled to 35 percent.[5] In California, 60 percent of the people admitted to prison in 1999 had been on parole. Four out of five of these were sent back not for committing new crimes but for technical violations of their parole.[6] The list of potential violations is long: testing positive for drugs use, drugs possession, failure to report for drug or alcohol treatment, leaving a jurisdiction without permission, failure to report for counseling, failure to maintain employment, failure to meet financial obligations, maintaining contact with known offenders, possessing a firearm. Any of these can earn a parolee a quick return ticket to prison.

Released prisoners face a daunting array of institutional barriers that make it incredibly difficult for them to find a place in society. Welfare reform legislation in 1996 banned anyone convicted of buying or selling drugs from receiving cash assistance or food stamps for life. No other offense resulted in a permanent loss of benefits.[7] Nobody was exempt from this blanket exclusion—not pregnant women, not people in treatment or recovery, not people suffering from HIV.

Legislation in 1996 and 1998 also excluded ex-felons and their families from federal housing. Under these provisions, a grandmother whose drug-using grandson was living with her could be evicted.[8] The law made it almost impossible for many women released from prison to reconnect with their children. Following its adoption, the number of people denied public housing virtually doubled overnight.

Ex-prisoners also face steep official and unofficial barriers when it comes to finding jobs. Most inmates leave prison with no money and few prospects. They may get $25 and a bus ticket home if they are lucky. Several states have barred parolees from working in a variety of professions, including real estate, medicine, nursing, engineering, education, and dentistry. In Illinois, released prisoners cannot work as hair dressers, cut the grass around medical centers, wash dishes in nursing homes, or work as hospital custodians. In 2003, the state had a list of 55 specified jobs ex-felons were not allowed to do. That year, it trimmed the list somewhat to 39.[9]

The Higher Education Act of 1998 bars people convicted of drugs offenses from receiving student loans. What we see here is the emergence of a permanent criminal class. Prisoners are told to reform, but they are given few tools to do so. Once they are entangled in the prison system, many belong to it for life. They may spend stretches of time inside prison and periods outside, but they are never truly free. Supreme Court Justice Anthony Kennedy commented, "A decent and free society, founded in respect for the individual, ought not to run a system with a sign at the entrance for inmates saying, 'Abandon Hope, All Ye Who Enter Here.'"[10]

In 2004, a group of lawmakers, Republicans and Democrats, introduced a bill designed to create a national resource center to provide training for officials dealing with prisoner reintegration, give aid to grandparents looking after the children of inmates, and allow some ex-prisoners to receive student loans if they remained off drugs. If passed, the bill would also provide grants to community organizations mentoring former inmates and money to states to pay for mental health services, substance abuse treatment and post-release housing. The bill died in committee but was reintroduced in 2005.[11]

Studies have found that a year after release, 60 percent of ex-inmates remain unemployed. A survey of employers in five cities found that two-thirds would not knowingly hire an ex-offender regardless of the crime they committed and up to 40 percent actually checked the records of their most recently hired employees.[12] Even if they get a job, former inmates' earning power is sharply limited. "Former inmates experience virtually no earnings growth. The best they can hope for is to find casual jobs in secondary labor markets without any benefits. Having a felony on your record is like having the mark of Cain on your forehead," said Bruce Western, a sociologist at Princeton University. Professor Western found that even when paroled inmates found legitimate jobs, they earned only half as much as people of the same background who had not been in prison. Unlike others, who begin their working lives with low paying jobs and work their way up, they have virtually no prospects of advancement.

Additionally, many inmates return to society burdened by owing thousands of dollars in unpaid child support. As soon as they get a job, no matter how low-paying, part of their salary is automatically deducted to make up the arrears.

In Los Angeles, thousands of parolees congregate in a 50-block area of downtown known as Skid Row, the largest concentration of homelessness in the United States.[13] The unwary visitor who stumbles on this part of the city might be excused for thinking he had suddenly been transported to Bangladesh. Thousands of people live in makeshift tents or cardboard boxes on the streets or crowd into cheap hotels or flophouses. Prostitutes ply their trade, looking for enough money for their next fix. People urinate and defecate in public; flies swarm over foul-smelling streets. Los Angeles County makes little effort to deal with its homeless population, which may reach as high as 100,000 on any given night. The county offers only 14,000 beds in homeless shelters.[14]

In November 2002, William Bratton, the newly appointed police chief, decided to crack down on Skid Row. More than 200 officers descended on the neighborhood, ordering people out of their tents and hotel rooms, arresting 130 people—60 percent on suspicion of parole violations. The next night, the police swooped again, picking up another 84 people. Two-thirds were described as parole violators who were not supposed to be in the area or who had been using drugs.[15]

In an article for the *Los Angeles Times*, cowritten with Rutgers University Professor George Kelling, Bratton denied he was targeting the homeless. "A good portion of those identified as homeless have problems that are far more severe than merely being without a home or job. Many are mentally disturbed or chronic alcohol or drugs abusers. This group is especially troubling. Many don't want help; many can't use help; many are incapable of holding jobs or maintaining a room or an apartment; and many don't want homes or shelters—they want to live on the streets," Bratton and Kelling wrote. "Clearly, Los Angeles has to find ways to manage its 'homeless' population in humane and legal ways. But the solutions also have to be realistic. The problem is a tangled web of homelessness, pathology, drugs and alcohol abuse and criminality. Allowing lawbreaking to continue serves neither the genuinely homeless nor the community."[16]

The article made some powerful points. However, Bratton and Kelling offered no real solutions other than aggressive policing. If people on Skid Row not only don't want but can't use any help, if indeed they are incapable of holding jobs or maintaining a room, then what is to be done with them?

Bratton's solution, it appears, is to arrest them and send them away. Then, when they are released from jail untreated and disturbed, arrest them and send them away again.

Bratton failed to persuade the courts that his method of managing the homeless was indeed humane and legal. In April 2003, U.S. District Judge Nora Manella issued an order barring the LAPD from indiscriminately seeking parole violators on Skid Row, saying the sweeps violated residents' Fourth Amendment rights against unreasonable search and seizure.[17]

California has taken a tougher attitude toward parolees than most other states. Elsewhere, parolees often get a second or third chance for minor violations such as failing to keep an appointment with an officer. In California, the policy is rigid and unforgiving. "Parole officers used to be trained to help ex-offenders stay straight. Now, they are an arm of law enforcement. The chief object is not reintegration into society but supervision," said Professor Western. In 2000, nearly 90,000 parolees were returned to prison in California, a 30-fold increase over 1980.[18] The state spends $900 million a year to house violators, who spend an average of five months in prison each time they are returned. Spending some of this money on transitional housing and job training for released inmates might benefit both the state budget and these individuals.

In Los Angeles, many law enforcement officials say they are fed up with sending parole violators back to prison for technical infractions, especially for drugs possession offenses. One assistant district attorney told me, "I'd like to understand the war on drugs as an effort to stop the wholesale importation of dangerous substances into our country. But if the frontline is busting small-time addicts on the street, it's not doing a lot of good. At best, it addresses the symptoms and not the causes of the problem."

There are some signs that California is beginning to understand this. Under Proposition 36, overwhelmingly adopted by California voters in 2000, first- and second-time nonviolent drugs possession offenders are directed to substance abuse treatment instead of prison. In its first year alone, the measure saved $275 million and diverted 37,000 people to treatment programs instead of state prisons.[19]

Nothing better illustrates the state's evolving approach toward drug addicts than its attitude to needle exchange programs designed to slow the spread of HIV and hepatitis C. Such programs are slowly spreading throughout the country but still face strong opposition, especially in suburban and rural areas. In 2002, after a fierce political battle, the city of San Diego voted to begin a test program over the strong opposition of both the mayor and police chief. But in neighboring San Diego County, needle exchange remained illegal. That did not stop Brent Whitteker from breaking the law every day, running a covert program for some 23,000 addicts in the county. When I met him in 2002, Whitteker was handing out 7,000 needles a week to 750 regular clients.

Some lived in upscale apartments in ritzy beach communities. Most he met in shabby mobile homes, parks, parking lots and on street corners. The police knew what he was doing but ignored him. A local hospital helped him dispose of used needles safely. The logic of such programs is clear. If addicts cannot get clean needles, they share dirty ones. Then, they discard them under bushes, on sidewalks, in garbage cans or on the beach, where they pose a huge public health hazard.

Every one of Whitteker's clients was breaking the law by using heroin. Many of them looked dreadful, with scars on their skinny arms and bloody tracks on their legs. Some had been injecting for 25 years or more while holding down jobs, paying taxes and functioning as members of society. Their behavior was clearly self-destructive, but who were they harming other than themselves?

The most powerful argument advanced by defenders of the U.S. prison system is that crime rates have dropped dramatically, especially since 1994. The Bureau of Justice Statistics report on criminal victimization for 2002 declared that crime had fallen to its lowest level since 1973, when the survey began. Between 1993 and 2002, violent crime decreased by 54 percent while property crime was cut in half.[20] The homicide rate, which also fell sharply during the 1990s, started to creep up again in 2001 and maintained a slight increase in 2002, when 16,100 people were murdered.

Contrary to popular opinion, crime rates for offenses other than murder are no higher in the United States than in many Western industrialized nations. Slightly fewer Americans than Canadians or Australians are assaulted each year proportionate to the size of the population. The auto theft rate is higher in Britain than in the United States. More Spaniards than Americans proportionately are victims of robberies.[21] But the U.S. homicide rate is five to seven times higher that of other industrialized nations, mostly due to deaths involving firearms.[22] Interestingly, 76 percent of homicide offenders in 2002 knew their victim, and guns were used in 63 percent of cases.[23]

The connection between incarceration and crime rates is a hotly debated academic issue. There certainly is some connection. However, as criminologist James Alan Fox noted, one should not commit the statistical sin of confusing correlation with causation. "Prison populations have been expanding long before the crime rate started its 1990s nose dive. From 1985 to 1991, the count of U.S. prisoners increased 63 percent while the crime rate rose 13 percent, including a 36 percent jump in violent crime," he wrote.[24] In fact, crime rates rose in the 1970s, fell from 1980 to 1984, rose again from 1985 to 1991 and then began their latest descent. Incarceration rates were rising steadily throughout this entire period.[25]

Nor was the decline in crime consistent throughout the nation. In some cities, crime rates fell dramatically. In others, they hardly budged or increased. New York City saw a particularly steep fall in violent crime. But the murder rate continued to rise in 16 of the 20 largest U.S. cities through 1997.[26] In a more rural setting, North and South Dakota are fairly similar states, socially and economically, but have widely different incarceration policies. South Dakota imprisons people at roughly three times the rate of North Dakota. Yet, crime in the two states is virtually the same and has been for decades.[27]

It would be absurd to argue that dramatically increased rates of incarceration had no effect on crime rates. Criminologists William Spelman and Richard Rosenfeld tried to quantify the effect of using a variety of data sources and statistical models. Working independently, both concluded that around a quarter in the drop in violent crime could be attributed to higher rates of incarceration.[28] The rest came from more effective and intensive policing, gun control legislation, changing demographics, the longest economic boom in history and the waning of the cocaine epidemic that caused so much mayhem in the 1980s.

It has long been known that males between ages 14 and 24 commit nearly half of all murders and account for a quarter of homicide victims.[29] In the 1990s, the number of young males declined as a proportion of the total population. As we move further into the 21st century, it is expected to increase once again, signaling perhaps a renewed rise in crime.

The crack wars were a huge factor in igniting public concern about crime. Yet as the 1980s ended, many young people, even in inner cities, came to see how devastating the drug was, and use of crack waned. At the same time, the Clinton economic boom opened new opportunities for employment and higher wages even among low-skill workers. Finally, sociologists point to a dramatic decline in the production of firearms starting around 1993 as a factor in lowering crime. From 1993 to 1998, production of semiautomatic pistols dropped 50 percent and production of cheap so-called "junk guns" fell by more than 75 percent. Homicides involving firearms by juveniles dropped by 70 percent from 1993 to 2000; among young adults, they fell by 40 percent.[30] Limiting the availability of guns would seem to be an effective way of fighting crime.

One effect of falling crime has been to concentrate criminal behavior more in inner-city ghettos. When prisoners are released, they typically must return to their old neighborhoods—the poorest in America. Police Sergeant Al Labrada of the Los Angeles gang unit said many parolees soon resumed their old criminal ways. "They come back but they are not rehabilitated. They soon go back to their old lifestyle," he said. "If they go into prison with the mindset of being part of a gang, they come out the same way or even more so." Some try to reclaim their place in the drugs trade, only to find it has been usurped by others. The result is violence. Washington, D.C., Police Chief Charles Ramsey said that almost half of the city's homicide victims in the first four months of 2003 had been released from prison within the previous two years.[31]

There is a growing body of research suggesting that when incarceration levels reach a certain tipping point, communities become so weakened that they lose the capacity to combat crime. As Urban Institute scholar Jeremy Travis has argued, strong families and financially viable, socially cohesive communities contribute to lower crime rates. Conversely, neighborhoods where the stable two-parent family has largely collapsed and where social institutions barely function become breeding grounds for crime. Children growing up without parents look for other structures to fill the void and invariably find them in youth gangs.[32]

Gangs are the production line for the next generation of prison inmates. Comparing the corrections industry to other industries, we see that it is incredibly efficient. First, through high recidivism, it recycles 60 percent of its raw material repeatedly through the system. Second, it has a reliable source of new raw material in the children of current prisoners who grow up in dysfunctional neighborhoods without family or social support. And so the groundwork is laid for continued, self-perpetuating growth in the prison system.

Talk to any gang member, and he will tell you the gang is his family. Take the case of 16-year-old Manuel, whom I met in Mesa, Arizona, in 2002.

An obviously intelligent young man, Manuel was trying to break away from the gang lifestyle, the only mode of living he had ever known. "I grew up in gangs. My father died of heroin when I was six. My mother was a junkie. My aunt and uncle tried to raise me but I liked to hang out with my two elder brothers. They were into the gang life. When I was just a little kid, they would take me cruising with them. I started helping them sell crystal meth. Pretty soon I was using it myself. When I was 10 or 11, I started doing stuff to show I was cool—beating up other kids on the street, scaring white folk. I got myself tattooed up. I have three dots over my eyes that stand for *Mi Vida Loca*, my crazy life. I have other tattoos on my arms and legs and a tear drop under my eye to remind me of a friend who was killed, shot nine times outside his house.

"I have three brothers and two sisters. My oldest sister has four kids and is hooked on meth. My oldest brother shoots up. He has seven kids with four different women. My second brother has just finished four years for armed robbery. The other brother was at a boot camp and he's on the run right now. The other sister is doing okay.

"Since I was 13, I've been in and out of juvenile detention. One time, I was caught in a stolen car going 85 miles per hour. They sent me to Adobe Mountain juvenile prison. Two weeks later, I overdosed. They took me to the hospital but I escaped. I was on the run for three months, living with different homies around the neighborhood, a few days with each. Eventually I got tired of it and I turned myself in. I wanted a different life. While I was in Adobe the last time, I started studying for my GED. I passed the exams in two months. I thought the drugs had rotted my brains but I found I was good at math and I like reading."

Last time I heard from him, Manuel was having his tattoos surgically removed by laser and had registered at a community college to become a nurse. It was not too late for him. Because he was still a juvenile, he had no criminal record.

Since the mid-1980s, youth gangs have spread to almost every large and medium-sized city in America and are establishing themselves in suburbs and rural areas as well.

In the sleepy farm town of Willows in California's Central Valley, at least 12 Hispanic and Asian gangs have appeared in recent years. The town has become the unlikely scene of a raging war between Mexican *Nortenos* and *Surenos*. Juan, who proudly wore tattoos on both wrists, had been in juvenile hall 21 times when I met him in 2001. He was just celebrating his 16th birthday and the birth of his first son but was not considering his new role as head of a family. "The gang is my family. I need it for protection. I've never not been in the gang," he said. Fellow gang member Cesar told me, "I fight people who piss me off. Whenever it happens, it happens. If they give me a wrong look, I fight them. I do bad but I do it real good."[33]

According to James Howell, a researcher at the National Youth Gang Center in Pinehurst, North Carolina, 93 percent of cities of 100,000 or more had active gangs in 2000. Two-thirds of cities of 50,000 to 100,000, 49 percent of towns of 25,000 to 50,000 and 23 percent of jurisdictions of less than 25,000 also reported gang activity. "Nearly nine out of 10 jurisdictions said their gang activities began between 1985 and 1995. Over half said their problem began in the 1990s," Howell said.[34]

Police are also worried about a relatively new phenomenon, the growth of violent Southeast Asian youth gangs. Providence, Minneapolis and Denver are just a few of the cities struggling with this problem. In Providence, just a couple of blocks from the city's newly refurbished downtown, the streets are ruled by Cambodian, Laotian and Hmong gangs who prey mainly on their own community. "We've had a dozen homicides and 50 to 60 shootings in the past 10 years attributable to Asian gangs," said John Reis, crime prevention adviser to the Rhode Island attorney general.[35]

In a youth detention center outside Providence, I met Samben Chet, a small slight boy who looked younger than his 15 years despite the large K for "Khmer" tattooed on one hand and the dragon emblazoned on the other. He also had the legend "Asian boy" tattooed on one leg and two stars on his chest. Chet admitted beating up and robbing people on the street, especially Hispanics. A fellow inmate, who identified himself with his street name, Cingh X Cutie, said he joined a gang called Laos Pride because, "I thought I would need backup." His hand was tattooed with five marks standing for the words "My Fucking Crazy Asian Life." The details of his crime could not be disclosed because he was a minor. Asked if he had learned anything from his incarceration, he said, "Next time I won't use a knife."

12

SOME MODEST SUGGESTIONS

---

*"Remember those who are in prison
as if you were in prison with them."*
Hebrews 3:13 ■

■

On August 9, 2003, Supreme Court Justice Anthony Kennedy delivered a remarkable speech to the annual meeting of the American Bar Association. Kennedy, who was appointed to the high court by President Reagan, is no liberal. In 2003, he was one of the five justices who upheld California's three strikes law as constitutional.

Kennedy began his speech by discussing the new challenges to America that arose after the 9/11 attacks, then moved to a general discussion about democratic values. "Embedded in democracy is the idea of progress. Democracy addresses injustice and corrects it. The progress is not automatic. It requires a sustained exercise of political will; and political will is shaped by rational public discourse," he said. For that reason, Kennedy declared, he felt impelled to speak out about the "inadequacies and injustices" of the U.S. prison system.

Addressing his audience of lawyers, Kennedy said they should be much more concerned with what was going on in the nation's prisons. "The focus of the legal profession, perhaps even the obsessive focus, has been on the process for determining guilt or innocence. When someone has been judged guilty and the appellate and collateral review process has ended, the legal profession seems to lose all interest. When the prisoner is taken way, our attention turns to the next case. When the door is locked against the prisoner, we do not think about what is behind it," Kennedy said.

"We have a greater responsibility. As a profession, and as a people, we should know what happens after the prisoner is taken away. To be sure, the prisoner has violated the social contract; to be sure, he must be punished to vindicate the law, to acknowledge the suffering of the victim, and to deter future crimes. Still, the prisoner is a person; still, he or she is part of the family of humankind."

In an indictment of the system, Kennedy noted the incredible size of the prison population and the fact that the United States incarcerates seven times as many people as a percentage of the population than countries like England, France and Germany. He spoke of the racial inequalities inherent in the system and its massive and rapidly mounting costs. "It requires one with more expertise in the area than I possess to offer a complete analysis, but it does seem justified to say this: Our resources are misspent, our punishments too severe, our sentences too long," Kennedy declared.

How would he address these problems? To begin with, he suggested revising federal sentencing guidelines downwards and getting rid of federal mandatory minimum sentences, which he called both unwise and unjust. Responsibility for sentencing ought to be returned to judges. It was absurd, Kennedy said, to send a young man to prison for 10 or 15 years for possession of five grams of crack cocaine. "Ladies and gentlemen, I submit to you that a 20-year-old does not know how long ten or fifteen years is. One day in prison is longer than almost any day you and I have had to endure."

Kennedy referred to the three strikes case, where his vote made a crucial difference. But, he argued, declaring that a law was constitutional did not make it right. "Few misconceptions about government are more mischievous than the idea that a policy is sound simply because a court finds it permissible. A court decision does not excuse the political branches or the public from the responsibility for unjust laws," he said.

Kennedy said states and the federal government should try to help those serving unreasonably long sentences under minimum sentencing guidelines by reviving the pardon process. "A people confident in its laws and institutions should not be ashamed of mercy.... I hope more lawyers involved in the pardon process will say to Chief Executives, 'Mr. President,' or 'Your Excellency, the Governor, this young man has not served his full sentence, but he has served long enough. Give him what only you can give him. Give him another chance. Give him a priceless gift. Give him liberty.'"

Kennedy argued that rehabilitation should be one of the chief goals of incarceration. He said prison authorities should not be in the business of degrading or demeaning inmates. Referring to Sheriff Joe Arpaio of Maricopa County, Kennedy said, "No public official should echo the sentiments of the Arizona sheriff who once said with great pride that he 'runs a very bad jail.'"

"It is no defense if our current prison system is more the product of neglect than of purpose. Out of sight, out of mind is an unacceptable excuse for a prison system that incarcerates over two million human beings in the United States. To that end, I hope it is not presumptuous of me to suggest that the American Bar Association should ask its president and the president-elect to instruct the appropriate committees to study these matters and to help start a new public discussion about the prison system. It is the duty of the American people to begin that discussion at once," Kennedy concluded.

My hope is that this book contributes to that debate. I believe the first 11 chapters point to some modest proposals that may help address a situation that has spiraled out of control. I say "modest proposals" because the issues are so deep-seated and so deeply embedded in the nation's political, economic and social fabric that there are no easy solutions. As I have argued, the growth of the U.S. prison system in the past quarter century has built up such momentum that it will be extremely hard to reverse course. There is nothing magic about the figure of two million people behind bars. It could well be headed for three million. Neither is there any quick and easy way to say, "Two million is enough; let's stop here." On the contrary, perpetual, self-generating growth is now largely built into the system. If existing processes are allowed to run their course, the prison population will continue to increase. Witness the past decade. Crime rates have declined dramatically yet the number of people behind bars continues to grow. With crime rates falling, one would expect the prison population to stabilize and eventually start to drop. Fewer crimes should mean fewer arrests, which should mean fewer people going to prison. That is not happening. Right now, the only real constraint on the growth of the prison population is fiscal. But even governors and state legislators struggling with unprecedented deficits find it difficult to cut their corrections budgets. Being labeled as "soft on crime" is still politically fatal. Moreover, releasing people just to cut costs is not a rational or considered way to proceed.

To tackle the root causes of the problem is beyond the scope of this book. Short of that, a pragmatic approach to prison reform might still produce tangible results. Such an approach could focus on three main tasks: first, shrinking the number of people entering the prison system; second, making sure that fewer of them come back once they are released; and third, eliminating some of the worst abuses within the system.

In the first category, Justice Kennedy's suggestion of abolishing mandatory sentences provides a good starting point. Additionally, states and the federal government might want to take a careful look at California's Proposition 36, under which people convicted of simple drugs possession are directed to drugs courts that impose treatment regimens. Prosecutors I spoke to in Los Angeles County were strongly supportive of this policy. They saw little risk that it would increase violent crime, while the financial benefits to the state were clear. An additional benefit was the drop in incarceration rates for women, allowing more mothers to stay with their children. When a mother is locked up, her entire family suffers and the seeds are planted for a new generation of prison inmates.

Drug courts have been spreading fast across the nation in recent years, to the point that there are now over 1,600 in existence. As Bush's drug czar, John Waters, has often said, they not only save taxpayer money— they also reduce recidivism and have a much better chance of healing those enslaved by drug addiction. Research on drug court graduates has shown they have a much lower recidivism rate than those incarcerated for drug charges.

A major theme of this book has been the treatment of the mentally ill. When the Los Angeles County Jail is the largest mental institution in the world, closely followed by Rikers Island, many Americans would say that something is seriously wrong. The problem is that the mentally ill have no voice. Who will speak for them? There is wide consensus throughout the criminal justice system that locking up the mentally sick is possibly the worst treatment option. Most would support a concerted effort to keep the mentally ill out of prisons and jails unless they have been convicted of violent felonies. Even then, their mental state should be weighed in deciding their sentence.

Likewise, there would be little disagreement to the idea of providing more support and follow-up for mentally ill inmates after their release. The problem is getting it done. Programs like Rochester's Project Renewal, where the mentally ill can learn to manage their illnesses without being incarcerated, have demonstrated their success both in reducing recidivism and saving money. To put it simply, the choice may be to invest in a better community mental health network or to build even more jails. Voters, confronted with such a choice, may well opt for the former and choose to close the revolving door between jail and the streets.

Rehabilitation has gotten a bad rap from American politicians. Yet prison wardens and corrections officers alike agree that it is crucially important if the cycle of recidivism is to be broken. But such programs are under even more pressure in cash-strapped prison systems. California's Department of Corrections fired 260 prison instructors in 2003 to save money because there was virtually nothing else to cut. "We can't cut security. We can't cut manpower. We can't cut health services to inmates. So we have to cut education, drug treatment programs and parole. It's a very shortsighted policy," Stephen Green, assistant secretary of the Department of Corrections, told me.

Ideally, prison administrators would like to see all inmates either working or studying while serving their sentences. Having them sitting idle is the worst option. Such inmates, when released, have little chance of staying straight. They need to be prepared for release. In the 18 months or year before their release date, they could be directed to educational or vocational instruction offering skills that give them a real chance of finding a job after they are freed.

Prisoners need more of an incentive to behave well. In recent years, many states have abolished parole or good time. Is this sensible? Has it deterred crime? Prisons work best when correctional officers and inmates see themselves in some sense as partners, working to maintain a peaceful, safe and positive environment. Correctional professionals all agree that rewarding good behavior with easier conditions and other privileges leads to calmer, less crowded prisons.

On a similar note, all prisoners should be offered anti-addiction programs and strongly encouraged to take part. Clearly, such programs will be wasted on some, who are determined to continue their unhealthy lifestyles. But even a 25 percent or 30 percent success rate would be tremendously cost effective if it reduced recidivism and kept more people out of hospital emergency rooms.

When examining ways of reducing recidivism, we need to look at what works. The evidence is clear that encouraging inmates to stay in touch with their families helps connect them to crucial social support networks after release. It follows therefore that prisoners should, wherever possible, be incarcerated within a reasonable distance from home so that family visits are possible. Where this is not possible, prisons might consider establishing onsite facilities, similar to those provided by Bedford Hills in New York, so family members who make the long trip can enjoy more extended visits with their loved ones. Some states are already taking steps to stop prisons and telephone companies from charging the families of prisoners excessively high call rates.

The way in which the Census Bureau counts inmates as citizens of the jurisdictions where they are jailed for purposes of drawing political boundaries or awarding federal grants seems like a clear case of inequity. The result is to drain money away from the inner cities that need help the most. Fixing this would send a strong signal of the nation's continued commitment to social justice.

If prisoners are to be reabsorbed into society after they are released, society at some point should stop punishing them. Those who have served their time should be allowed to vote. In recent years, several states have recognized this argument and have taken steps to allow ex-felons to regain their voting rights. By the same logic, they should also qualify for federal housing, health and education assistance. Pushing ex-felons to the margins of society vastly increases the chance they will re-offend. Parole officers might also exercise a little more latitude before returning ex-felons to prison for technical, nonserious violations.

When it comes to inmates' health care, again there is evidence to show what works. One example is Hampden County in Massachusetts, where inmates are connected to health practitioners from their own neighborhoods so they can continue to seek services after release. Prisoners who have a stake in their own health are less likely to re-offend.

Medical care in the United States is tightly regulated and monitored by professional boards that set and maintain minimum standards. Given that inmates have a constitutional right to proper care, it is difficult to see why prisons should be an exception. All prisons and jails should be required to seek and receive accreditation from the National Commission on

Correctional Health Care. If an institution fails to meet the necessary standards or loses its accreditation, it would face mandatory fines and other sanctions. The result might well be fewer lawsuits, saving taxpayer dollars.

Health professionals worry about the role of prisons and jails as incubators of infectious diseases. They would like to see all such institutions keeping much more comprehensive data on the physical and mental health of their prison populations. Offering preventive care, such as hepatitis B vaccines, treatment for sexually transmitted diseases and tuberculosis testing and treatment, would be a tremendous social benefit.

As a first step, all prisoners entering the system could receive comprehensive information on the dangers of hepatitis C and be offered the opportunity to be tested. Peer counseling programs, such as San Quentin's Centerforce, could be established in more prisons.

Working in a prison is tough and takes a toll on even the most dedicated professional. Medical staff working in correctional institutions need to be offered frequent counseling to guard against the danger of professional burnout. They could also be required to complete continuing education requirements focusing on the special challenges of health care in prison.

Prisons should reexamine the system of charging inmates co-payments to see medical staff. The evidence suggests that such schemes are not cost-effective and that they encourage inmates to neglect medical conditions that could be more easily and cheaply treated at an early stage. Authorities might also take a more generous approach to granting seriously sick inmates compassionate reprieves, which would also save enormous amounts of money.

The mentally ill, wherever possible, need to be housed away from the general prison population. The principle that they should not be incarcerated in supermax prisons has now been established by two federal courts of appeal but has not yet been implemented nationwide.

Women's medical needs in prison have to be more fully met. Where appropriate, they should be offered timely mammograms and other preventive tests. Mammograms may be expensive but they are surely cheaper than treating inmates who develop breast cancer.

Authorities should make it easier for inmates to receive the drugs they require every day and ensure that they complete courses of antibiotics and take their medication. This is simple commonsense and would help protect against the emergence of more drug-resistant bacteria.

Courts have ruled that all prisoners—even those in segregation or on death row—should be offered appropriate conditions and sufficient time for physical exercise. Departments of corrections need to implement these rulings.

In discussing general prison conditions, let me begin by again quoting from the corporate credo of Wackenhut Corrections Corporation as stated on its Internet site:

"WCC knows that the loss of freedom, and not the conditions of confinement, is the only punishment that an offender should face."

This is a tremendously important statement of principle. Deliberately creating intolerably miserable conditions for inmates is not part of a prison's mission. Abuse is an aberration, not a norm. How might we tackle abuse? A start might be to require all institutions to gain accreditation from the American Correctional Association. While not perfect, this would at least provide a baseline for prisons to meet and expose some of the worst offenders. Any institution failing to meet ACA standards for three years in a row would be fined and placed under new management.

The United States badly needs an independent prison inspectorate to monitor abuses within the system. Short of that, more states could establish citizens' organizations similar to the Pennsylvania Prison Society. Founded in 1787, with Benjamin Franklin among its early members, its lay members, by an act of the Pennsylvania General Assembly, are guaranteed access to all correctional facilities in the state and make around 5,000 visits to jails and prisons each year. All states need their own equivalent of the Pennsylvania Prison Society.

Failing that, making prisons more accessible to journalists and academic researchers would be a good first step. All too often, reporters are allowed access to prisons where the authorities have a positive story to tell, but denied when abuses are taking place. Prison wardens have a free hand in whether or not to allow reporters into their facilities.

The onus should be on them to justify each and every decision to deny entrance to the media.

One of the biggest problems that has emerged in recent years in the U.S. prison system has been the overuse of supermax facilities. Let me repeat the words of Chase Riveland, a former head of corrections in the state of Washington: "Prison staff have always had to deal with uncooperative inmates. They continuously test the limits, frequently break minor rules and consume an inordinate amount of staff time. As comforting as it may be to an institution staff to be rid of such persons, the use of costly high-custody beds for this population is probably not only inefficient, but arguably overkill. These facilities are inappropriate for the nuisance inmate."

Professionals like Riveland believe that incarceration in a supermax is appropriate only for the most dangerous inmates with a proven record of violence behind bars and multiple offenses. The decision to send an inmate to such a facility needs to be taken on an individual basis at the highest level and reassessed every six months. Even in segregation, prisoners have rights, including the right to have adequate human contact and recreational time. Many supermax prisons could be shut down or partially converted to regular maximum security facilities.

When it comes to the use of electronic stun guns, four- and five-point restraints and the hog-tying of prisoners, it is hard to justify such means in a society that values human rights in the 21st century. Similarly, holding prisoners naked for extended periods violates our sense of human dignity. Chain gangs are part of a shameful past and have no part in modern corrections.

As argued by Justice John J. Noonan of the 9th Circuit Court of Appeals in an opinion I quoted in Chapter Seven, wherever possible, female corrections officers should supervise female inmates. The judge strongly argued that male officers ought not to conduct intrusive bodily searches of female inmates and ought to be accompanied by female guards on their duties wherever possible.

Fulfilling the terms of legislation passed in 2003 and signed by President Bush, prison authorities have been ordered to collect detailed data on both male and female rape. All such cases need to be taken seriously and investigated. During such investigations, the victim has the right to be protected from the alleged rapist, whether he is a fellow inmate or a guard.

Common decency demands that women ought not have to give birth while shackled and should be allowed to spend time with their babies to bond with them after birth. A mother who is educated in the techniques of responsible parenting and recognizes her duty to her children is less likely to re-offend. More efforts need to be made to keep women inmates in contact with their children. Allowing weekend visits within prison grounds, similar to those offered in trailers at Bedford Hills, has a positive payoff for mothers, children and society.

Faith groups do a tremendous job in prisons and, as advocated by President Bush and others, should be encouraged to expand their operations. However, it is hard to see why intense rehabilitation programs such as that operated by the Prison Fellowship Ministry could not also be offered to nonreligious inmates, many of whom could benefit.

Such reforms would certainly not end America's prison crisis. But they would be a start. If adopted, they would begin to put the brakes on the unbridled growth of the prison population and they would lessen the abuse and suffering visited on those within the system.

In his speech to the ABA, Justice Kennedy stated why the subject of prisons should be of concern to all Americans. Let me end with his words:

"The subject of prisons and corrections may tempt some of you to tune out. You may think, 'Well, I am not a criminal lawyer. The prison system is not my problem. I might tune in again when he gets to a different subject.' In my submission you have the duty to stay tuned in. The subject is the concern and responsibility of every member of our profession and of every citizen.

"This is your justice system; these are your prisons."

ENDNOTES

Chapter 1

1. Radio Address to the Nation on Proposed Crime Legislation, February 18, 1984.

2. Court TV's page on *Inside Cell Block F.* http://www.courttv.com/onair/shows/hege/.

3. Sheriff Hege's personal Web site. http://www.hegecountry.com/.

4. Quotes without endnotes throughout are from interviews with the author.

5. Schiraldi, Vincent, and Jason Ziedenberg, "The Punishing Decade." The Justice Policy Institute. Washington, April 1999.

6. CNN, "Judge: Sheriff Can't Stream Jailhouse Images on the Internet." March 13, 2003.

7. Bittner, Emily, "Tent City Inmates Strip to Pink Skivvies." *Arizona Republic*, July 10, 2003.

8. Grossfield, Stan, "Chain of Pain." *Boston Globe*, May 31, 1998.

9. Amnesty International, "Ill-Treatment of Inmates in Maricopa County Jails, Arizona." August 1, 1997.

10. Justice Department Press Release, "Jails in Maricopa County, Arizona, to Take Steps to Reduce Excessive Force and Use of Improper Restraints Under Justice Department Agreement." October 31, 1997.

11. Ortega, Tony, "The $8 Million Victim." *Arizona New Times*, January 14, 1999.

12. Ibid.

13. Graham, Barry, "On the Job with America's Toughest Sheriff." *Harper's*, April 2001.

14. Interview on KAET TV, September 4, 2001.

15. Rouse, Mike, "Tough Sheriff, the Poor Fellow Needs Help." *Goldsboro News Argus*, November 21, 2001.

16. Damico, Dana, "Cocky, Controversial, Tough-on-Crime Sheriff Says Making Waves Is the Best Way He Knows to Turn the Tide." *Winston-Salem Journal*, June 13, 1999.

17. Roig-Franzia, Manuel, "15-Count Indictment Puts Heat on Hege." *Washington Post*, September 29, 2003.

18. Giovanelli, Laura, "Hege Pleads Guilty in Deal." *Winston Salem Journal*, May 18, 2004.

19. Tomlinson, Tommy, "'Star' Sheriff Deals with Poetic Justice." *Charlotte Observer*, September 17, 2003.

Chapter 2

1. Interview on "America's Drug Forum," 1991.

2. Bureau of Justice Statistics, *Prison and Jail Inmates at Midyear 2002*. Washington, April 2003.

3. National Center for Juvenile Justice, *Juvenile Offenders and Victims: National Report*. Washington, September 1999.

4. Bureau of Justice Statistics, *Source book on Criminal Justice Statistics 2001*, Table 6.1. Washington, 2001.

5. Bureau of Justice Statistics, *Justice Expenditure and Employment in the United States, 2001*. Washington, April 2004.

6. Lipton, Eric, "Budget Increase Tied to Rise in Fees." *New York Times*, Feb. 8, 2005.

7. Bureau of Justice Statistics, *Justice Expenditure and Employment in the United States, 2001*. Washington, April 2004.

8. Jackson, Rev. Jesse L., Sr., "Liberty and Justice for Some." *Mother Jones*, July 10, 2001.

9. Huling, Tracy, "Building a Prison Economy in Rural America." In Marc Mauer and Meda Chesney-Lind (Eds.), *Invisible Punishment: The Collateral Consequences of Mass Imprisonment*. The New Press, New York, 2002.

10. Ziedenberg, Jason, "Quantifying the Effect of Prison Expansion in the South." Justice and Police Institute, April 2003.

11. U.S. Census Bureau. http://www.census.gov/population/cen2000/phc-t5/tab01.pdf.

12. Bureau of Justice Statistics, *Prison and Jail Inmates at Midyear 2004*. Washington, April 2005.

13. Human Rights Watch, "Race and Incarceration in the United States." New York, February 2002.

14. Bonczar, Thomas O., and Allen J. Beck, "Lifetime Likelihood of Going to State or Federal Prison." Bureau of Justice Statistics, Washington, March 1997.

15. Conover, Ted, *Newjack: Guarding Sing Sing*. Knopf, New York, 2000, p. 19.

16. Street, Paul, *Mass Incarceration as Reverse Reparations*. The Urban League, Washington, September 2001.

17. Shakur, Sanyika, *Monster: The Autobiography of an L.A. Gang Member*. Penguin Books, New York, 1994, p. 163.

18. Butterfield, Fox, "As Inmate Population Grows, So Does a Focus on Children." *New York Times*, April 7, 1999.

19. The Sentencing Project, *Felony Disenfranchisement Laws in the United States*. Washington, 2001.

20. Mahlberg, Bob, "State Will Help Felons Regain Voting Rights." *Orlando Sentinel*, July 25, 2003.

21. Centers for Disease Control, "HIV/AIDS Counseling and Testing in the Criminal Justice System." August 2001.

22. Milton S. Eisenhower Foundation, "What Doesn't Work." http://www.eisenhowerfoundation.org/policy/fr_dsntwork.html.

23. Brennan, Justice William, *O'Lone* v. *Estate of Shabazz*, 482 U.S. 342, 354–55 (1987).

24. Mauer, Marc, *Race to Incarcerate*. The New Press, New York, 1999, p. 16.

25. Bureau of Justice Statistics, *Prison and Jail Inmates at Midyear 2004*. Washington, April 2005.

26. Kings College, London, International Centre for Prison Studies, "Highest Prison Population Rates." http://www.kcl.ac.uk/depsta/rel/icps/worldbrief/highest_rates(manual.html); and The Sentencing Project, *U.S. Surpasses Russia as World Leader in Rates of Incarceration.* Washington, 1997.

27. Fink, Micah, "Don't Forget the Hype: Media, Drugs and Public Opinion." *Fairness and Accuracy in Reporting* (Extra), September 1992.

28. Haney, Craig, and Philip Zimbardo, "The Past and Future of U.S. Prison Policy." *American Psychologist,* July 1998.

29. Drug Police Alliance, *Crack/Cocaine Disparity.* New York, 2001.

30. Bureau of Justice Statistics, *Total Estimated Drug Law Violation Arrests in the United States, 1980–01.* http://www.oip.usdoj.gov/dcf/tables/arrtot.htm.

31. King, Ryan S. and Marc Mauer, *"The War on Marijuana: The Transformation of the War on Drugs in the 1990s."* The Sentencing Project, Washington, May 2005.

32. Bureau of Justice Statistics, *Estimated Number of Arrests by Type of Drug Law Violation, 1982–01.* http://www.oip.usdoj.gov/bjs/dcf/tables/salespo.htm.

33. Madigan, Nick, "Judge Questions Long Sentence in Drug Case." *New York Times,* Nov. 11, 2004.

34. Richey, Warren, "Is 'Three Strikes' Law Cruel and Unusual Punishment?" *Christian Science Monitor,* November 25, 2002.

35. Greenhouse, Linda, "Justices Uphold Long Sentences in Repeat Cases." *The New York Times,* March 3, 2003.

36. Substance Abuse and Mental Health Services Administration, *2001 National Household Survey on Drug Abuse.* Washington, September 5, 2002.

37. Hilfiker, David, *Urban Injustice: How Ghettos Happen.* Seven Stories Press, New York, 2002, p. 39.

38. Katz, Jesse, "Prejudice & Punishment: Blacks Unfairly Targeted in 'War on Drugs.'" *Los Angeles Times,* June 8, 2000.

39. McCaffrey, Barry R., Keynote Address, National Conference on Drug Abuse Prevention Research. Washington, 1996.

40. Office of National Drug Control Policy, FY 2003 Budget Summary. http://www.whitehousedrugpolice.gov/publications/policy/03budget/.

41. McNamara, Joseph D., "The War America Lost." *Hoover Digest,* Palo Alto, 2001.

42. Mauer, *Race to Incarcerate,* p. 152.

43. Cole David, *No Equal Justice: Race and Class in the American Justice System.* The New Press, New York, 1999, p. 146.

44. Zimring, Franklin E., Gordon Hawkins, and Hank Ibser, "Estimating the Effect of Increased Incarceration on Crime in California," Policy Research Program of the California Policy Seminar, 1995.

45. Texas Department of Criminal Justice, Statistical Summary, Fiscal Year 2002.

46. Mauer, *Race to Incarcerate,* p. 1.

47. Parenti, Christian, *Lockdown America: Police and Prisons in the Age of Crisis.* Verso Books, London, 1999, p. 212.

48. Conover, *Newjack,* p. 25.

49. Eisenhower Foundation, "What Doesn't Work."

50. Parenti, *Lockdown America,* p. 176.

51. Knights, Roger, "Misbehave and You Get Food for Thought." *Seattle Times*, April 4, 2002.

52. Mumola, Christopher J., "Substance Abuse and Treatment, State and Federal Prisoners, 1997." Bureau of Justice Statistics, Washington, January 1999.

53. Centers for Disease Control, "HIV/AIDS Counseling and Testing in the Criminal Justice System." August 2001.

54. Centers for Disease Control, "Drug Use, HIV, and the Criminal Justice System." August 2001.

55. Greifinger, Robert B., et al., "Health Status of Soon-To-Be-Released Inmates: A Report to Congress." National Commission on Correctional Care, April 2002.

56. Clemetson, Lynette, "Links Between Prison and AIDS Affecting Blacks Inside and Out." *New York Times*, Aug. 6, 2004.

57. Famer, Paul, "Tuberculosis and Incarceration." In Marc Mauer and Meda Chesney-Lind (Eds.), *Invisible Punishment: The Collateral Consequences of Mass Imprisonment*. The New Press, New York, 2002.

58. Douglas, Lee, "Oregon Debates Kidney Transplant for Death Row." Reuters, May 27, 2003.

59. Oregon: Death Row Inmate Will Not Get Kidney Transplant. *Transplant Week*, June 15, 2003.

60. The Sentencing Project, "Mentally Ill Offenders in the Criminal Justice System." Washington, January 2002.

61. Bureau of Justice Statistics, *Eighty Nine Percent of State Adult Correctional Facilities Provide Mental Health Services*. Washington, July 15, 2001.

62. Bureau of Justice Statistics, *Prison and Jail Inmates at Midyear 2004*. Washington, April 2005.

63. Chesney-Lind, Meda, "Women in Prison." In Marc Mauer and Meda Chesney-Lind (Eds.), *Invisible Punishment: The Collateral Consequences of Mass Imprisonment*. The New Press, New York, 2002.

64. Bureau of Justice Statistics, *Prison and Jail Inmates*, p. 88.

65. Bureau of Justice Statistics, *Source book on Criminal Justice Statistics 2002*, Table 6.37. Washington, 2002.

66. Richie, Beth E., "The Social Impact of Mass Incarceration on Women." In Marc Mauer and Meda Chesney-Lind (Eds.), *Invisible Punishment: The Collateral Consequences of Mass Imprisonment*. The New Press, New York, 2002.

67. Bureau of Justice Statistics, *Almost 1.5 Million Minor Children Have a Mother or Father in Prison*. Washington, August 30, 2000.

68. Mauer, Marc, and Meda Chesney-Lind (Eds.), *Invisible Punishment: The Collateral Consequences of Mass Imprisonment*. The New Press, New York, 2002, p. 4.

69. Butterfield, "As Inmate Population Grows."

70. Durhams, Sharif, "N.C. Faces Budget Buster on Prisons." *The Charlotte Observer*, December 1, 2002.

71. Presley, Robert, "Releasing Prisoners Is No Way to Cut the Budget." *North Country Times*, February 9, 2003.

72. California Department of Corrections, Facts and Figures, Second Quarter 2003. http://www.cdc.state.ca.us/Communications Office/facts_figures.asp.

73. Gladstone, Mark, "Lawmakers from Both Sides Criticize Plan." *San Jose Mercury News*, May 15, 2003.

74. Corrections Independent Review Panel, "Reforming California's Youth and Adult Correctional System." Sacramento, June 2004. http://cpr.ca.gov/report/indrpt/corr/.

75. Human Rights News, "Gov. Schwarzenegger Backs Away from Commitment to Prison Reform." New York, Oct. 4, 2004. http://hrw.org/english/docs/2004/10/04/usdom9483.htm.

76. Institute of Governmental Studies, University of California, "California Correctional Peace Officers Association." http://www.igs.berkeley.edu/library/htlCaliforniaPrisonUnion.htm#topic3.

77. *Los Angeles Times*, "Cop-Out on Parole Reform." May 4, 2005.

78. Associated Press, "Budget Slashing Lawmakers Propose Leaner Prison Menu." March 8, 2003.

79. Warren, Jennifer, and Dan Morgan, "Budget Cuts Threaten Prison Literacy Program." *Los Angeles Times*, May 3, 2003.

80. Associated Press, "Inmates Kept In Cells 24 Hours Per Day to Save Funds." June 3, 2003.

81. Travis, Jeremy, "Prisoner Reentry Seen Through a Community Lens." The Urban Institute, Washington, August 23, 2001.

82. Bureau of Justice Statistics, *Source book on Criminal Justice Statistics 2001*, Table 6.42. Washington, 2001.

83. "Making Crime Pay—Triangle of Interest Created Infrastructure to Fight Lawlessness." *Wall Street Journal*, May 12, 1994.

84. Bonnerman, Jennifer, "The Riot Academy." *The Village Voice*, May 24th, 2000.

85. Bureau of Justice Statistics, *Justice Expenditures and Employment in the United States, 2001*. Washington, May 2004.

86. The corporate Web sites of General Motors, Ford and Wal-Mart. http://gm.com; http://ford.com; http://walmartstores.com.

Chapter 3

1. *Farmer* v. *Brennan*, 1994.

2. Zimbardo, Philip, Stanford Prison Experiment, Slide Show. http://www.prisonexp.org/.

3. Stanford University News Service, "The Stanford Experiment: Still Powerful After All These Years." Palo Alto, August 1997.

4. Haney, Craig, and Philip Zimbardo, "The Past and Future of U.S. Prison Policy." *American Psychologist*, June 1998.

5. Haney, Craig, and Philip Zimbardo, "The Past and Future of U.S. Prison Policy."

6. Haney, Craig, "Psychology and the Limits to Prison Pain." *Psychology, Public Policy and Law*, 3, 499–588, 1997.

7. Reuters, "Suit Charges Cruelty to Infirm in Alabama Prison." Feb. 24, 2005.

8. Brook, Daniel, "A History of Hard Time: Solitary Confinement Then and Now." *Legal Times*, February 2003.

9. Dickens, Charles, "American Notes." Chap. 7. London 1868. Electronic text on http://www.wsrv.clas.virginia.edu~jlg4p/dickens/mainpg.html.

10. A site providing information about prison movies. http://www.prisonflicks.com/.

11. Glenn, Lon Bennett, *The Largest Hotel Chain in Texas*. Eakin Press, Austin 2001, p. 17.

12. Lerner, Jimmy A., *You Got Nothing Coming: Notes from a Prison Fish*. Random House, New York, 2002, p. 36.

13. Enkoji, M. S., "Judge: Race-Based Lockdowns are Illegal." *Sacramento Bee*, December 21, 2002.

14. Lane, Charles, "Justices Rule Against Prisoner Segregation." *Washington Post*, Feb. 24, 2004.

15. Potter, Gary W., "Organized Crime." Eastern Kentucky University. http://www.policestudies.eku.edu/POTTER/crj401_10.htm.

16. United States Attorney, Western District of Texas, "Barrio Azteca Gang Members Sentenced to Federal Prison." U.S. Department of Justice, June 19, 2002.

17. Walker, Robert, "Gangs or Us, Black Guerrilla Family." http://www.gangsorus.com/.

18. United States District Court for the Central District of California, *United States* v. *Barry Byron Mills et al.* February 2002 Grand Jury Indictment.

19. Ibid.

20. Interview with Thom Mrozek, public affairs officer for United States District Attorney, Central District of California, May 5, 2005.

21. Cauvin, Henri E., and Serge F. Kovaleski, "Suspect in Slaying of Transit Officer Attacked in DC Jail." *Washington Post*, June 12, 2003.

22. Cauvin, Henri E., "Transit Officer's Killer Gets Life," *Washington Post*, July 31, 2004.

23. Ibid.

24. California Correctional Peace Officers Association, "Behind the Walls: The Toughest Beat in California." Video. 1996.

25. California Dept. of Corrections, "Inmate Incidents in Institutions, Calendar Year 2001." Sacramento, May 2002.

26. Geniella, Mike, "Web of Gang Terror Stretches Wide." *San Jose Press Democrat*, April 21, 2001.

27. Bromwich, Michael R., Inspector General, "Criminal Calls: A Review of the Bureau of Prisons' Management of Inmate Telephone Privileges." Dept. of Justice, August 1999.

28. American Friends Service Committee, "Equitable Telephone Campaign—Background." http://www.grassrootsvoices.org/prback.html.

29. Cahill, Tom, President of Stop Prisoner Rape, Interview. May 1, 2001. http://www.alertnet.org/story.html?storyID=10818.

30. Abbott, Karen, "Keep Letters Out of Prison Sex Trial, Defense Urges." *Rocky Mountain News*, November 29, 2002.

31. Hughes, Jim, "Officials Get Probation for Inmate Sex." *Denver Post*, May 16, 2003.

32. Glenn, *Largest Hotel Chain*, p. 252.

33. Abbott, Karen, "Cousins Face Death Penalty." *Rocky Mountain News*, August 17, 2002.

34. Crowder, Carla, "Inside Colorado's Deadliest Prison." *Rocky Mountain News*, February 11, 2001.

35. Williams, Bob, "Murder, Mayhem, Corruption and Snitches: BOP Florence Exposed." *Prison Legal News*, April 2003.

36. Abbott, Karen, "Jurors Acquit Four Ex-Prison Officers." *Rocky Mountain News*, June 25, 2003.

37. McAndrew, Ron, Testimony to the Commission on Safety and Abuse in America's Prisons, Tampa, April 19, 2005.

38. Glenn, *Largest Hotel Chain*, p. 250.

39. Justice Dept. Office of the Inspector General, "The Federal Bureau of Prisons' Drug Interdiction Activities." Washington, January 2003.

40. Ibid.

41. Dayton, Kevin, "Oklahoma Prison Called Drug Haven by Inmates." *Honolulu Advertiser*, August 15, 2001.

42. Ross, Jeffery Ian, and Stephen C. Richards, *Behind Bars: Surviving Prison*. Alpha Books, Indianapolis, 2003.

43. Prison Fellowship Ministries, About PFM. http://www.pfm.org/.

44. Ibid.

45. Glenn, *Largest Hotel Chain*, p. 321.

46. Adler, Margot, "Pagans Behind Bars." http://www.beliefnet.com/story/70/story_7060.html.

47. Statewide Interactive, Perspective, "Nebraska's New Prison and Its Anxious Neighbors." November 9, 2001.

48. Southern Poverty Law Center, "Behind the Walls." Intelligence Report 108, Winter 2002.

49. Schumer, Charles, "Growing Influence of Wahhabi Islam over Military and Prisons Pose Threat." Testimony to Senate Judiciary Subcommittee hearing on terrorism, technology and homeland security, June 26, 2003.

50. Weber, David, "Inmate Planned Geoghan Murder, Says DA Conte." *Boston Herald*, August 26, 2003.

51. Conover, Ted, "Prisoners of Hate." *New York Times*, August 28, 2003.

52. Conover, Ted, *Newjack: Guarding Sing Sing*. Vintage Books, New York, 2002, p. 20.

53. Southern Poverty Law Center, "Behind the Wire." SPLC Intelligence Report, Fall 2000.

54. Southern Poverty Law Center, "Behind the Walls."

55. Ulferts, Alisa, "Prison Study Finds No Signs of Bias." *St. Petersburg Times*, August 29, 2001.

56. Commission on Human Rights and Opportunities, Report on the Transfer of Connecticut Inmates to Wallens Ridge State Prison. Hartford, February 2001.

57. Fahthi, David, Declaration in Support of Motion for Class Certification. *Robert Joslyn et al.* v. *John J. S. Armstrong*, United States District Court, District of Connecticut. June 29, 2001.

58. Steven J. Martin, Testimony to Commission on Safety and Abuse in America's Prisons, Tampa, April 20, 2005.

59. First Amended Class Action Complaint for Injunctive and Declaratory Relief. *Robert Joslyn et al.* v. *John J. S. Armstrong*, United States District Court, District of Connecticut. March 14, 2001.

60. Names withheld by author.

61. Serious Incident Report, Wallens Ridge State Prison. June 29, 2000.

62. Reuters, "Virginia Move Puts Focus on Use of Stun Guns." May 22, 2001.

63. Hammack, Laurence, "$1.1 Million Settlement for Prison Stun Gun Death." *Roanoke Times*, March 15, 2002.

Chapter 4

1. Wilde, Oscar, "The Ballad of Reading Gaol."

2. Bruntmyer, Linda, Testimony Before the Senate Committee on the Judiciary, Washington, July 31, 2002.

3. Gabriel Media, Rodney Hulin Suicide Note. http://www.gabrielfilms.com/prisonrapefilm/documentation/hulin_6.html.

4. Human Rights Watch, "No Escape: Male Rape in U.S. Prisons." New York, 2001.

5. As part of the Prison Rape Elimination Act of 2003, the Bureau of Justice Statistics was empowered to conduct annual surveys of inmates to analyze the incidence and effects of prison rape. As of the time of writing, the first of these surveys had still not been published.

6. Wolf, Frank, Testimony Before the Senate Committee on the Judiciary, Washington, July 31, 2002.

7. Tucker, Neely, "Reform Plan Targets Prison Rape." *Washington Post*, July 26, 2003.

8. Stop Prisoner Rape, Update on Prison Rape Elimination Act, May 2005.

9. Bureau of Justice Statistics, *Date Collections for the Prison Rape Elimination Act of 2003*, Washington, June 30, 2004.

10. Arizona Correctional Peace Officers Association, Corrections USA Update, March 31, 2005.

11. Stop Prisoner Rape, op cit.

12. Struckman-Johnson, Cindy and David, "Sexual Coercion Rates in Seven Midwestern Prison Facilities for Men." *The Prison Journal*, December 1994.

13. Donaldson, Stephen, "Rape of Incarcerated Americans: A Preliminary Statistical Look." July 1995; "Stop Prisoner Rape," July 1995.

14. Dumond, Robert W., Hearing Before the Senate Committee on the Judiciary, July 31, 2002.

15. Human Rights Watch, "No Escape."

16. *David Ruiz et al.* v. *Gary Johnson*, No. CIV.A. H-78-987, United States District Court. S.D. Texas, March 1, 1999.

17. Cunningham, Garrett, Testimony to Commission on Safety and Abuse in America's Prisons, Tampa, March 19, 2005.

18. U.S. Department of Justice, Office of the Inspector General, Deterring Staff Sexual Abuse of Federal Inmates, Washington, April 2005.

19. Qutb, Sabrina, and Lara Stemple, "Selling a Soft Drink, Surviving Hard Time." *San Francisco Chronicle*, June 9, 2002.

20. *Roderick Keith Johnson* v. *Gary Johnson, Executive Director, Texas Department of Criminal Justice et al.* Preliminary Statement. United States District Court for the Northern District of Texas, Wichita Falls Division.

21. I have withheld the names of alleged gang members and corrections officers identified in the deposition.

22. "Prisoner Rape." ACLU fact sheet, April 2002.

23. ACLU Press Release, "ACLU Hails Important Step Forward in Shocking Prison Sex Slave Case," Washington, Sept. 9, 2004.

24. *David Ruiz et al.* v. *Gary Johnson*, No. CIV.A. H-78-987, United States District Court. S.D. Texas, March 1, 1999.

25. Ibid.

26. Lockette, Tim, "Officials: Overcrowding Led to Alleged Jail Rape." *Gainesville Sun*, June 11, 2003.

27. Earley, Mark, Testimony Before the Senate Committee on the Judiciary, Washington, July 31, 2002.

28. Parenti, Christian, *Low-down America*. Verso, New York, 2000, pp. 182–183.

29. Arax, Mark, "Stakes High as Prison Guards Go on Trial." *Los Angeles Times*, October 4, 1999.

30. Arax Mark, "Guards Acquitted of Setting Up Prison Rape." *Los Angeles Times*, November 9, 1999.

Chapter 5

1. Nietzsche, Friedrich, *Beyond Good and Evil*.

2. Pages on the Internet site of the Powell County Chamber of Commerce. Old Montana Prison, http://www.powellpost.com/aOldMontanaPrison.htm.

3. Pages on the Internet site of the Powell County Museum & Arts Foundation. Old Prison Museum, http://www.pcmaf.org/prison.htm.

4. *State of Montana* v. *Mark Edward Walker*, No. 01-528, Appellant's Brief.

5. *Mark Edward Walker* v. *State of Montana*, No. 01-528, Supreme Court of Montana, April 29, 2002.

6. Kupers, Terry, *Prison Madness*. Jossey-Bass, San Francisco, 1999.

7. Montana Dept. of Corrections, "Corrections Responds to Montana Supreme Court Decision." May 1, 2003.

8. *David Ruiz et al.* v. *Gary Johnson*, No. CIV.A. H-78-987, United States District Court. S.D. Texas, March 1, 1999.

9. Ibid.

10. Kupers, *Prison Madness*, p. 20.

11. Conover, Ted, *Newjack: Guarding Sing Sing*. Vintage Books, New York, 2000, p. 138.

12. "More Than a Quarter Million Prison and Jail Inmates are Identified as Mentally Ill." Bureau of Justice Statistics, Washington, July 11, 1999.

13. Walsh, Denny, "Prisons Lack Staff to Aid Mentally Ill." *Sacramento Bee*, December 11, 1998.

14. Ibid.

15. United States District Court, District of Connecticut, *R. Bartley Halloran* v. *John J. Armstrong et al.* Complaint for Damages, April 11, 2001.

16. Levine, Dan, "$2.9 Million Settlement for Death of Mentally Ill Man." *Hartford Courant*, May 2, 2002.

17. Office of Protection and Advocacy, "The Death of Timothy Perry." Hartford, August 2001.

18. Superior Court, Judicial District of Hartford, *Elaine Wiseman* v. *John J. Armstrong et al.* Complaint. November 15, 2002.

19. *Madrid* v. *Gomez*, 889 F. Supp. 1146 (N.D. Cal. 1995). Thelton E. Henderson, Opinion, *Alejandro Madrid et al.* v. *James Gomez*, United States District Court for the Northern District of California, January 10, 1995.

20. "Former Inmate at Pelican Bay Wins Judgment Against State." *San Francisco Chronicle*, March 1, 1994.

21. President's New Freedom Commission on Mental Health, "Achieving the Promise: Transforming Mental Health Care in America." Executive Summary. Washington, July 22, 2003. http://www.mentalhealthcommission.gov/.

22. The Sentencing Project, "Mentally Ill Offenders in the Criminal Justice System." Washington, January 2002.

23. National Alliance for the Mentally Ill et al., Amici Brief in *Brad H. et al.* v. *City of New York*. New York Supreme Court, Appellate Division, First Department, 1999.

24. Brannigin, William, and Leef Smith, "Mentally Ill Need Car, Find Prison." *Washington Post*, November 25, 2001.

25. Sentencing Project, "Mentally Ill Offenders."

26. Ibid.

27. Faust, Thomas N., "Shift the Responsibility of Untreated Mental Illness Out of the Criminal Justice System." *Corrections Today*, April 2003.

28. NBC4.TV, *Trapped Inside*, May 8, 2003.

29. "Mentally Ill Inmates at Risk in L.A. County Jails." ACLU, March 31, 1997.

30. Department of Justice, Memorandum of Agreement Between the United States and Los Angeles County, California, Regarding Mental Health Service at the Los Angeles County Jail. Washington, December 19, 2002.

31. Boyd, Ralph F., Jr., Santa Fe County Adult Detention Center, Department of Justice, Civil Rights Division, March 6, 2003.

32. Ibid.

33. Faust, "Shift the Responsibility."

34. Ibid.

35. Leonard, Christina, "Nurse Quits Over Mental Care in Jails." *Arizona Republic*, June 30, 2003.

36. Harris, Dan, "Suing for Sanity." ABCNews.com, January 2, 2001.

37. Fry, Steve, "Jury Finds Officers Negligent in Suicide." *Topeka Capital-Journal*, April 23, 2003.

38. Kupers, *Prison Madness*, p. 175.

39. Hayes, Lindsay M., "Prison Suicide: An Overview and Guide to Prevention." National Center on Institutions and Alternatives. Mansfield, MA, June 1995.

40. Ross, Jeffery Ian, and Stephen C. Richards, *Behind Bars: Surviving Prison*. Alpha Books, Indianapolis, 2002, p. 126.

41. Schmitt, Ben, "Wayne County Jail Suicides Spur Suit." *Detroit Free Press*, December 19, 2001.

42. Adams, Jim, and Sara Shipley, "State Acts to Improve Care." *Louisville Courier-Journal*, March 3, 2002.

43. Hayes, Lindsay M., "Prison Suicide: An Overview and Guide to Prevention."

44. National Center on Institutions and Alternatives and National Institute of Corrections, Special Issue: Preventing Suicides Through Prompt Intervention. Volume 10, Number 3, Summer 2001.

45. Boyd, Santa Fe County Adult Detention Center.

46. Ibid.

47. Strickland, Ted, "Mentally Ill Don't Belong in Prison." *Psychiatric News*, December 17, 1999.

48. Wynn, Jennifer, *Inside Rikers: Stories from the World's Largest Penal Colony*. St. Martin's Press, New York, 2001, p. 35.

49. Kolker, Robert, "Diagnosis Insanity." *City Limits*, May 2002.

50. Budnick, Nick, "Public Enemy No. 4." *Willamette Week*, February 19, 2003.

Chapter 6

1. Hall, Douglas Kent, and Richard Stratton, *Prison Tattoos*. St. Martin's Press, New York, 1997.

2. Grinberg, Emmanuella, "Canada to Open Prison Tattoo Parlors," Court TV, May 4, 2004.

3. Maruschak, Laura M., "HIV in Prison, 2000." Bureau of Justice Statistics, Washington, February 24, 2003.

4. Greifinger, Robert B., et al., "The Health Status of Soon-To-Be-Released Inmates." National Commission on Correctional Health Care, Chicago, April 2002.

5. Anderson, Christopher, "Maryland: Hepatitis Epidemic Looms in Prisons." *CDC News Update*. Centers for Disease Control, Atlanta, November 13, 2002.

6. Allen, Scott, M.D., "Developing a Systematic Approach to Hepatitis C for Correctional Systems: Controversies and Emerging Consensus." HEPP Report, HIV & Hepatitis Prison Project, April 2003.

7. "Corrections Announce TB, HIV and Hepatitis Test Results." PR Newswire, Sacramento, September 29, 1995.

8. Greifinger, "Health Status of Soon-To-Be-Released Inmates."

9. Anderson, "Maryland: Hepatitis Epidemic."

10. "Hepatitis C Spreads Mostly Unchecked in Prisons." Reuters, April 5, 2001.

11. Allen, "Systematic Approach to Hepatitis C."

12. Reuters, "Hepatitis C Spreads."

13. Galloway, Angela, "System Examined in Death of Washington Prisoner," *Prison Legal News*, September 2002; "Washington DOC Settles HEP C Death Suit for $1 Million," *Prison Legal News*, September 2002.

14. "Tainted Blood: Poison from the Prisons." *The Economist*, March 13–19, 1999.

15. Thompson, Justin, "Canada's Tainted Blood Scandal: A Timeline." CBC News Online, November 20, 2002. http://www.cbc.ca/news/features/blood_scandal_timeline.html.

16. Greifinger, "Health Status of Soon-To-Be-Released Inmates."

17. "Poor Health Status of Prison Inmates a Threat to Public Health." *Forensic Nurse*, January 28, 2003. http://www.forensicnursemag.com/hotnews/31h28162918.html.

18. Ibid.

19. Greifinger, "Health Status of Soon-To-Be-Released Inmates."

20. Center for Infectious Disease Prevention and Control, "Tuberculosis in Prison." *Health Canada*, March 2001.

21. Ibid.

22. Ibid.

23. National Center for HIV, STD and TB Prevention, "Tuberculosis Outbreak in Prison Housing Units for HIV-Infected Inmates—California, 1995–1996." Centers for Disease Control, February 5, 1999.

24. Rigby, Michael, "Prisons Experience Outbreaks of Infectious Disease." *Prison Legal News*, May 2003.

25. Pfeiffer, Mary Beth, "Prison Is Riskiest for the Sick." *Poughkeepsie Journal*, January 5, 2003.

26. "A Public Health Model for Correctional Health Care" and "The Public Health Burden in Correctional Facilities." Massachusetts Public Health Association, http://www.mphaweb.org/.

27. *Estelle* v. *Gamble*, 429 U.S. 97 (1976).

28. *David Ruiz et al.* v. *Gary Johnson*, No. CIV.A. H-78-987, United States District Court. S.D. Texas, March 1, 1999.

29. Ibid.

30. Galloway, Angela, "Failings in the System Go Back Many Years." *Seattle Post-Intelligencer*, August 21, 2002.

31. Hodges, Sam, "Inmate Deaths: A Fact of Life." *Mobile Register*, May 11, 2003.

32. Reuters, "Suit Charges Cruelty to Infirm in Alabama Prison," Feb. 24, 2005.

33. Pfeiffer, Mary Beth, "Prison Doctor's Record Arouses Concerns." *Poughkeepsie Journal*, January 6, 2003.

34. "State Pays Double for Temp Agency RNs in Prisons." *Forensic Nurse*, June 12, 2003.

35. Ibid.

36. Shenon, Philip, "Report on U.S. Antiterrorism Law Alleges Violations of Civil Rights." *New York Times*, July 21, 2003.

37. Zahn, Mary, and Jessica McBride, "Secrecy Veils More Than 100 Deaths." *Milwaukee Journal Sentinel*. October 21, 2000.

38. Pfeiffer, Mary Beth, "Prison Doctor's Record."

39. Pfeiffer, Mary Beth, "Prison Is Riskiest."

40. Ibid.

41. Zahn and McBride, "Secrecy Veils More Than 100 Deaths."

42. Ibid.

43. Lackeos, Nick, "Judge Orders Inmate Care." *Montgomery Advertiser*, December 12, 2002.

44. Mentor, Marvin, "$2.5 Million Verdict in California Medical Neglect Case." *Prison Legal News*, March 2003.

45. Prison Health Services, Inc., Company Overview. http://www.prisonhealth.com/overview.html.

46. Bridges, Tony, "Jail's Provider Has Mixed Record." *Tallahassee Democrat*, June 30, 2003.

47. Straub, Jim, "PHS: Prison Health Scam." *Philadelphia Weekly*, February 28, 2001.

48. Sentementes, Gus, "Health Firm Says It Lost Md. Prison Contract," *Baltimore Sun*, May 10, 2005.

49. Bykowicz, Julie, "Grand Jury to Study City's Jail Health Care," *Baltimore Sun*, May 10, 2005.

50. U.S. Department of Justice, Civil Rights Divison, Report on Baltimore City Detention Center, Washington, Aug. 13, 2002.

51. Hodges, "Inmate Deaths."

52. Boyd, Ralph F., Jr., Assistant U.S. Attorney General, Letter to Jack Sullivan, Santa Fe County Commission Chairman. Dept. of Justice, Civil Rights Division, March 6, 2003.

53. Ibid.

54. Ibid.

55. Hunter, Gary, "Medical Care Still Deficient in Texas Prisons." *Prison Legal News*, December 2002.

56. McDaniel, Deangelo, and Holly Hollman, "Observer: State Prison HIV Care 'Inhuman.'" *Decatur Daily*, February 28, 2003.

57. "ACLU of Washington Sues to Remedy Inhumane Conditions at County Jail." ACLU press release, February 26, 2002.

58. Hunter, "Medical Care Still Deficient."

59. Staples, Brent, "Treat the Epidemic Behind Bars Before it Spreads to the Population." *New York Times*, June 22, 2004.

60. Polk County Sheriff's Office, Cyber Sub-Station, Personal Hygiene and Personal Responsibility. http://www.polksheriff.org/detention/hygiene.html.

61. "Senate Passes Bill Requiring Prisoner Co-Pay." *News from the Senate Republican Majority*, Albany, March 18, 2002.

62. Friends Committee on Legislation of California, Analysis of SB 396: Health Care for Prisoners. June 11, 2001.

63. Reutter, David M., "Florida's Private Food Service Demonstrates that Profit Overrides Sanitary Practice." *Prison Legal News*, March 2003.

64. "State Cuts the Cost of Prison Meals." Associated Press, May 25, 2001.

65. "Prisons Need Better Food." Editorial, *St. Petersburg Times*, July 2, 2002.

66. Reutter, "Florida's Private Food Service."

67. Massachusetts Public Health Association, Introduction to the Public Health Model for Correctional Health Care. http://www.mphaweb.org/.

68. Warren, Jennifer, "Quadriplegic Possibly State's Most Expensive Prisoner." *Los Angeles Times*, May 15, 2003.

69. Warren, Jennifer, "The Graying of the Prisons." *Los Angeles Times*, June 9, 2002.

70. Campos, Carlos, "Medical Reprieves, Ill Prisoners Pay Dearly for Freedom." *Atlanta Journal Constitution*, July 21, 2003.

Chapter 7

1. *The Columbia World of Quotations*, 1996. First quoted in *The Observer*, London, March 29, 1981.

2. *Linda Laube et al. v. Michael Haley et al.* Civil Action No. 02-T-957-N.U.S. Middle District of Alabama, Northern Division.

3. Harrison, Paige M., and Allen J. Beck, "Prison and Jail Inmates at Midyear 2004." Bureau of Justice Statistics, Washington, April 2005.

4. Ibid.

5. "When Mothers Are in Prison Kids Pay High Price." Reuters, June 6, 2001.

6. Wolf Harlow, Caroline, "Prior Abuse Reported by Inmates and Probationers." Bureau of Justice Statistics, April 1999.

7. Lambert, Craig, "The Women of Cell Block B." *Harvard Magazine*, September–October 1999.

8. Browne, Angela, Brenda Miller, and Eugene Maguin, "Prevalence and Severity of Lifetime Physical and Sexual Victimization Among Incarcerated Women." *International Journal of Law and Psychiatry*, 1999.

9. National GAINS Center for People with Co-Occurring Disorders in the Justice System, The Wicomico County (Maryland) Phoenix Project. Summer 1999.

10. Cooper, Cynthia, "Medical Treatment in Women's Prisons Ranges from Brutal to Non-Existent." *The Nation*, May 6, 2002.

11. Pierson, Cassie, "LSPC Mourns the Loss of Sherrie Chapman." Legal Services for Prisoners with Children. http://prisonerswithchildren.org/news/chapman.htm.

12. Institute for Law, Psychiatry and Public Policy, "Incarcerated Women in the United States: Facts and Figures." University of Virginia, Charlottesville, September 10, 2001.

13. Kupers, Terry, *Prison Madness*. Jossey-Bass, San Francisco, 1999, p. 116.

14. Not her real name.

15. Amnesty International, *Abuse of Women in Custody: Sexual Misconduct and Shackling of Pregnant Women*. London, 2001.

16. Ibid.

17. Center for Reproductive Rights, "Prison Inmate Denied Right to an Abortion in Louisiana." April 9, 2002. http://www.crlp.org/pr_00_0705lainmate.html.

18. "Courthouse Tug-of-War Keeps Woman in Jail Waiting for Abortion." *Cleveland Plain Dealer*, October 11, 1998.

19. Public Information Office: Opinions and Case Summaries, "Former Judge Loses Law License for Six Months." 01-412. *Cleveland Bar Assn.* v. *Cleary*. September 19, 2001.

20. Amnesty International, "Not Part of My Sentence"—Violations of the Human Rights of Women in Custody, London, 1999.

21. Farmer, Ann, "Mothers in Prison Losing All Parental Rights." *Women's E-News*, June 21, 2002.

22. Foreshaw, Bonnie, "Faith, Power and Pants." In Wally Lamb (Ed.), *Couldn't Keep It to Myself*. Regan Books, New York, 2003.

23. Institute for Law, Psychiatry and Public Policy, "Incarcerated Women in the United States."

24. Delgado, Diana, Testimony to Illinois Senate Judiciary Committee, April 23, 2002.

25. Thompson, Carla, "Alabama Moves Female Prisoners Away from Children." *Women's E-News*, July 18, 2003.

26. Associated Press, "Louisiana DA Pursuing Charges Against Guards Involving Alabama Inmates," April 7, 2004.

27. O'Shea, Doreen, "Woman Behind Bars Reveals the Hardship of Her World." *Standard-Times*, New Bedford, Mass., July 17, 2003.

28. Amnesty International, "Not Part of My Sentence."

29. Jarvis, Angela, *Skurstenis* v. *Jones*, 236 F.3d 678 (11th Cir., 2000), http://www.forensic-evidence.com/site/Police/Pol_stripsearch.html.

30. Law Offices of Howard Friedman, *Mack et al.* v. *Suffolk County*, http://www.lawyers.com/civil-rights-law/cases.jsp.

31. "Judge Allows Suit in Strip Searches." Associated Press, February 19, 2000.

32. Sebok, Anthony J., "New York City's $50 Million Strip-Search Lawsuit Settlement." CNN.com, January 15, 2001.

33. Associated Press, "Miami-Dade settles strip search lawsuit," April 19, 2005.

34. Haney, Judith, "Testimony to Commission of Safety and Abuse in America's Prisons, Tampa," April 19, 2005.

35. *Jordan* v. *Gardner*, 986 F.2d (9th Cir., 1993).

36. Ibid.

37. Author's italics.

38. Amnesty International, "Not Part of My Sentence."

39. Ibid.

40. Ibid.

41. "When Can Male Officers See Naked, Violent, Unruly Female?" *Correctional Law Reporter*, April/May 2003.

42. "Justice Department Sues Arizona Over Conditions at Women's Prisons." U.S. Department of Justice, Press Release, March 10, 1997.

43. "Justice Department Settles Litigation to End Sexual Misconduct and Invasions of Privacy in Arizona State Women's Prisons." U.S. Department of Justice, Press Release, March 12, 1999.

44. Rigby, Michael, "Arizona Guards Continue to Rape Prisoners." *Prison Legal News*, April 2003.

45. "Male Officers Cannot Be Excluded from Working in Female Housing Units." *Correctional Law Reporter*, April/May 2003.

46. *Everson* v. *Michigan Department of Corrections*, 232 F. Supp. 2d 864 (E.D. Mich., 2002).

47. Ibid.

48. "Women in Prison: Sexual Misconduct by Correctional Staff." United States General Accounting Office, Washington, June 1999.

49. *Lucy Amador et al.* v. *Department of Correctional Services.* Class Action Complaint. U.S. District Court for the Southern District of New York, 2003.

50. Amnesty International, "Public Statement: USA (Michigan)." Press Release, London, October 29, 1998.

51. Brasier, L. L., "Prison Hero Gets a New Day in Court." *Detroit Free Press*, August 9, 2001.

52. Brasier, L. L., "Woman Gets 21–70 Years in New Murder Sentence." *Detroit Free Press*, December 6, 2001.

53. Latour, Francie, and Thomas Gallagher, "Sexual Abuse in Suffolk Prison." *Boston Globe*, May 23, 2001.

54. Clarke, Matthew T., "Sex, Drugs and Beatings at Boston Jails." *Prison Legal News*, February 2003.

55. Brink, Betty, "Opening the Doors on Carswell." *Fort Worth Weekly*, June 19, 2003.

56. Heinzi, Toni, "Rape Victim Wins Suit Against Prison Guard." *Fort Worth Star-Telegram*, June 24, 2003.

57. *Lucy Amador et al.* v. *Department of Correctional Services*, Class Action Complaint. U.S. District Court for the Southern District of New York, 2003.

Chapter 8

1. *Rhodes* v. *Chapman*, 452 U.S. 337 (1981).

2. The Gideons International. http://www.gideons.org/.

3. Callender, David, "Thompson Says Supermax Does What It Should." *Capital Times*, October 11, 2000.

4. Riveland, Chase, "Supermax Prisons: Overview and General Considerations." U.S. Department of Justice, National Institute of Corrections, January 1999.

5. Brook, Daniel, "A History of Hard Time: Solitary Confinement, Then and Now." *Legal Affairs*, February 2003.

6. Lueders, Bill, "Sizing Up Supermax." *The Isthmus*, August 15, 2000.

7. Pettigrew, Charles A., "Comment: Technology and the Eighth Amendment: The Problem of Supermax Prisons." *North Carolina Journal of Law & Technology*, 2002.

8. *Jones'El et al.* v. *Berge and Litcher*, U.S. District Court, Western District of Wisconsin (164 F. Suoo. 2d 1096).

9. Callender, "Thompson Says Supermax."

10. Lueders, "Sizing Up Supermax."

11. Florida Corrections Commission, Florida's Need for a Special Management Unit, 2000 Annual Report.

12. Riveland, "Supermax Prisons."

13. Riveland, "Supermax Prisons." (Italics added by author.)

14. Timberg, Craig, "Documents Show Use of Force at Wallens Ridge." *Washington Post*, July 31, 2001.

15. Hammack, Laurence, "Connecticut Settles Lawsuits in Supermax Deaths." *Roanoke Times*, March 15, 2002.

16. Sizemore, Bill, "Prison Chief Aims to Punish, Not Rehabilitate." *Virginian-Pilot*, May 1, 2000.

17. *Jones'El et al.* v. *Berge and Litcher*.

18. Callender, David, "In Over His Head—Teen's Survival Tactics at Supermax Cost Him Dearly." *Capital Times*, August 16, 2001.

19. Name withheld at her request.

20. *Jones'El et al.* v. *Berge and Litcher*.

21. Wilson, Colleen M., "Rethinking Supermax." *Eye on the Capitol*. March 14, 2001.

22. Associated Press, "Would Consider Changes at Supermax, Doyle Says." November 29, 2002.

23. Woodman, Robert, "U.S. District Court Finds Supermax Placement at Ohio Prison 'Atypical and Significant Hardship.'" *Prison Legal News*, February 2003.

24. *Charles Austin et al.* v. *Reginald Wilkinson et al.*, U.S. District Court, Northern District of Ohio (Case No. 4:01-CV-71), Opinion and Order, February 25, 2002.

25. McGough, Michael, "Ohio Defends Ohio Supermax Transfer Policy." *Toledo Blade*, March 31, 2005.

26. *Wilson* v. *Seiter*, 510 U.S., 294 (1991).

27. Letter to author.

28. "Isolation of Mentally Ill Inmates Criticized." *Chicago Tribune*, September 30, 2002.

29. Name withheld by attorney.

30. Cabana, Donald, Testimony to Commission on Safety and Abuse in America's Prisons, Tampa, April 19, 2005.

31. Florida Corrections Commission, "Florida's Need."

32. Brook, "A History of Hard Time."

33. Haney, Craig, "The Psychological Impact of Incarceration: Implications for Post-Prison Adjustment." From Prison to Home Conference, January 30–31, 2002.

34. Florida Corrections Commission, "Florida's Need."

35. Kupers, Terry, "The SHU Syndrome and Community Mental Health." American Association of Community Psychiatrists, Summer 1998.

36. Timberg, "Documents Show Use of Force."

37. Human Rights Watch, Red Onion State Prison. New York, May 1999.

38. Topham, James H., "Correctional Response Teams: 5 Officer Cell Extraction." http://www.corrections.com/cert/topham1.html.

39. *Madrid* v. *Gomez*, 889 F.Supp. 1146 (N.D. Cal. 1995). Thelton E. Henderson, Opinion, *Alejandro Madrid et al.* v. *James Gomez*, United States District Court for the Northern District of California, January 10, 1995.

40. Turley, Jonathan, "Torture at the Push of a Button." *Washington Post*, August 28, 2003.

41. Rigby, Michael, "Virginia Guards Acquitted of Assaulting Prisoner." *Prison Legal News*, January 2003.

42. Serious Incident Report, Wallens Ridge State Prison. April 5 & 7, 2001.

43. Rigby, "Virginia Guards Acquitted."

44. Arax, Mark, "8 Prison Guards Are Acquitted in Corcoran Battles." *Los Angeles Times*, June 10, 2000.

45. "Not Guilty On All Charges." *The Standard*, February 20, 2002.

46. "Inmate Says Texas Death Row a Living Hell." Reuters, January 7, 2001.

47. "Harsh Prison Conditions Prompt Inmates to Opt for Execution." Reuters, January 8, 2002.

48. Phillips, Robert Anthony, "Volunteering for Death: The Fast Track to the Death House." *Crime Magazine*, January 7, 2002.

49. Trial Transcript, *Willie Russell et al.* v. *Robert L. Johnson et al.*, U.S. District Court, Northern District of Mississippi Eastern District. Day Two, Volume Two, February 13, 2003.

50. Harden, Clay, "Miss. Told To Clean Up Death Row." *Jackson Clarion-Ledger*, May 22, 2003.

51. ACLU Press Release, Appeals Court Reaffirms that Mississippi Death Row Conditions are Unconstitutional, June 30, 2004.

Chapter 9

1. *San Francisco Daily Morning Call*, September 21, 1864.

2. "Retarded Boy Seeking U.S. Asylum Is Jailed, Abused." Reuters, March 13, 2002.

3. Young, Wendy, Testimony to Senate Judiciary Committee. March 5, 2001.

4. Montgomery, Lori, "Rural Jails Profiting from INS Detainees." *Washington Post*, November 24, 2000.

5. Singer-Bart, Susan, "Neighbors Say No to Federal Prisoners." *Rockville Gazette*, May 14, 2003.

6. Human Rights Watch, "Locked Away: Immigration Detainees in Jails in the United States." New York, September 1998.

7. Women's Commission for Refugee Women and Children, "Behind Closed Doors: Abuse and Refugee Women at the Krome Detention Center." Washington, October 5, 2000.

8. Boyd, Ralph F., Jr., Assistant Attorney General, Letter to Mr. L. Russell Molnar, President Wicomico County Council, September 9, 2002.

9. Montgomery, "Rural Jails Profiting."

10. Office of the Inspector General, "The September 11 Detainees: A Review of the Treatment of Aliens Held on Immigration Charges in Connection with the Investigation of the September 11 Attacks." Washington, June 2003.

11. "Report Critical of Treatment of Sept. 11 Detainees." *USA Today*, June 2, 2003.

12. "Retarded Boy Seeking U.S. Asylum."

13. Singo, Kopandru, Statement. February 19, 2002.

14. Names withheld by author.

15. Bureau of Justice Statistics, "Prison and Jail Inmates at Midyear 2002." Washington, April 2003.

16. Ibid.

17. New York City Correction Department, General Facts and Figures. http://www.ci.nyc.ny.us/html/doc/html/gnlstats.html.

18. Bureau of Justice Statistics, "Prison and Jail Inmates."

19. Ibid.

20. Thomas Russell, Wendy, "Officials: 'It's Not Filthy.'" *Long Beach Press Telegram*, June 30, 2003.

21. Porter, Arlie, "Detainees Face Rats, Overcrowding in County's Jail." *Charleston Post and Courier*, July 13, 2003.

22. "Marion County Officials Wrestle with Jail Overcrowding." Associated Press, July 12, 2003.

23. Fonce-Olivas, Tammy, "County Found Liable in Jail Death." *El Paso Times*, May 20, 2003.

24. Budnick, Nick, and Philip Dawdy, "The Strong Arm of the Law." *Willamette Week*, August 23, 2000.

25. Southern Poverty Law Center Intelligence Report, "Behind the Wire." Fall 2000.

26. Upmeyer, Nick, "$56.5 Million for Death in Drunk Tank." *National Law Journal*, May 20, 2002.

27. Walker, Don, "Construction Begins on Shreveport Jail." *Shreveport Times*, June 11, 2003.

28. Huddy, John T., "Jail Target of Justice Department." *Albuquerque Journal*, May 8, 2002.

29. Hannah, Jim, "Lawsuit Tells of Jail Brutality." *Cincinnati Enquirer*, June 11, 2003.

30. Wasilewski, Vince, "Use of Force: Let's Be Reasonable." http://www.corrections.com/cert/.

31. Mills, Steve, and Maurice Possley, "Mass Jail Beating Covered Up." *Chicago Tribune*, February 27, 2003.

32. Discovery deposition of Roger Fairley, Chicago, January 17, 2003.

33. Names withheld by author.

34. Long, Ray, and Steve Mills, "Prison Chief Quits Amid Jail Furor." *Chicago Tribune*, March 15, 2003.

35. Discovery deposition of Roger Fairley.

36. Snyder, Jean, Letter to Richard A. Devine, State's Attorney of Cook County. August 7, 2003.

37. Stern, Daniel K., Report of the Special Commission on the Suffolk County Sheriff's Department. October 15, 2002.

38. Farragher, Thomas, and Francie Latour, "Guard Brutality Called Rampant." *Boston Globe*, May 24, 2001.

39. Estes, Andrea, "Jury Awards Former Guard $500,000." *Boston Globe*, May 17, 2003.

40. Farragher and Latour, "Guard Brutality."

41. United States Department of Justice, District of Massachusetts, Nashua Street Jail Officers Convicted for Beating of Pre-Trial Detainees. March 31, 2003.

42. Ibid.

43. Farragher and Latour, "Guard Brutality."

44. Stern, Special Commission on the Suffolk County Sheriff's Department.

45. Latour, Francie, "Report Blasts Operation of Suffolk Sheriff's Office." *Boston Globe*, July 19, 2001.

46. Latour, Francie, "Strip-Search Settlements Hit Road Block." *Boston Globe*, February 27, 2003.

47. Wynn, Jennifer, *Inside Rikers: Stories from the World's Largest Penal Colony*. St. Martin's Press, New York, 2001, pp. 68, 95.

48. "Rikers Island Guards Beat Inmates for Years." Associated Press, August 16, 1998.

49. Hernandez, Daisy, "Seven Jail Workers Face Bribery and Drug Charges." *New York Times*, July 3, 2003.

50. McPhee, Michele, "Gang Boss in Jail Sex Scandal." *New York Daily News*, June 26, 2003.

51. "City Corrections Chief Resigns." WABC TV, November 27, 2002.

52. New York City Department of Investigation, Grand Jury Charges High Ranking Correction Department Officials with Grand Larceny and Other Offenses. February 13, 2003.

Chapter 10

1. The Internet site of the Canon City Public Library. http://ccpl.lib.co/us/lhc.html.

2. King, Ryan S., Marc Mauer, and Tracy Huling, "Big Prisons, Small Towns: Prison Economics in Rural America." The Sentencing Project, February 2003.

3. Norment Security Group, "Arizona State Prison Complex." http://www.normentsecurity.com/jobs/5116.htm.

4. Salomon Smith Barney, Buckeye, Arizona. http://www.livinginclarkston.com/buckeye.html.

5. Huling, Tracy, "Prisoners of the Census." *Mother Jones*, May 10, 2000.

6. Kahn, Chris, "Appalachia Rejuvenated by Prison Building Boom." *Cincinnati Enquirer*, December 23, 2001.

7. Doyle, Zanetta, "Does Crime Pay? Pros and Cons of Rural Prisons." *Economic Development Digest*, July 2002.

8. Huling, Tracy, "Building a Prison Economy in America." In Marc Mauer and Meda Chesney-Lind (Eds.), *Invisible Punishment: The Collateral Consequences of Mass Imprisonment*, The New Press, New York, 2002.

9. Sizemore, Bill, "New Prisons Bring Much-Needed Jobs to Rural Areas." *Virginian-Pilot*, March 7, 2000.

10. Huling, "Prisoners of the Census."

11. Parenti, Christian, *Lockdown America: Police and Prisons in the Age of Crisis*. Verso, London, 1999, p. 211.

12. King, Mauer, and Huling, "Big Prisons."

13. Ibid.

14. Harrison, Paige M., and Allen J. Beck, "Prisoners in 2002." Bureau of Justice Statistics, Washington, July 2003.

15. Holmes, Alexander, "The Role of Private Prisons in Oklahoma." Oklahoma Criminal Justice Resource Center, January 20, 2003.

16. Austin, James, and Garry Coventry, "Emerging Issues on Privatized Prisons." Bureau of Justice Assistance, Washington, February 2001.

17. Huling, "Building a Prison Economy."

18. Holmes, "Role of Private Prisons."

19. Clark, John L., Report to the Attorney General: Inspection and Review of Northeast Ohio Correctional Center. Washington, 1998.

20. Greene, Judith, "Bailing Out Private Jails." *The American Prospect*, September 10, 2001.

21. Florida Corrections Commission 1997 Annual Report: Out-of-State Inmates Housed in Private Correctional Facilities. Tallahassee, November 1, 1997.

22. ABC TV Nightline, "Prison Abuse: Is It Just As Bad Here?" Aug. 26, 2004.

23. Gallegos, Gilbert, "Prison Report Raps Politics, Fast Move to Privatization." http://www.abqtrib.com/archives/news00/011800_prisons.shtml.

24. Greene, Judith, "Prison Privatization: Recent Developments in the United States." Presented at International Conference on Penal Abolition, Toronto, May 12, 2000.

25. Gallegos, Gilbert, "Prison Report Raps Politics, Fast Move to Privatization." *Albuquerque Tribune*, January 19, 2000.

26. Greene, "Bailing Out."

27. Wackenhut Corrections Corporation, Fast Facts About WCC. http://www.wcc-corrections.com/wcc-corrections/facts-about-wcc.asp?id=1.

28. Butterfield, Fox, "Privatized 'Prison for Profit' Attacked for Abusing Teenage Inmates." *New York Times*, March 16, 2000.

29. "Justice Department Sues, Files for Emergency Relief to Protect Juveniles in Louisiana's Jena Juvenile Justice Center." U.S. Department of Justice press release, March 30, 2000.

30. Pounds, Stephen, "Private Operator Makes Corrections to Expand." *Palm Beach Post*, August 24, 2003.

31. Gruley, Bryan, "Building Spree Creates Glut of Lockups." *Wall Street Journal*, September 6, 2001.

32. Pounds, "Private Operator."

33. "Corrections Corporation of America Announced 2003 Second Quarter Results." *Business Wire*, August 6, 2003.

34. Wackenhut, Fast Facts.

35. Maclean, Pamela, "The Strong Arm of the Law." *California Lawyer*, November 2002.

36. Ibid.

37. "Davis Gets $251,000 From Prison Guards Union After Big Pay Raises." Associated Press, March 31, 2002.

38. Arax, Mark, "Union Crushed Bill to Let State Prosecute Guards." *Los Angeles Times*, July 19, 1999.

39. Rao, Lotta, "Fair Trade or Convict Leasing: Dissecting the Prison Labor Debate. Correctional Forum," June 2005.

40. "Legislation Limiting Inmate Lawsuits Signed by Governor." State of Oklahoma press release, August 27, 2002.

41. Plunkett, Chuck, "Crowded Powder Kegs." *Denver Post*, August 24, 2003.

42. Scutari, Chip, "New Prisons Chief Hasn't a Moment to Lose." *Arizona Republic*, August 13, 2003.

43. "If It's Prisons, We're Suddenly Big Spenders." *Tallahassee Democrat*, August 15, 2003.

44. Office of State Planning and Budgeting, Fact Sheet, Colorado Department of Corrections. Boulder, July 2003.

45. Mitchell, Kirk, "Sterling Prison Strike Ends Quietly as Leaders Transferred." *Denver Post*, July 12, 2003.

Chapter 11

1. King, Martin Luther, Jr., *Chaos or Community*. Hodder & Stoughton, New York, 1968.

2. Petersilia, Joan, *When Prisoners Return to Communities: Political, Economic and Social Consequences*. National Institute of Justice, Washington, 2000.

3. Butterfield, Fox, "Often, Parole Is One Stop on the Way Back to Prison." *New York Times*, November 29, 2000.

4. Petersilia, *When Prisoners Return*.

5. Ibid.

6. Butterfield, "One Stop on Way Back to Prison."

7. "Life Sentences: Denying Welfare Benefits to Women Convicted of Drug Offenses." The Sentencing Project, Washington, 1999.

8. Rubinstein, Gwen, and Debbie Mukamal, "Welfare and Housing, Denial of Benefits to Drug Offenders." In Marc Mauer and Meda Chesney-Lind (Eds.), *Invisible Punishment: The Collateral Consequences of Mass Imprisonment*, The New Press, New York, 2002, p. 44.

9. Reuters, "U.S. Lawmakers Launch Effort to Help Released Felons," Feb. 2, 2005.

10. Kennedy, Anthony M., Speech at the American Bar Association Annual Meeting. August 9, 2003.

11. Reuters, op cit.

12. Petersilia, *When Prisoners Return*.

13. LeDuff, Charlie, "In Los Angeles, Skid Row Resists an Upgrade." *New York Times*, July 15, 2003.

14. Ryan, John, "Police Sweeps on Skid Row Raise Concerns." *Daily Journal*, November 25, 2003.

15. Blankstein, Andrew, "Police Arrest 84 More in Second Skid Row Sweep." *Los Angeles Times*, November 23, 2002.

16. Brattton, William, and George L. Kelling, "The LAPD Is Targeting Crime on Skid Row, Not the Homeless." *Los Angeles Times*, March 11, 2003.

17. "In a Victory for ACLU/SC, National Lawyers Guild, Federal Judge Grants Temporary Restraining Order Against Police Sweeps in Skid Row Area." ACLU press release, April 3, 2003.

18. Travis, Jeremy, and Sarah Lawrence, "California Parole." Urban Institute, August 2002.

19. California Proposition 36. http://www.prop36.org/.

20. Rennison, Callie Marie, and Michael Rand, "Criminal Victimization, 2002." Bureau of Justice Statistics, Washington, August 2003.

21. Donziger, Steven R., *The Real War on Crime*. Harper Collins, New York, 1996, p. 10.

22. Mauer, Marc, *The Race to Incarcerate*. The New Press, New York, 1999, p. 290.

23. Rennison, "Criminal Victimization."

24. Fox, James Alan, "The Many Purposes of Prisons." *Boston Herald*, September 4, 2001.

25. Mauer, *Race to Incarcerate*, p. 82.

26. Ibid., p. 84.

27. Donziger, *Real War on Crime*, p. 440.

28. Travis, Jeremy, and Michelle Waul, "Reflections on the Crime Decline: Lessons for the Future." Urban Institute, Washington, August 2002.

29. Ibid.

30. Ibid.

31. Tucker, Neely, "Study Warns of Rising Tide of Release Inmates." *Washington Post*, May 21, 2003.

32. Travis, Jeremy, "Prisoner Reentry Seen Through a Community Lens." Urban Institute, Washington, August 23, 2001.

33. "U.S. Youth Gangs Spread Violence to Quiet Rural Area." Reuters, August 23, 2001.

34. "U.S. Gangs Spreading Overseas, Conference Hears." Reuters, June 11, 2002.

35. "Asian Youth Gangs Prey on Rhode Island." Reuters, August 12, 2002.

INDEX

Moral Intelligence
Enhancing Business Performance and Leadership Success
BY DOUG LENNICK AND FRED KIEL

Through a combination of research, and original thought leadership, the authors demonstrate how the best performing companies have leaders who actively apply moral values to achieve enduring personal and organizational success. These individuals exhibit moral intelligence: a strong moral compass and the ability to follow it, even in a world that may reward bad behavior in the short run. Lennick and Kiel reveal how dozens of companies benefit from the moral intelligence of their leaders. The authors help you build the specific moral competencies leaders need: integrity, responsibility, compassion, forgiveness, and more.

"The authors offer a timely, important, and practical personal guidance system that anyone in the business world would do well to adopt. The world of business would be vastly improved if *Moral Intelligence* became required reading."

- Daniel Goleman, Author of *Emotional Intelligence*

ISBN 0131490508, © 2005, 304 pp., $25.95

The Rise of the Rogue Executive
How Good Companies Go Bad and How to Stop the Destruction
BY LEONARD R. SAYLES AND CYNTHIA J. SMITH

Financial scandals aren't unknown in US business history, but today's growing problem of executive excesses and self serving behavior is unprecedented in both its persistence and pervasiveness. Executives continue to plunder their companies and rip off their stockholders. This book reveals the true breadth and depth of corporate corruption—including flagrant new cases that haven't received the publicity they deserve. More important, it answers the questions that matter most: Why now? And how can we stop it? Sayles is one the world's most honored management experts. As in-house corporate anthropologist at Arthur Andersen, Smith had a unique vantage point on the cultural changes that led to Andersen's collapse. Together, they identify powerful forces that cut across management, finance, the economy, politics, even psychology. Along the way, they identify rarely-discussed contributing factors such as the consulting boom, new technologies used by accounting and auditing professionals, the transformation of b-schools, journalism, and the media in general. This book addresses both criminal activity and the not-quite-illegal abuses that are now endemic in the executive suite—abuses that challenge the underpinnings of capitalism. Its deep insights will help both leaders and citizens understand exactly what's happened and what is needed to stem the tide of destructive behavior.

ISBN 0131477722, © 2006, 288 pp., $26.99